Language Independent Design
An Introduction

S. P. Maj

British Library Cataloguing in Publication Data
Maj, S. P.
Language independent design : an introduction
1. Software
I. Title
005.3

ISBN: 1–85554–001–0

First published in 1991 by:

NCC Blackwell Limited, 108 Cowley Road, Oxford OX4 1JF, England.

Editorial office: The National Computing Centre Limited, Oxford House, Oxford Road, Manchester M1 7ED, England.

Typeset in Palatino/Futura by Bookworm Typesetting; and printed and bound in Great Britain by Biddles Ltd, Guildford and King's Lynn
ISBN 1 – 85554 – 001–0

Preface

Studying from a book is perhaps not one of the easiest or most efficient ways of learning. The ideal environment, for many, is one lecturer and a small group of students. In this interactive situation the lecturer can respond to any difficulties for each student as they occur, but only after letting them struggle for a little while! As the students will learn from each other the lecturer can also gain insights into the subject being taught. Perhaps you have read prefaces 'to the students of class PTCS ...'. A good group of students will be supportive of each other through those 'dark nights of the soul' in the learning experience.

If you get stuck whilst reading a book it may be some time, if ever, before you can overcome the difficulty. Momentum is lost, help may not be on hand and the dynamic, supportive and interactive environment is not there. This is especially the case with a skill such as programming. What seems the most intractable problem to the reader can sometimes be solved by the simplest explanation from a lecturer. Attempts by an author to assume no previous knowledge are invariably flawed as readers start from such varied backgrounds. What is obvious to the author can be muddy waters to another.

This book is the result of several years' lecturing and using a language independent design methodology. It is important to note that the illustrative examples are by design simple. They were developed in a teaching environment where the emphasis, in the first instance, was on teaching efficiency rather than algorithmic efficiency, the idea being to encourage concentration on the concepts being taught rather than on the detail of a variety of complex problems. This also serves the purpose of allowing the user to quickly progress through the text. Once a program has been typed in then the following program will often be a logical progression. It is then easier to observe the pattern and hence learn the principles. The reader is very much encouraged to try all the programs and to experiment with the designs and associated code. I would encourage readers, especially those new to programming, to be rigorous in the use of the design principles taught. Then with experience and practice, the rules can be relaxed as the reader develops a style. This can be summarised by the saying 'Learn the rules before you break the rules'. In the final analysis what is needed is the intelligent application of the rules.

Every year that I have lectured on this topic the graph of learning experienced by students has been the same. A slow, sometimes very slow, initial progression; then the concepts become a reality and the beautiful simplicity is apparent. Using this method students, even those completely new to computing, have produced excellent designs and programs after about forty to sixty hours' tuition. Smiles, self satisfaction etc abound. It has all been worth it! I hope you will be able to say the same.

Acknowledgements

Dedication
To my parents, Dominic, Tosh and to Sharon who 'just kept going' and finally made it.

With thanks to
Due tribute must be given to the following. The help and humour given by some of those mentioned was far away and long ago, but has not been forgotten.

The students I have taught, in particular A level Computing and PTCS students – the problems that they gave me led to this book. I wish them all well.

Mr M Marriage, a senior systems programmer, for his patient assistance over the years.

Dr N Wilson, a research fellow at the University of East Anglia, for his critical comments and suggestions. In some cases we have agreed to disagree.

Mr A Day who for some years was head of computing at a comprehensive school and is now a Senior Lecturer in computing in the further and higher education sector.

The Fellowship of Engineers for the grant from the Matsushita Trust.

Professor Symons FRS of Leicester University for his unstinting help in the early years of my research career.

Dr Tsing Chen for his friendship and assistance with some difficult experimental work.

Mr P Hunt, a senior computer training manager. We had our differences but he stood by his word.

Though my proof readers have conscientiously read and re-read the manuscript (or so they told me!), in the final analysis I accept full responsibility for any mistakes that remain.

The programs are all available on a floppy disc from the following address:

Mr M Marriage
56 Avenue Rd
Norwich
Norfolk
NR2 3HN
UK

In order to cover administration, cost of the disc, postage and packing the cost is £10 made payable to Mr M Marriage. Do please specify the format, ie 5.25 inch (360K or 1.2M) or 3.5 inch (720K or 1.44M).

Contents

Introduction

This book has been designed and written to help the reader to produce better programs. It may be used to learn the principles of the language Pascal but it is assumed that the reader has a knowledge of BASIC.

It is a book concerned with program design rather than programming languages. It is suitable for BTEC National/Higher level courses, first-year undergraduates and will be of use to practising programmers. In view of the recent changes in some 'A' level Examination Board marking schemes, in favour of the project, the more complex treatment presented in this text may now be more appropriate.

The traditional methods – flowcharts, pseudocode, keyboard design etc, are demonstrably unsatisfactory for large system solutions. Typically the code produced lacks cohesion. Related operations are scattered throughout the program. The code will tend to have high coupling in the form of unnecessary interdependence between sections of code. Finally, there will often be a low consistency between the data structures of the system and the code. The result will be software solutions that are hard to maintain. This should be considered in the light of software costs which can represent up to 80% of the total budget of a new system, with DP departments spending over 50% of their time, and effort, on maintenance.

This book is about design, language independent design. For this to be meaningful it is important in the first instance to see the relationship between the principles of design and the solution in the form of target code. The target code will be Pascal and BASIC. It is assumed that the reader has some knowledge of programming and computers so the basic principles in the use of a computer, compilers etc are not addressed. The fundamentals of Pascal are quickly covered along with our design method. The Pascal is strict ISO code, but, where appropriate, different enhancements are included. After studying this book you should be able to think, that is analyse and design, in a language independent design method. The conversion to the target language will then be the simple mechanical application of the rules associated with that language. Data validation, screen handling etc, though important topics, are not addressed. The design principles learnt here can be applied to these subjects and the reader is fully encouraged to do so.

1 Software Engineering

1.1 INTRODUCTION

Rapid advances in electronic device fabrication have taken us from the thermionic valve – large, expensive, inefficient and unreliable – to solid state transistors, integrated during manufacture onto a single piece of semiconductor, ie integrated circuits. Advanced fabrication techniques now employ submicron lithography. Future trends can be clearly identified as higher packing densities, higher operating speeds and new semiconductor materials.

As a programmable, general purpose device the microprocessor is made application specific only by the associated software. General purpose devices command large production volumes with minimal unit cost. The same microprocessor chip may be found in a desktop computer, arcade machine or a guided missile! Over the years there has been a rapid decrease in the cost of hardware but an increase in performance.

Why then do software costs represent 80% of the total system cost? The problem is that as the sophistication and power of the hardware has increased so the size of the associated application system has also increased. The complexity of large systems is such that it is impossible for any single individual to hold and maintain the details of each aspect of the project, the result being a cost escalation for unreliable software delivered behind schedule.

1.2 SYSTEMS ANALYSIS AND DESIGN

The term software engineering was introduced in the late 1960s in response to the software crisis generated by the introduction of third-generation computers based on integrated circuits. These machines increased, by an order of magnitude, the size and complexity of possible computer based applications. Techniques applicable to smaller systems could not be scaled up resulting in computer based data processing systems which were overdue, unreliable, expensive and difficult to maintain. The production of complex systems requires the use of the software or system life-cycle. This consists of a series of distinct stages, with each stage consisting of clearly defined activities.

Typically the stages are:

- 1. Statement of requirements
- 2. Requirements analysis
- 3. System specification
- 4. System design
- 5. Detailed design
- 6. Coding
- 7. Integration
- 8. Implementation
- 9. Maintenance.

Many other methods with varying degrees of complexity have since been developed such as Information Engineering, Structured Design and Analysis, Structured Systems Analysis and Design Method (SSADM). Most methods, however, employ the basic principles of stepwise, top-down decomposition in which the stepwise refinement allows the deferment of detailed considerations by the use of abstraction to suppress and emphasise detail as appropriate. They all attempt to be understandable, expressive, implementation independent and generally applicable. Progression through the system development life-cycle consists of a series of transformations from the user statement of requirements to the detailed design. This involves documentation employing various notations appropriate to the requirements of each stage. The statement of requirements document will be in natural language with some graphics for clarity. This document will, as a result of the complex semantics of English (or any other natural language) be ambiguous, incomplete and contain contradictions. From this document the requirements analysis stage has to produce a requirements specification to be used as a reference document for all subsequent work and for final acceptance testing prior to handover. As such it has to be complete, consistent and unambiguous. Progression through the development cycle reduces the natural language content with a subsequent increase in more diagrammatic notations. The output of each stage is a specification for the following stage from which the appropriate design is made. Verification is the process of ensuring that the design of each stage is correct with respect to the specification of each preceding stage ie, is the product right? Validation ensures design integrity in that the final design should satisfy the initial user requirements, ie is it the right product?

For further details on systems analysis and design, please refer to *Introducing Systems Analysis*, S Skidmore and B Wroe, NCC Publications, 1988 and *Introducing Systems Design*, S Skidmore and B Wroe, NCC Blackwell, 1990.

1.3 GOOD PROGRAMMING DESIGN

Here the aims are to design programs which are easy to read, understand and modify, all within an acceptable timescale. To do this it is necessary to improve the design and associated documentation of program logic, ie structured or language independent design. For this we can use modular programming. Modular programming is the means by which a problem/program is divided into separately identified and addressable elements called modules that are integrated to satisfy the program requirements.

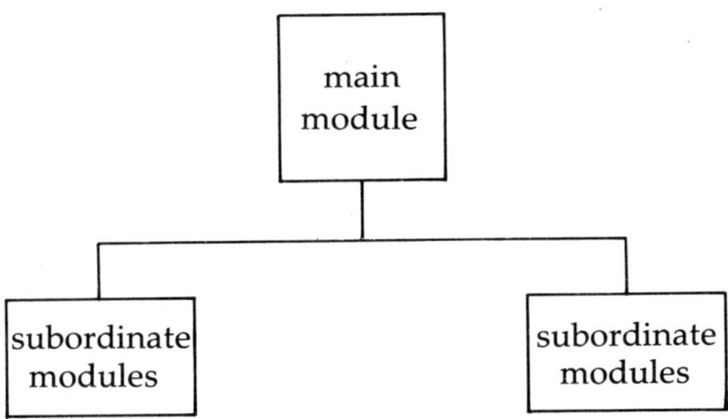

This modular approach allows us to employ a stepwise, top-down decomposition of the problem. The stepwise refinement allows the deferment of detailed considerations by the use of abstraction to suppress or emphasise detail as appropriate. More simply, you leave out the detail until it is required. Consider for a moment saying 'Let's go for a coffee' to a friend. Here you are using abstraction. You do not have to supply the details of how to walk, open the door, etc. It may be necessary to clarify when and where the coffee is to be taken, but only as appropriate. If you are talking to someone new it may be necessary to provide more detail. But from then on you can revert to "Let's go for a coffee".

Traditional design methods are not a suitable vehicle for high level language design. They very quickly become both complex and unmanageable. Our design method should represent the real problem with only logically correct programs being converted to the target language. The coding process should only be the mechanical application of the rules of syntax of the target language. The code is only the means by which to communicate with the computer in order to execute the design. With incorrect or incomplete designs it becomes necessary to solve each problem as it arises – often generating other problems.

1.4 SOFTWARE RELIABILITY

The reliability of any system will depend on:

- 1. The completeness of the analysis of the current systems and its associated problems.
- 2. The correctness of the system design.
- 3. The correctness of the mapping between the system design and the implementation – sometimes called interpretation.
- 4. The reliability of the components of the system.

We therefore depend on correct design and implementation. Our program should meet its specification, never produce incorrect output, never allow itself to be corrupted and take meaningful actions in unexpected situations – certainly a tall order!

1.5 CRITERIA FOR GOOD PROGRAMS

What do we mean by a good program? Criteria for evaluation include:

- 1. Readability; programs should use meaningful variable names with the controlled use of comments and should therefore be easy to understand. The code should be structured and modular.
- 2. Reliability; the program should be tested to demonstrate that it will serve the task it is designed for. Designing and testing will be to a specification.
- 3. Maintainability; is the code easy to maintain? Types of maintenance include perfective, adaptive and corrective. *Corrective measures* entail correcting any errors; note the correction of one error should not lead to any others! *Perfective changes* provide new facilities that were not previously available. *Adaptive modifications* encompass environmental changes ie, a change in the supporting hardware, operating systems or target language. It is worth stressing that about 50% of the resources of a given computer department will be for maintenance.
- 4. Robustness; 'press any key to continue', what if the user presses the Break key? ie, does the program deal sensibly with unusual data?
- 5. Portability; is the design specification portable between

    a. different machines?

    b. different operating systems?

    c. different languages?

  It is important to isolate the code from the effects of external modifications. In the final analysis it should be easier to port than rewrite the code.
- 6. Performance; this is not usually a consideration except for critical, real-time applications.

1.6 SUMMARY

– 1. Rapid advances in computer technology have meant decreasing cost of the computer hardware yet increases in performance.

– 2. Software typically represents the major cost in computer based solutions.

– 3. Software Engineering was the response to the software crisis that includes the use of the system life cycle.

– 4. The quality of software depends on the design method used. Traditional design methods, such as flow charts, are not suitable for the production of large software engineering projects.

1.7 PROBLEMS

– 1. To illustrate the rapid advances in computer technology obtain a series of cost/specification tables for a range of computers from 5 years ago and perhaps 10 years ago. Compare these to what can be obtained today.

– 2. If the opportunity arises, speak with a computer systems manager to get some idea of the budget for maintenance.

– 3. Obtain the source code for programs written by other people. See how quickly you can understand how the program works.

– 4. If you can obtain copies of the source code for someone else's programs, try and modify what the program can do. Does the modified program work? Are you sure there are no side effects?

– 5. With a program you have written, port it to another machine working under a different system. Is it easier to modify your program or rewrite it?

– 6. Give a program you have written to someone else and ask them to test it against your program specification.

2 Pascal

2.1 INTRODUCTION

Why Pascal? This is best introduced by a quote from Nilaus Wirth, the author of Pascal, at the Turing Award Lecture, 1984:
'The subject (ie computer languages) seemed to consist of 1% science and 99% sorcery, and this tilt had to be changed.'

also

'Programs should be designed according to the same principles as electronic circuits, that is, clearly subdivided into parts with only a few wires going across the boundaries. Only by understanding one part at a time would there be hope of finally understanding the whole.'

Modern structured languages, such as Pascal, have as their cornerstones the principles of modularity and communication. Using these principles it is possible to divide a problem into subproblems and then solve each subproblem accordingly – Divide and Conquer. Pascal aids the programmer to keep track of all the subcomponents by using representative names that become part of the program itself. These facilities, as we will see, complement language independent design.

2.2 A SIMPLE PASCAL PROGRAM

Pascal is a high level programming language that is characterised by its block-structure and data-typing, both of which we will employ to our full advantage. The syntax or structure of Pascal is described by means of examples, discussion and more formal definitions. The complete syntax of Pascal in the form of Pascal syntax diagrams is given in Appendix 1. Primarily this is a text about design, and sufficient Pascal will be considered to support this aim. For a fuller explanation of syntax diagrams and Pascal the reader is referred to one of the many excellent books on the market.

Upper case is used to highlight keywords such as BEGIN, with variable names and other user defined objects appearing in lower case. Do note, the compiler is not case sensitive and does not therefore distinguish between upper and lower case. Upper case is only distinguished in character strings.

By definition a Pascal program consists of two major components, heading and block:

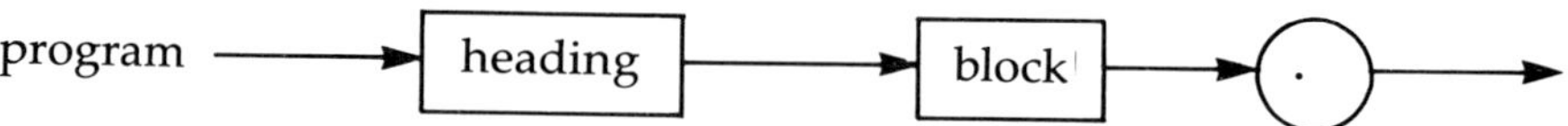

where heading is defined by:

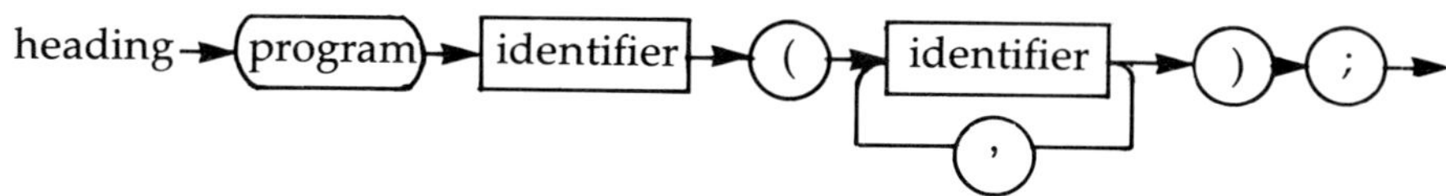

and block is defined by:

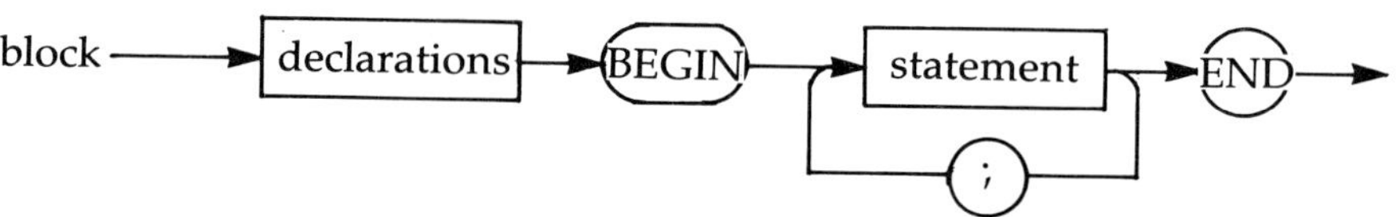

The declarations syntax diagram allows us to select our definitions and declarations as appropriate.

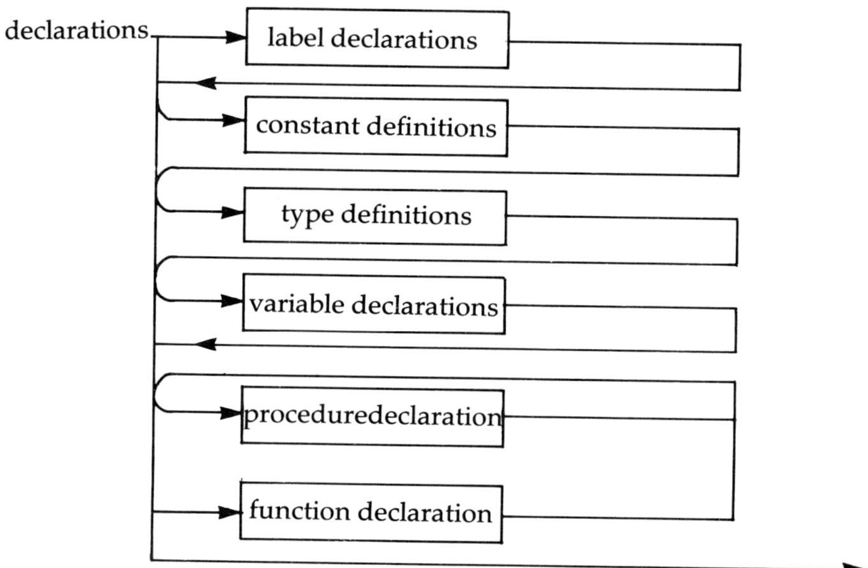

What this means is a program consists of a heading, followed by a block which consists of declarations, definitions and statements terminating in a period – all rather abstract! Here then is a simple Pascal program:

```
PROGRAM Ch2P1 (OUTPUT);                    (* Program heading *)
                                              (* Block *)
BEGIN                                           (* Statement(s) *)
        WRITE('Basearea')
END.
```

Points to note are:

– 1. The heading identifies the name of the program, Ch2p1, and lists its files. This program uses a standard Pascal file, OUTPUT, in order to display the result on a screen. For ease of reference, Ch2p1 means Chapter 2, Program 1. There will be more on files later.

– 2. In this simple program there are no declarations – more on this later. From our syntax diagrams we can see that declarations are optional.

– 3. The Block part consists of a single statement enclosed by the reserved words BEGIN and END.

– 4. A period terminates the program.

– 5. Comments may be placed anywhere in the program and are enclosed within parentheses – asterisk pairs. Always remember the programmer's lament 'When I wrote this program only God and I knew how it worked. Now, six months later, only God knows!'.

– 6. WRITE causes the contents in the quotes to be displayed on your screen ie, Basearea.

2.3 PROGRAM ELEMENTS

The Pascal character set, a subset of ASCII or EBCDIC, consists of:

letters:

A B C D E F G H I J K L M N O P Q R S T U V W X Y Z

decimal digits:

0 1 2 3 4 5 6 7 8 9

and special characters:

+ – / * ( ) › ‹ # ^ [ ] { } @ = . : ; , ' (blank)

Characters other than these may only appear in comments. The special characters are symbols with a particular use, see Appendix 4.

Reserved words, or keywords, such as BEGIN, have a predefined meaning and are listed in Appendix 2. To assist the reader all reserved words will be in upper case.

Pascal is not field-dependent or line-oriented. A Pascal statement may begin in any position on a line and can continue over many lines. We can free-format the code to our best advantage. The following program would work equally well!

```
PROGRAM Ch2P2 (OUTPUT); (* Program heading *)

(* Block *) BEGIN (* Statements *) WRITE('Basearea') END.
```

Column indentation is conventionally used to make a program more readable. Nesting is illustrated by indenting to different levels and aligning equivalent levels.

Let us now make our computer do some work.

```
PROGRAM Ch2P3 (OUTPUT);                       (* Program heading *)

(* The use of arithmetic evaluation *)              (* Block *)

BEGIN                                                  (* Statements *)

        WRITELN('Basearea', 10 * 10);

        WRITELN('Perimeter', 2*(10 + 10));

        WRITELN('Volume', 10 * 10 * 10)
END.
```

Further points to note are:

- 1. The entire statement part, enclosed by the BEGIN and END reserved words, is now a compound statement.
- 2. A compound statement consists of one or more statements separated by semicolons. The last statement is not followed by a semicolon.

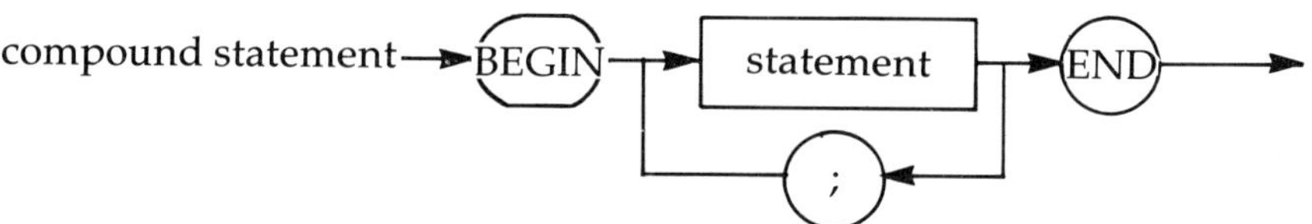

- 3. The arithmetic expressions are evaluated.
- 4. WRITELN causes the comments to be displayed on the screen and then go to a new line. Modify the above program by

changing WRITELN to WRITE and observe the effect. Typically WRITELN is used in conversation mode.

2.4 THE USE OF VARIABLES

The problem with the programs so far is that there is no interaction with the user. The values associated with Basearea, etc are fixed within the machine. We must be able to vary values according to the needs of the user. A variable declaration allocates a memory area for each variable and associates each area with an identifier or variable name. The size of the memory area depends on the data type of the variable. All variables must be declared. Variables allow the description of a calculation in more general terms. They can be considered as place holders or memory locations, the contents of which can be changed. Typically only the first eight characters are significant; hence datalogging1 and datalogging2 would be treated as the same variable. However do check with your compiler. Variable names should start with a letter and consist of letters and digits.

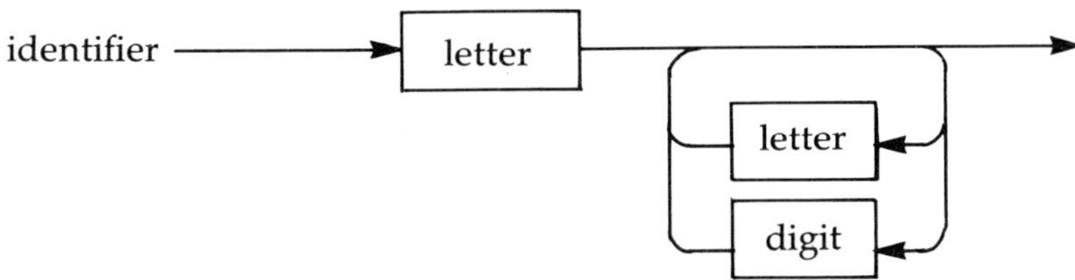

Where possible use meaningful names. All variables must be declared and 'typed' to define what values they may assume, valid operations and their storage requirements.

Data types are categorised as simple, structured or dynamic, see Appendix 5. For the moment we are only interested in simple data types ie, INTEGER, REAL, CHAR (CHARacter) and BOOLEAN.

Hence we have:

- 1. A description of the values that may be used and hence the storage requirements.
- 2. A description of the way the elements of the data structure are related.
- 3. A specification of the methods of access to the elements.
- 4. A specification of the permitted operations.

Programs consist of two parts, data and operations (also called statements) on data.

The simple data types are either ordinal or non-ordinal. For ordinal types the successor or predecessor to a value is known eg, the successor

SIMPLE DATA TYPES

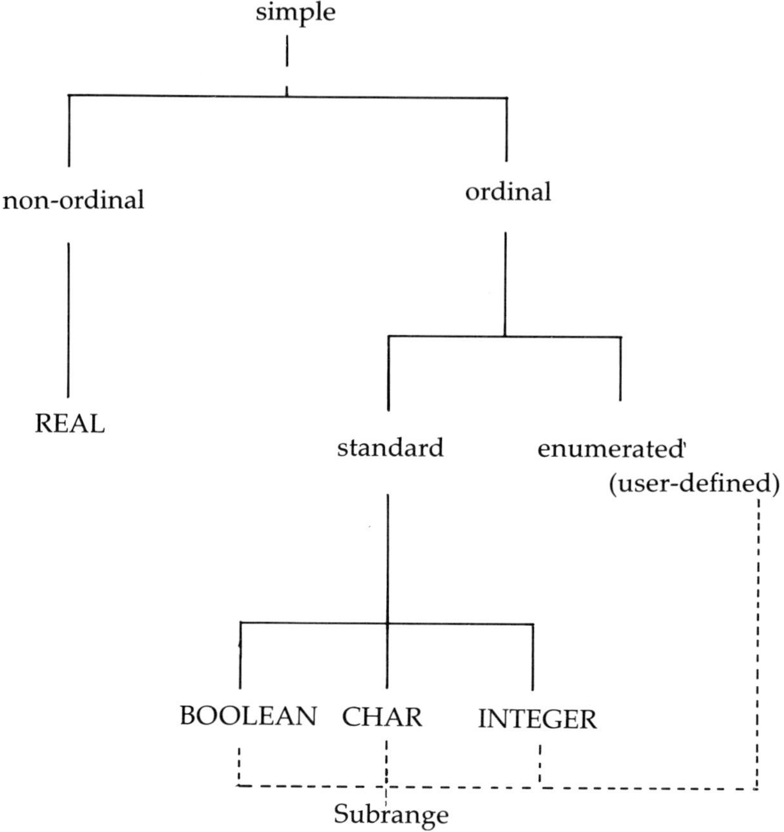

to 1 is 2, the predecessor to 2 is 1. For non-ordinal types this is not the case eg, what is the successor to 3.142? Is it 3.15 or 3.1421?

Variables allow a much more interactive system. We can read into the computer a quantity associated with length. The computer will process this data and produce the associated output. Depending on the program, it may be possible to enter another data value resulting in another output (see Figure 2.1 on the use of variables).

2.4.1 Type INTEGER

An INTEGER is a signed or unsigned whole number eg, 123, with a range that will depend on the word length of the computer being used. Valid operations on INTEGER operands include:

*	multiplication
DIV	integer division

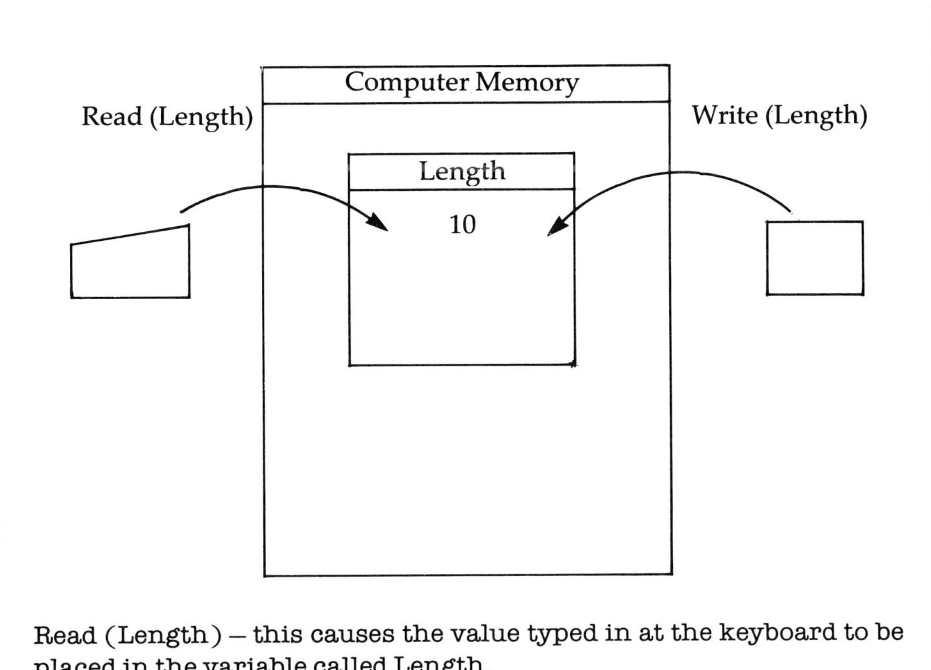

Read (Length) – this causes the value typed in at the keyboard to be placed in the variable called Length.
Write (Length) – this causes the value in the variable called Length to be displayed on the screen.

Figure 2.1

MOD	modulus (gives remainder of division)
+	addition
—	subtraction

Recall that:

Expression	Result
9 DIV 2	4
9 MOD 2	1

Each operation results in an INTEGER when the operands are of type INTEGER. REAL division may be performed on INTEGER operands but the resulting operand must be of type REAL. Relational operators may also be applied to INTEGER operands to give a BOOLEAN result.

```
PROGRAM Ch2P4 (Input, Output);

(* The use of INTEGER variable declarations *)

VAR Length, Width, Height : INTEGER;
```

```
BEGIN
      READ(Length);
      READ(Width);
      READ(Height);
      WRITELN('Basearea', Length * Width);
      WRITELN('Perimeter', 2*(Length + Width));
      WRITELN('Volume', Length * Width * Height)
END.
```

Points to note are:

- 1. The syntax diagram for variable declarations is:

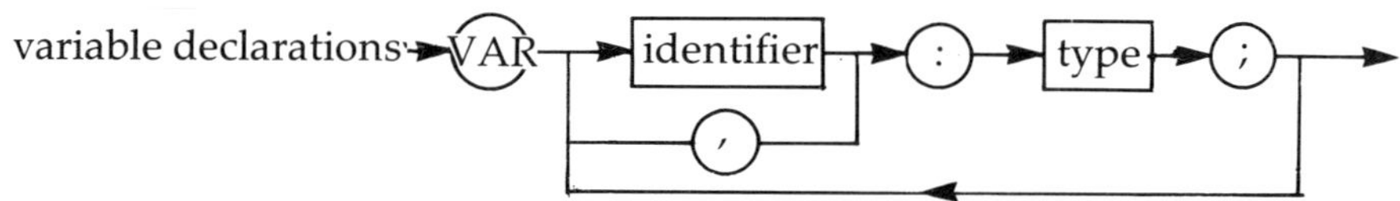

- 2. READ will take the value input to the keyboard and place it in the associated variable ie, stored in memory. (See Figure 2.1.)
- 3. The data input must be consistent with the type of the variable. Try typing in 1.23 for the length and observe the effect.
- 4. READ(Length) expects only one value.
- 5. READ(Length) initiates the reading of a sequence of characters that form, in this case, an INTEGER. The reading is terminated by the encounter of a character that cannot be converted to type INTEGER.
- 6. READLN(Length) performs a READ and then skips to the next line, the remainder of the current line is ignored. All three variable values must be on separate lines.
- 7. It is possible to READ(Length, Width, Height) and READLN (Length, Width, Height). Modify your program and observe the effects.
- 8. This program will allow the user to type in three values relating to the length, width and height.

User prompts

The most obvious limitation of the above program is that the user may not have written it. User prompts are essential.

```
PROGRAM Ch2P5 (Input, Output);
(* The use of user prompts *)
VAR Length, Width, Height : INTEGER;
BEGIN
        WRITELN('Please enter Length, Width and Height');
        READ(Length);
        READ(Width);
        READ(Height);
        WRITELN('Basearea', Length * Width);
        WRITELN('Perimeter', 2*(Length + Width));
        WRITELN('Volume', Length * Width * Height)
END.
```

2.4.2 Type REAL

A REAL is a signed or unsigned number consisting of an integer and a fractional part, rather like scientific notation. The magnitude of the number will depend on the machine being used. REAL numbers can be represented in conventional decimal notation:

1.23   0.123

or in exponential notation

1.23E1

where E denotes 'power of ten' in denary scientific notation and 'power two' in floating point notation. A REAL variable will accept an INTEGER assignment and in doing so the integer is converted to type REAL, but the reverse is not true. Valid operations on REAL operands include:

*	multiplication
/	REAL division
+	addition
–	subtraction

These operations give a REAL result when one or more of the operands is REAL. The INTEGER operators DIV and MOD cannot be applied to REAL operands. Relational operators may be used. Reals are non-ordinal in that the members of its set cannot be defined.

```
PROGRAM Ch2P6 (Input, Output);
```

```
(* The use of REAL variable declarations *)
VAR Length, Width, Height : REAL;
BEGIN
    WRITELN('Please enter Length, Width and Height');
    READ(Length);
    READ(Width);
    READ(Height);
    WRITELN('Basearea', Length * Width);
    WRITELN('Perimeter', 2*(Length + Width));
    WRITELN('Volume', Length * Width * Height)
END.
```

Due to the way these types of number are stored it is necessary to format the output.

```
WRITELN('Basearea', Length * Width :6 :2);
```

The first value, 6, is the field width and defines the column the value will be placed in. The second value, 2, defines the number of decimal places to be used. Vary these values and observe the effect on your screen.

Mixing the REAL and INTEGER data types, which is a common occurrence, produces the following results:

Data types	Resultant data type
INTEGER only	INTEGER
REAL only	REAL
INTEGER and REAL	REAL

Do note that assigning a variable of type INTEGER to a variable of type REAL is valid. However the converse is not true. To assign a variable of type REAL to one of type INTEGER it is necessary to first either TRUNC or ROUND. Where:

TRUNC(1.2) = 1, TRUNC(–1.2) = –1

ROUND(1.2)=1, ROUND(–1.2)= –1

Appendix 6 gives the arithmetic operators and the resultant type.
Appendix 7 gives the relational operators and the resultant type.

2.4.3 Type CHARacter

Characters are members of the set of type CHAR, which is either the

ASCII or EBCDIC character set eg 'A'. We will assume the machine is working with ASCII, but check with your manual. A variable of type CHAR can be assigned any ASCII character. Arithmetic operators cannot be applied to character operands. Relational operators can be used. Character strings may be written with as many characters as desired.

In the ASCII character set, characters are stored using a seven bit binary code.

Character	ASCII code	Binary value
A	65	1000001
B	66	1000010
C	67	1000011

It is therefore possible to use relational operators on type CHARacter. Do note that the basic unit of manipulation in a computer is the byte (eight bits). Our seven bit ASCII code is converted to eight bits by incorporating a parity bit for error detection.

2.4.4 Type BOOLEAN

Only two values exist in the BOOLEAN data type, FALSE and TRUE. The following logical operators can be applied to BOOLEAN operands to give a BOOLEAN result.

NOT logical negation

AND logical conjunction

OR logical disjunction

The relational operators yield BOOLEAN results and may be applied to BOOLEAN operands. We will use this type in section 2.6.2 and when we consider structured statements in Chapter 5.

2.5 CONSTANTS

It is often useful to define constant values, eg pi = 3.142. A constant definition gives a symbolic name (identifier) to a constant and assigns it a permanent value. The name pi can be used throughout the program. If however we wish to alter the value to say pi = 3.1423 only one line has to be changed. Constants have an implicit data type, for example, the constant 100 is INTEGER, 3.142 is REAL, 'a' is CHAR and TRUE is BOOLEAN. From our declaration syntax diagram we can see that CONSTANT definitions must be made before VAR declarations.

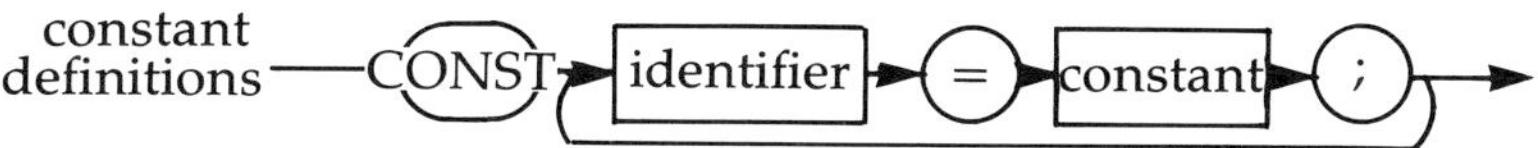

```
PROGRAM Ch2P7 (Input, Output);
(* The use of the constant definition *)

CONST Density = 5.0;
VAR Length, Width, Height: REAL;

BEGIN
        WRITELN('Please enter Length, Width and Height');
        READ(Length);
        READ(Width);
        READ(Height);
        WRITELN('Basearea', Length * Width :6 :2);
        WRITELN('Perimeter', 2*(Length + Width) :6 :2);
        WRITELN('Volume', Length * Width * Height :6 :2);
        WRITELN('Mass', Length * Width * Height * Density:6 :2)
END.
```

A TYPE definition defines new data types which can be attributes of variables, more on this in Section 2.8. The standard data types INTEGER, REAL, BOOLEAN and CHAR are predefined.

2.6 ASSIGNMENTS

One of the most elementary actions is an assignment. This evaluates an expression and assigns the result to a variable. The data type of the result must be compatible with the type of the variable. The assignment operator is the symbol: = .

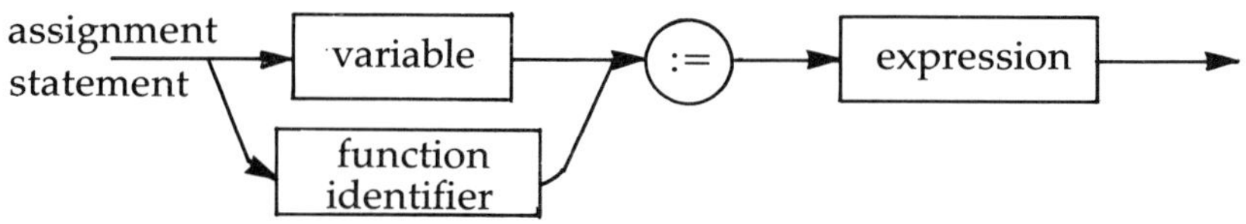

Do note that after the execution of the expression x := x + 1, if the initial value of x is 9, then the final value will be 10.

```
PROGRAM Ch2P8 (Input, Output);
```

```
(* The use of the assignment statement *)
CONST Density = 5.0;
VAR Length, Width, Height, Mass, Basearea, Perimeter, Volume :
REAL;
BEGIN
    WRITELN('Please enter Length, Width and Height');
    READ(Length);
    READ(Width);
    READ(Height);
    Basearea := Length * Width;
    Perimeter := 2 * (Length + Width);
    Volume := Perimeter * Height;
    Mass := Density * Volume;
    WRITELN('Basearea', Basearea :6:2);
    WRITELN('Perimeter', Perimeter :6:2);
    WRITELN('Volume', Volume :6:2);
    WRITELN('Mass', :6:2)
END.
```

2.6.1 Arithmetic Operations

Arithmetic expressions are evaluated with the normal rules of precedence ie a hierarchy that determines which operations are performed first.

Operator	Priority
Unary + –	Highest
Binary * / MOD DIV + –	Lowest

The operator with the highest priority is performed first. When operators have the same priority then the expression is evaluated from left to right. The priority may be raised by using parenthesis.

2.6.2 BOOLEAN Operations

A BOOLEAN operation is a logical computation on one or more BOOLEAN operands. The BOOLEAN operations are negation, disjunction and conjunction; see Appendix 7. BOOLEAN expressions evaluate to one of the values TRUE or FALSE. Relational operations also yield BOOLEAN results.

BOOLEAN operators that can be applied to give a BOOLEAN result are:

NOT logical negation

AND logical conjunction

OR logical disjunction

We will be considering these in detail when we look at structured statements in Chapter 5.

2.6.3 Relational Operations

A relational operation involves a comparision of operands. The operands in a relational operation must be of the same data type, with the one exception that REAL and INTEGER operands may be compared. The INTEGER value will be converted to type REAL; see Appendix 6.

Relational operators can be applied to character strings. In this case the ordinal values of the characters are compared.

2.7 SUBRANGE TYPES

Subrange types are subranges of previously defined data types thereby more exactly defining legal limits. As we will see later in Chapter 16, input data can be partitioned. Consider the case of

```
VAR Materialcost : INTEGER;
```

Here the acceptable value of materialcost depends on the word length of your machine, but will typically be quite large. Modifying this to

```
TYPE Pricerange : 1..5;

VAR Price : Pricerange;
```

restricts the value materialcost can take to between 1 and 5 inclusive.

```
PROGRAM Ch2P9 (Input, Output);

(* The use of type definitions *)

(* Subrange *)
```

```
CONST Density = 5.0;
TYPE Pricerange : 1..5;
VAR Price : Pricerange;
        Length, Width, Height, Mass, Basearea,
        Perimeter, Volume, Materialcost : REAL;
BEGIN
        WRITELN('Please enter Length, Width, Height and Price');
        READLN(Length);
        READLN(Width);
        READLN(Height);
        READLN(Price);
        Basearea := Length * Width;
        Perimeter := 2 * (Length + Width);
        Volume := Perimeter * Height;
        Material Cost := Volume*Price;
        Mass := Density * Volume;
        WRITELN('Basearea', Basearea : 6 :2);
        WRITELN('Perimeter', Perimeter : 6 : 2);
        WRITELN('Volume', Volume :6 :2);
        WRITELN('Cost', Materialcost :6 :2);
        WRITELN('Mass', Mass :6 :2)
END.
```

Points to note:

– 1. Depending on the compiler an error may or may not occur if the value of price is outside of the range 1 to 5 inclusive. It may be possible to select compiler options such as strict ISO Pascal.

– 2. Selection of the strict mode will result in an error if the value of price is outside of the defined range.

2.8 ENUMERATED TYPES

Pascal provides the above four predefined data types. User-defined types may be used. These enumerated data types are similar to BOOLEAN in that they may assume only a relatively small range of values. The possible values are enumerated in a type definition or variable declaration.

For example, a type MONTH could be declared and defined as the set of values JAN, FEB, MAR, APR, MAY, JUN, JUL, AUG, SEP, OCT, NOV, DEC.

The relational operators can be applied to values of an enumerated type.

2.9 SUMMARY

– 1. Pascal is a block structured high level language with strong data typing.

– 2. Syntax diagrams are a convenient means of defining and using the Pascal language.

– 3. Programs can be said to consist of two parts, data and statements.

– 4. Data types can be categorised as ordinal or non-ordinal and provide a specification of data storage and handling.

– 5. Variables are a convenient method of data manipulation and typing.

2.10 PROBLEMS

– 1. Write a program to display your name on the screen, something like this:

– 2. Write a program that will prompt the user to input his/her gross annual salary. The program will then return the net amount after tax – in Denmark the tax rate is 68%. Assume INTEGER values only. Obviously you will use a variable, but don't use the assignment statement – yet.

– 3. Modify the above program to handle REAL values.

– 4. Modify the program again this time using the CONST definition.

– 5. Finally write the program using the assignment statement.

3 Simple Statements

3.1 INTRODUCTION

We have been using statements, it is important to consider what they are and how they can be classified. Statements are the executable part of a program, where things are done. This can be contrasted with the data structures that are manipulated by the statements. The statement part of a program, following the declarations and definitions, usually consists of simple and structured statements. Simple statements are single statements, no part of which constitutes another statement. This can be contrasted with structured statements which are compound, conditional or iterative. Consecutive statements are separated by semi-colons.

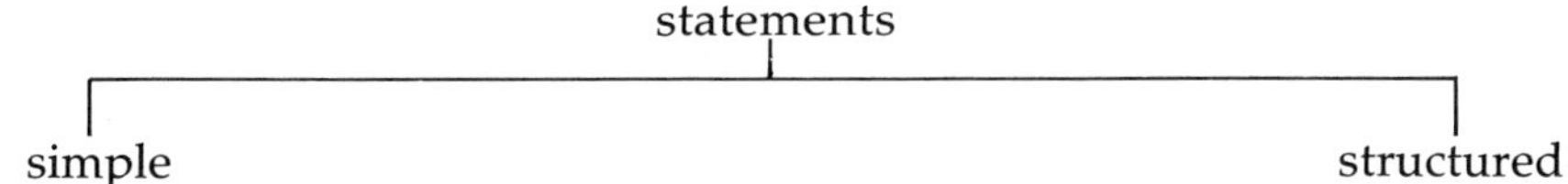

3.2 SIMPLE CONTROL STATEMENTS

There are:

- 1. Assignment and operation statements.
- 2. Output statements, which allows data output using the reserved words WRITE and WRITELN.
- 3. Input statements, which allows data input using the reserved words READ and READLN.
- 4. PROCEDURE or FUNCTION statement, which invokes a predefined or a user defined PROCEDURE or FUNCTION.
- 5. EMPTY statements, which takes no action.
- 6. GOTO statements, which transfers control to another statement.

We have previously considered assignment, output (WRITE and WRITELN), input (READ and READLN). Now we will consider PROCEDURE and FUNCTION calls, the EMPTY statement and GO TO.

3.3 PROCEDURE STATEMENTS

Procedures and functions are relatively independent subprograms which may be invoked to perform certain tasks. They are the basic components of Structured Programming. A procedure is equivalent to a program. Standard procedures and functions are supplied with the compiler. WRITE, for example, is a predeclared procedure. The

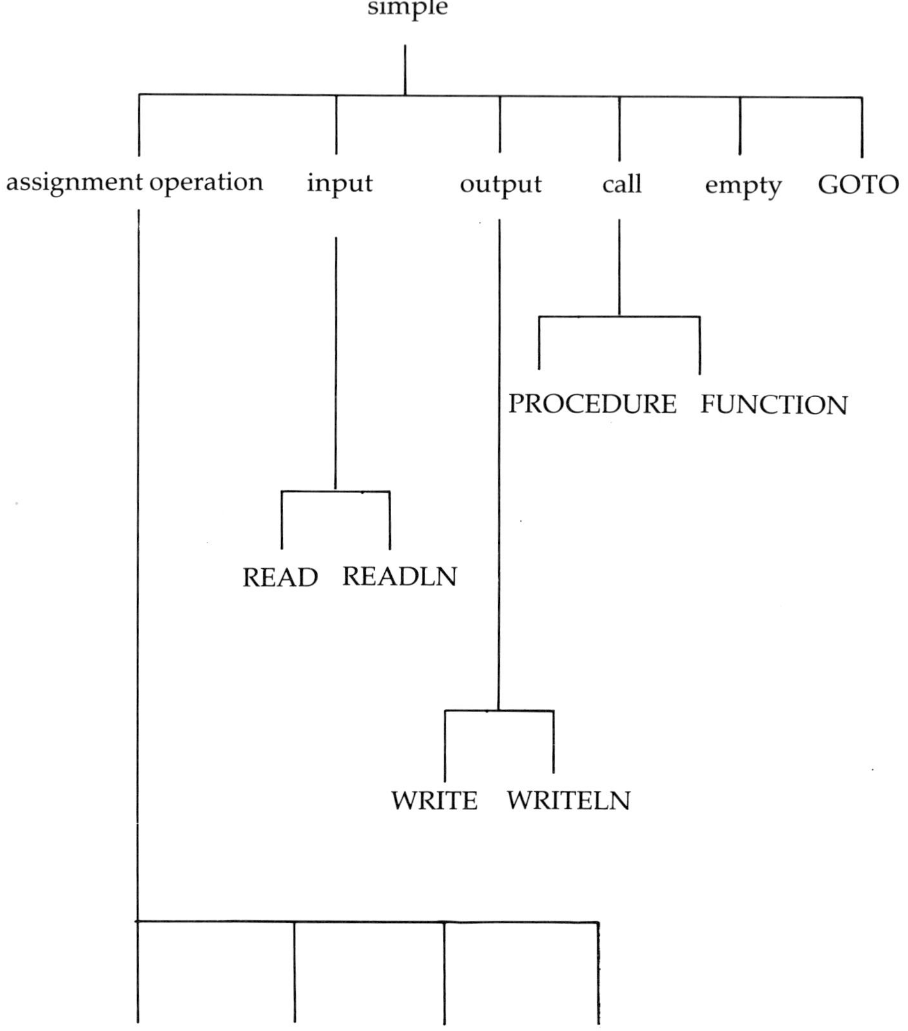

structure of a subprogram is similar to that of a main program – the main program, identified in program heading, itself is known as the main procedure. All programs consist of one main procedure and zero or more subsidiary procedures and functions.

Procedures and functions appear as the last declarations in the main program. All procedures and functions invoked within the program must be declared. A procedure or function declaration consists of a heading identifying the subprogram and listing its parameters, followed by a block. As with a program, a procedure or function block consists of label declarations, constant and type definitions, variable declarations and a statement part.

There are three ways data may be made available to procedures:

– 1. Local variable declarations. These variables are only 'known' to the procedure that declares them.

– 2. In order to communicate data between procedures it is possible to pass data, ie parameter passing.

– 3. Variables declared at the start of the main program are available for all the procedures in the program, ie global variables. Though undesirable, for the time being we will be using global variables. Later chapters will present a more rigorous treatment.

The syntax diagram for a procedure statement is:

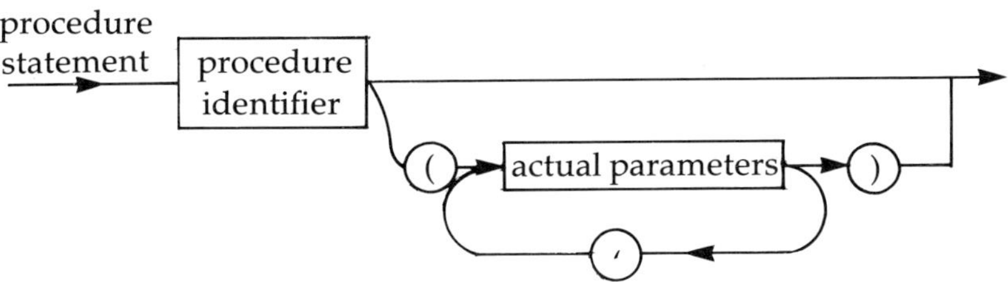

Procedures and functions are executed only when invoked, either directly or indirectly, by the main procedure. They can be executed as many times as desired, repetitively or recursively, as we will see later. Similarly we will be looking at data availability in Chapter 14 on Modular Programming.

We have previously seen the following program:

```
PROGRAM Ch2P6 (Input, Output);

(* The use of REAL variable declarations *)

VAR Length, Width, Height : REAL;

BEGIN

        WRITELN('Please enter Length, Width and Height');

        READ(Length);

        READ(Width);

        READ(Height);

        WRITELN('Basearea', Length * Width);
```

```
        WRITELN('Perimeter', 2*(Length + Width));
        WRITELN('Volume', Length * Width * Height)
END.
```

It is possible to rewrite the above program using procedures. There are different ways of doing this but one way is as follows:

```
PROGRAM Ch3P1 (Input, Output);
(* The use of procedures *)
VAR Length, Width, Height : REAL;

PROCEDURE Inputdata;
BEGIN
        WRITELN('Please enter Length, Width and Height');
        READ(Length);
        READ(Width);
        READ(Height);
END;

PROCEDURE Outputdata;
BEGIN
        WRITELN('Basearea', Length * Width);
        WRITELN('Perimeter', 2*(Length + Width));
        WRITELN('Volume', Length * Width * Height)
END;

BEGIN
        Inputdata;
        Outputdata
END.
```

Here the procedures Inputdata and Outputdata are called and excuted in that order. The boxes are not part of the program and are for clarification only.

One of the great strengths of Pascal is that it allows users to embed programs within programs by means of procedures and functions. As we progress through this text, we will see that procedures are useful in the following ways:

– 1. Abstraction: detail is supplied only as appropriate. The procedure name will indicate what it will do, eg Inputdata.

– 2. Re-usable: procedures can be used (called) as many times as needed. Inputdata can be called again.

– 3. Communications: procedures help establish necessary communications between parts of the program.

3.4 FUNCTION STATEMENTS

Sometimes we wish to generate a single calculated value eg square root. Functions compute a single value which is assigned to the function name and returned to the invoking expression. Points to note are:

– 1. The function designator activates a function to produce (return) a single result.

– 2. A function designator consists of a function identifier and a parameter list. The parameter list details how many data items are supplied and what the data types are.

– 3. A function designator can never appear by itself, it must always be part of a larger instruction.

– 4. A function identifier is limited to a scalar or pointer type (simple, enumerated, subrange or pointer). We thus define the value that will be returned after the function call.

– 5. The function names always gets assigned the result produced by the function.

This is expressed in the function syntax diagram:

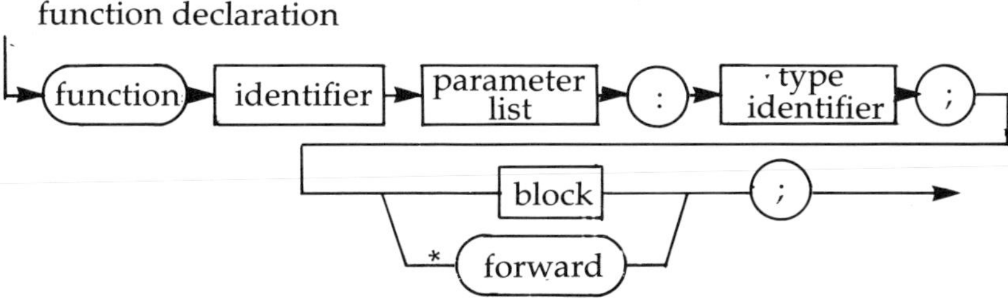


```
PROGRAM Ch3P2 (INPUT, OUTPUT);
VAR Number : INTEGER;
```

```
PROCEDURE Inputdata;
BEGIN
        WRITELN('Input a number');
        READLN(Number)
END;
```

```
PROCEDURE Outputdata;
BEGIN
        WRITELN('Number squared is', Number := SQR(Number)
END;
```

```
BEGIN
        Inputdata;
        Outputdata
END.
```

Points to note:

- 1. SQR is a predefined arithmetic function.
- 2. The value in the variable Number is passed to the function SQR which then squares it. The resulting value is then assigned to Number.
- 3. There are other predefined arithmetic functions such as SIN, COS, TAN etc.
- 4. It is possible to write your own function, but more on functions later.

3.5 EMPTY STATEMENT

The empty statement is a 'dummy' statement which takes no action but can be used as a place holder. More of this in Chapter 5 on Selection.

3.6 GOTO

This is never mentioned in polite company! The GOTO statement transfers control to a labelled statement elsewhere in the same program. This must only be used in exceptional circumstances.

3.7 SUMMARY

– 1. Procedures are relatively independent subprograms with similar structure to the main program. Procedures can be 'called' as many times as needed.

– 2. Data may be made available to procedures in three ways: local, global and parameter passing.

– 3. Functions generate a single value that is then assigned to the function name and returned to the invoking expression. As such a function must be part of a larger expression.

3.8 PROBLEMS

– 1. In Chapter 2, if you did the problems, you wrote a series of programs to calculate net salary given the gross salary. Modify one of your programs so that it is in a procedure based format.

– 2. Write a program that prompts the user to input an integer value and returns that value cubed. Write the function to do this.

4 Sequences

4.1 INTRODUCTION

Structured statements are composed of statements which are executed in sequence, either conditionally or repetitively or with an expanded scope. Structured statements are Sequence or Compound, Selection and Iteration. The expanded scope is the WITH statement; we will examine this further when we look at records and files.

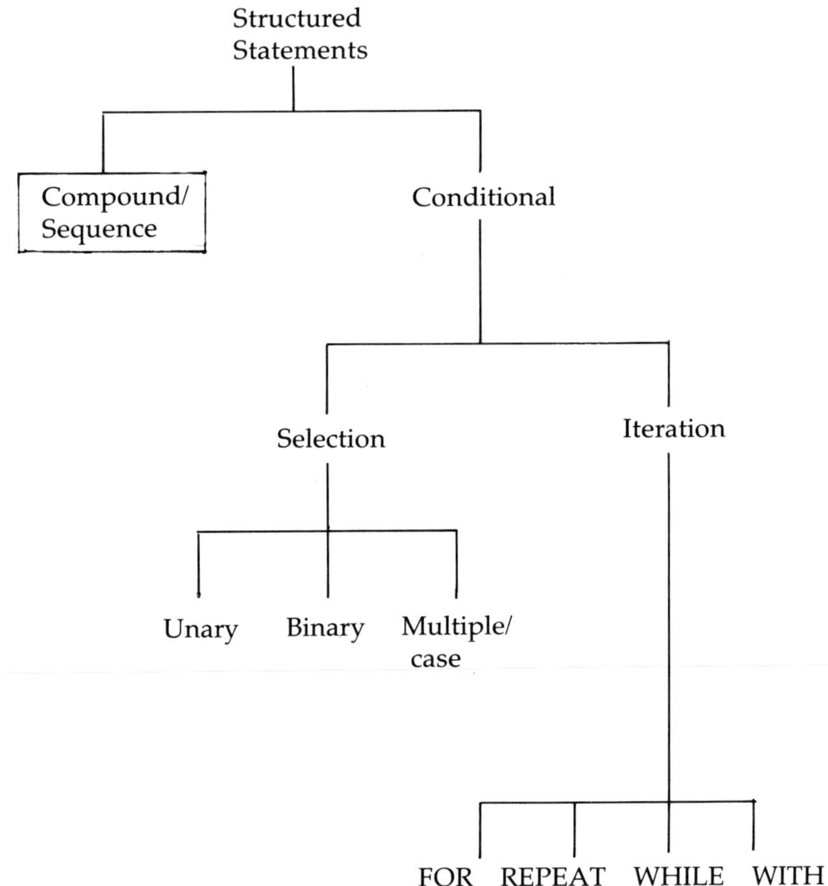

4.2 SEQUENCE

A Sequence or Compound statement is a sequence of statements executed in the order in which they appear (subject to any branching) and enclosed by BEGIN and END. The statements can be simple or structured.

The following points should be noted:

– 1. All statements must be separated by a semicolon.

– 2. The reserved words BEGIN and END are not separate statements but part of a single compound statement. Hence, no semicolon follows BEGIN or precedes END. A semicolon in this position would not be in error but would create an empty statement.

– 3. Indentation within the compound statement has no effect on the compiler and can be used to considerable advantage to aid readability.

The syntax diagram for a compound statement is:

compound statement

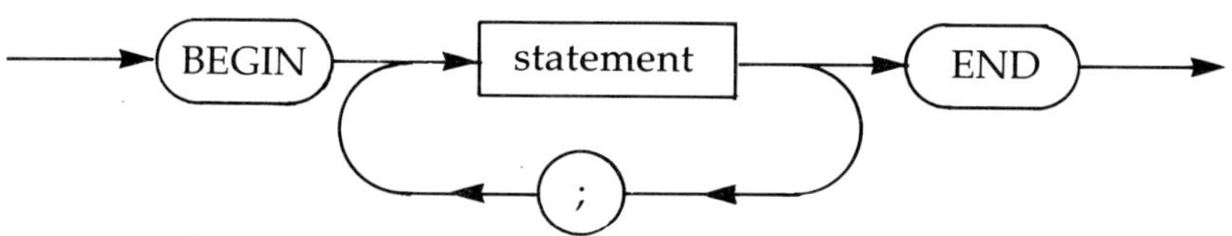

4.3 SEQUENCE DIAGRAMS

Let us consider the simple problem of calculating the dimensions of a room.

As we will see most programs can be written in a standard format – sometimes called the universal program (see diagram below).

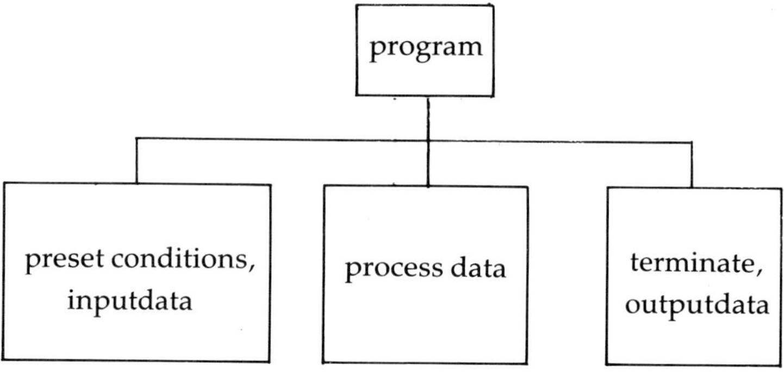

This illustrates what is called the 'top-down, stepwise refinement' approach. At the top is the overall problem; we work step-by-step, to refine the design by putting in more and more detail as appropriate.

Consider the program we have seen before:

```
PROGRAM Ch2P8 (Input, Output);

(* The use of the assignment statement *)

CONST Density = 5.0;

VAR Length, Width, Height, Mass, Basearea,

        Perimeter, Volume : REAL;

BEGIN

        WRITELN('Please enter Length, Width and Height');  (*1*)

        READ(Length);                                      (*2*)

        READ(Width);                                       (*3*)

        READ(Height);                                      (*4*)

        Basearea := Length * Width;                        (*5*)

        Perimeter := 2 * (Length + Width);                 (*6*)

        Volume := Perimeter * Height;                      (*7*)

        Mass := Density * Volume;                          (*8*)

        WRITELN('Basearea', Basearea : 6 :2);              (*9*)

        WRITELN('Perimeter', Perimeter : 6 : 2);           (*10*)

        WRITELN('Volume', Volume :6 :2);                   (*11*)

        WRITELN('Mass', Mass :6 :2)                        (*12*)

END.
```

In essence we have a sequence of twelve instructions, that we can label one to twelve.

The instructions are executed in the order given and each simple statement is called. Control is only passed to the next statement when the preceding statement has been completed. We have here a sequential control structure.

This can be rewritten in the form of a sequence of procedure calls:

```
PROGRAM Ch4P1 (Input, Output);

(* Sequential procedure calls *)

CONST Density = 5.0;
```

SEQUENTIAL PROGRAM

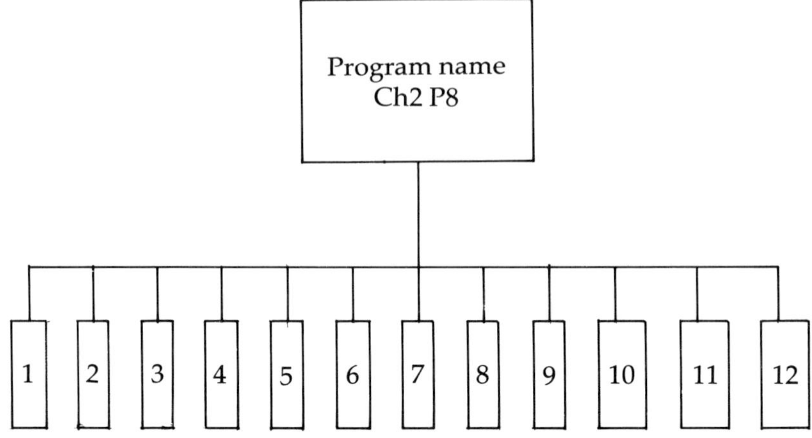


```
VAR Length, Width, Height, Mass, Basearea,
    Perimeter, Volume : REAL;
```

```
PROCEDURE Inputdata;
BEGIN
    WRITELN('Please enter Length, Width and Height');
    READ(Length);
    READ(Width);
    READ(Height)
END;
```

```
PROCEDURE Processdata;
BEGIN
    Basearea := Length * Width;
    Perimeter := 2 * (Length + Width);
    Volume := Perimeter * Height;
    Mass := Density * Volume
END;
```

```
PROCEDURE Outputdata;
BEGIN
        WRITELN('Basearea', Basearea : 6 :2);
        WRITELN('Perimeter', Perimeter : 6 : 2);
        WRITELN('Volume', Volume :6 :2);
        WRITELN('Mass', Mass :6 :2)
END;

BEGIN
        Inputdata;
        Processdata;
        Outputdata
END.
```

The boxes are meant as an aid to the reader. It is important to see the relationship between the code and the associated structured diagrams. Why have we done this? If we include blank lines we have increased the number of lines of code from 22 to 33. There are however some important concepts in this simple program. (Do recall we are keeping the examples simple in order to better concentrate on the principles being taught. In a working environment it is unlikely our program would be written in the above form. It does however serve us well as an illustrative example.) The main body of the program calls the procedure Inputdata, Processdata and then Outputdata in sequence.

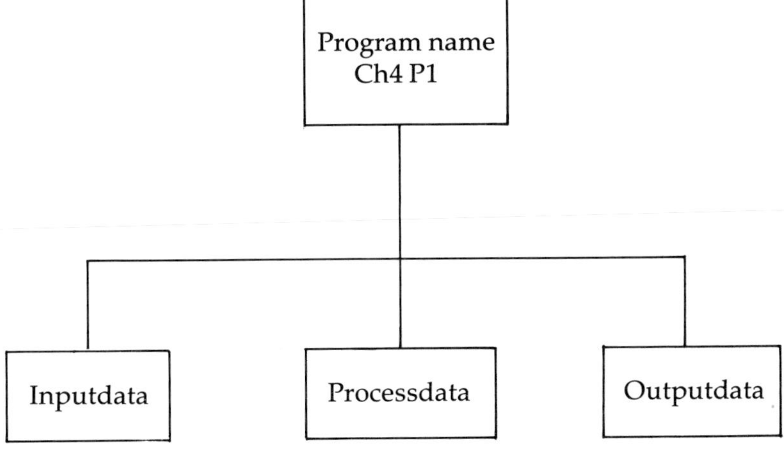

We here have an overview of the program and what it will do:

> The code associated with a procedure is invoked by calling that procedure.
>
> We have employed the principle of abstraction.
>
> A process has been named allowing us to suppress the detail.
>
> We know what Inputdata will do.
>
> Inputdata can be called as many times as we wish. A good procedure is written once but can be used many times.
>
> Should we require further detail we can examine the appropriate code.

Using this principle we can break problems up by stepwise refinement, deferring detailed considerations until appropriate. Do try and see the relationship between the code and structured diagram.

Let us now formalise our diagram a little more by including what are sometimes called terminal functions. These are operations that we do not decompose any further in our given procedure, although they may be broken down further in other procedures.

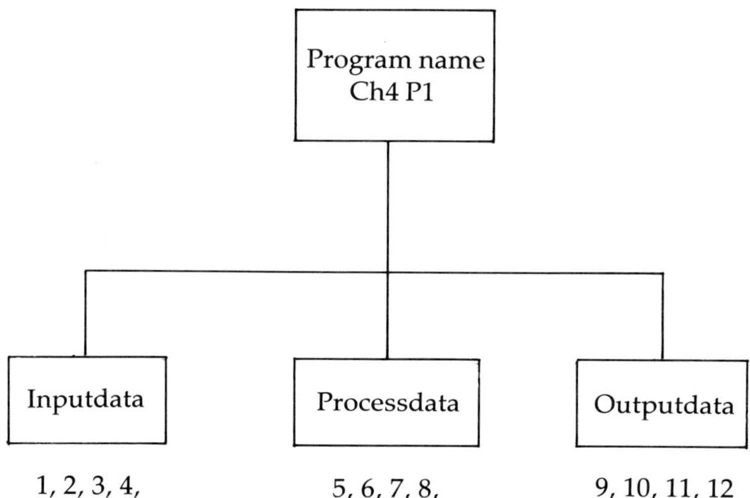

Functions list

1. User prompt 'Please enter Length, Width and Height'
2. Read in the Length
3. Read in the Width
4. Read in the Height

5. Calculate Basearea
6. Calculate Perimeter
7. Calculate Volume
8. Calculate Mass
9. Write to screen Basearea
10. Write to screen Perimeter
11. Write to screen Volume
12. Write to screen Mass.

The total number of terminal functions executed is the same, ie twelve. The instructions are now in groups of closely related operations so there is greater cohesion.

What have we done? The diagrams have the following advantages:

- 1. Graphical representation. Graphical techniques have a greater visual impact than words. More information can be transferred in a shorter period of time.
- 2. Modules. The actions of the program are divided into modules that can be described by one word. Hence the detail is available only as required.
- 3. Relationships. The relationships between the modules are clearly defined.
- 4. Documentation. Structured diagrams are a means of documentation.
- 5. Maintenance. The diagrams are an aid to maintenance. Recall that for code to be maintainable it is important to be able to quickly understand the current system and define the effects of the modifications on the rest of the system. The modules are relatively independent sections of code that can be easily replaced.
- 6. Portability. The design is largely language independent hence it can easily be converted to another target language should it be necessary.

4.4 SUMMARY

- 1. A sequence is a structured statement that is executed in the order in which it appears.
- 2. The universal program is a format suitable for many programming problems and indicates how problems can be broken down into progressively more detail.

– 3. Sections of code can be grouped together in a meaningful manner and given a suitable name. This grouping is called cohesion. Thus we have abstraction which allows the suppression of detail. We can therefore specify what is required without commitment to detail.

– 4. Programs can be represented graphically with the relationships between modules clearly defined.

– 5. Terminal functions are not decomposed any further.

4.5 PROBLEMS

– 1. Draw the structured diagrams for all of the programs, including your own, so far.

– 2. Investigate other graphical methods of representation.

– 3. What are the advantages and disadvantages of graphical methods over structured English?

5 Selection

5.1 INTRODUCTION

Programs can be made to respond to alternatives. In purely sequential coding, only a sequence of instructions is followed. A conditional statement allows selection of options for execution, with the selection dependent on a condition (or set of conditions). The types of conditional statement are unary, binary and multiple.

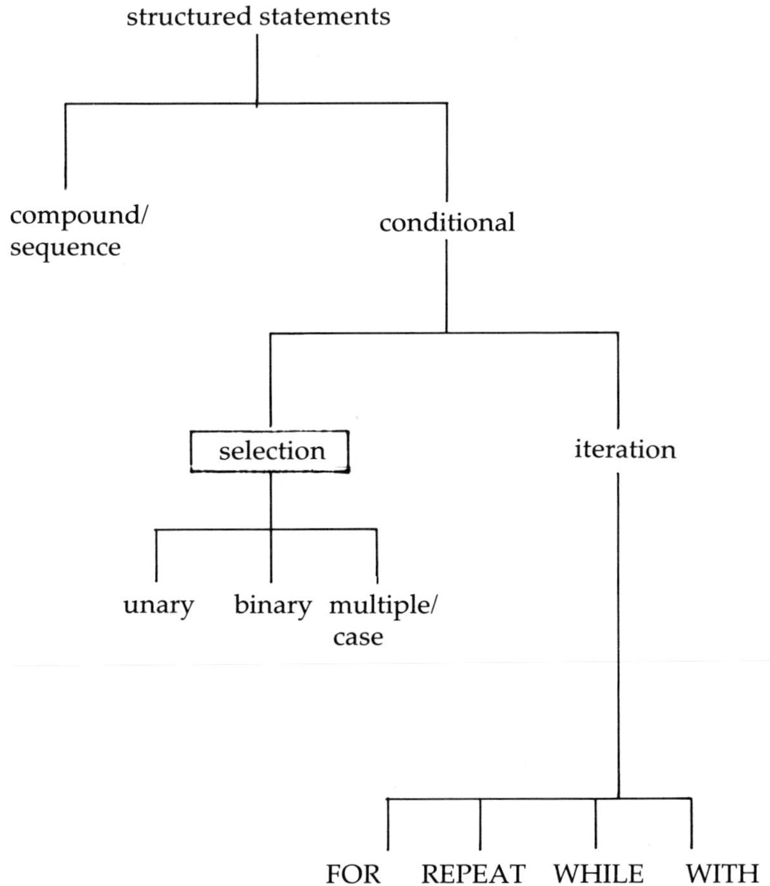

5.2 BOOLEAN OPERATORS AND EXPRESSIONS

In order to make decisions we need to be able to express logical statements. We do this using BOOLEAN expressions. A BOOLEAN operator is a logical computation on one or more BOOLEAN operands. The BOOLEAN operators are AND, OR and NOT. Truth tables can be used to define all the possible conditions that can occur. For two input variables there are four possible input combinations (2 exp 2). Similarly for three input variables there are eight input combinations (2 exp 3).

5.2.1 AND operator (logical conjunction)

Condition A	Condition B	A AND B
FALSE	FALSE	FALSE
FALSE	TRUE	FALSE
TRUE	FALSE	FALSE
TRUE	TRUE	TRUE

The final output is only TRUE when both input conditions are TRUE.

5.2.2 OR operator (logical disjunction)

Condition A	Condition B	A or B
FALSE	FALSE	FALSE
FALSE	TRUE	TRUE
TRUE	FALSE	TRUE
TRUE	TRUE	TRUE

The final output is TRUE when either input condition is TRUE.

5.2.3 NOT operator (logical negation)

Condition A	NOT A
FALSE	TRUE
TRUE	FALSE

NOT is a unary operator and reverses the value of a condition.

5.3 BOOLEAN EXPRESSIONS

A BOOLEAN expression can be defined by the following syntax diagram :

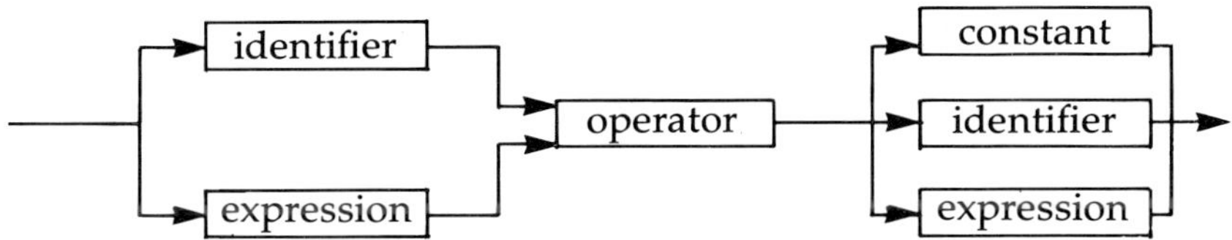

with our operator being defined from the following:

Operator	Symbol Name	General Usage
<	less than	relational operators
>	greater than	
=	equals	
<>	not equal	
#	not equal	
<=	less than or equal	
>=	greater than or equal	

The following are examples of BOOLEAN expressions. The value of each expression is either TRUE or FALSE depending on the value assumed by the variables.

BOOLEAN expression	A B C	Value
A = 1	1	TRUE
A = 1	2	FALSE

5.4 UNARY SELECTION – THE IF...THEN STATEMENT

The IF . . . THEN statement specifies a statement to be executed if a BOOLEAN expression evaluates to TRUE. If FALSE, either no statement (empty statement) or the statement following the symbol ELSE is executed. This is also known as the Unary and Binary selection.

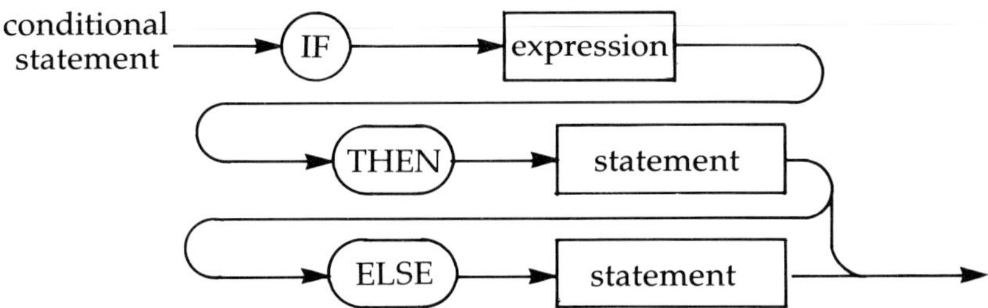

Note the keyword ELSE is optional but THEN is required.

```
If condition = TRUE THEN Statement1;
```

The THEN-statement may be compound:

```
IF condition
   THEN BEGIN
          statement1;
          statement2;
          statement3;
     END;
```

Do note that the semicolons separate simple statements within the compound statement but do not appear within the IF statement itself.

Consider the problem of reading-in two numbers from the keyboard. Whatever the order in which they are typed in they will be displayed in ascending order.

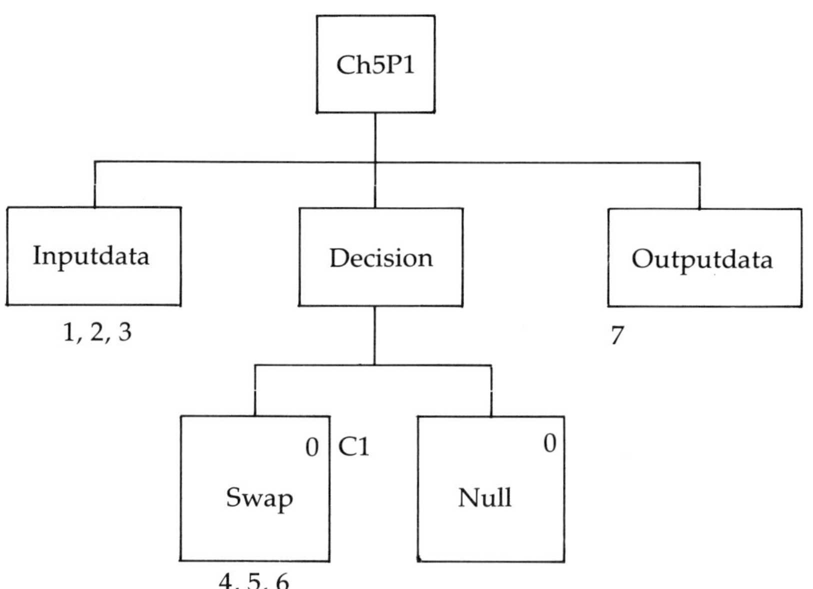

Functions	Conditions
1. User prompt, 'Input two numbers'	C1 if X is greater than Y select procedure Swap
2. Read X	
3. READ Y	
4. Assign X to Temporary	

5. Assign Y to X

6. Assign Temporary to Y

7. Write to screen 'Numbers in ascending order', Numbers

The procedures Inputdata, Decision and Outputdata are called sequentially. The procedure Decision holds the conditional statement that controls the selection, or not, of the procedure Swap. Procedures that are selected conditionally are indicated by a superscript of zero. For Swap to be selected the condition C1 must be TRUE. Control is not given to Outputdata until Decision has been completed. Note the absence of GOTO, as there is intrinsic control.

```
PROGRAM Ch5P1 (INPUT, OUTPUT);

(* Unary selection *)

(* Program reads in two numbers and outputs them in order *)

VAR X, Y, Temporary: INTEGER;

PROCEDURE Inputdata;

BEGIN

        WRITELN('Input two numbers');

        READLN(X);

        READLN(Y)

END;

PROCEDURE Decision;

        PROCEDURE Swap;
        (*Procedure to swap data values*)
        BEGIN

                Temporary := X;

                X := Y;

                Y := Temporary
        END;

BEGIN

        IF X < Y THEN

        Swap

END;
```

```
PROCEDURE Outputdata;
BEGIN
        WRITELN('Numbers in ascending order', X, Y)
END;
```

```
BEGIN
        Inputdata;
        Decision;
        Outputdata
END.
```

As we have seen before it is possible to produce more efficient code but do recall we are trying to demonstrate the principles of structured programming.

```
PROGRAM Ch5P2 (INPUT, OUTPUT);
(* Unary selection *)
(* Program reads in two numbers and outputs them in order *)
VAR X, Y, Temporary: INTEGER;
BEGIN
        WRITELN('Input two numbers');
        READLN(X);
        READLN(Y)
        IF X > Y THEN
             BEGIN
                Temporary := X;
                X := Y;
                Y := Temporary
             END;
        WRITELN('Numbers in ascending order', X, Y)
END.
```

The structured diagram still applies in principle.

5.5 BINARY SELECTION – THE IF...THEN...ELSE STATEMENT

In this case the full syntax diagram is implemented. If the expression is TRUE, statement1 is executed; if FALSE, statement2 is executed.

The THEN-statement and ELSE-statement may be compound:

```
IF condition
    THEN
        BEGIN
            statement1;
            statement2;
            statement3
        END
    ELSE
        BEGIN
            statement4;
            statement5;
            statement6
        END
```

Again, note the use of semicolons. IF statements may be nested, but an apparent ambiguity can arise if each is not paired with an ELSE, eg

```
A := 0;
IF B > 1 THEN IF B < 10 THEN A := 1 ELSE A := –1;
```

This statement, whilst syntactically correct, appears to be semantically ambiguous. The ELSE could perhaps refer to the first THEN or the second THEN. If the first condition fails, ie if B is not greater than one, the value of A could become –1 or remain at zero, depending on the interpretation of the statement. Pascal resolves this 'dangling else' by always pairing an ELSE with the nearest preceding unpaired THEN. Hence

```
A := 0;
IF B > 1 THEN
    BEGIN
        IF B < 10
```

```
                THEN A := 1
        ELSE
                A := –1
    END;
```

The ELSE is paired with the inner IF and thus is never reached if the first test fails. If B is greater than one is FALSE, A remains at zero.

A simplified structure diagram would be:

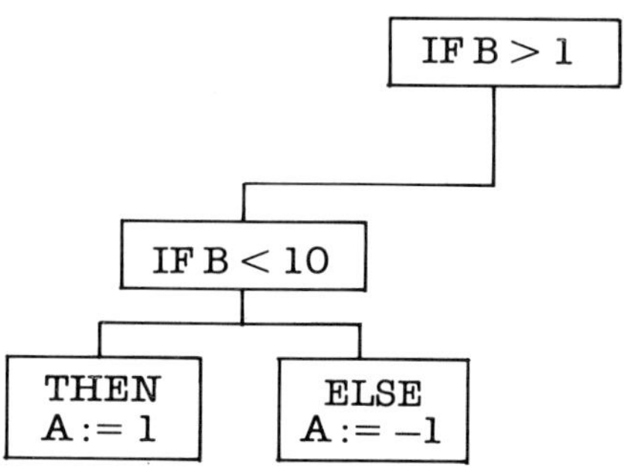

Let us modify the previous program to indicate to the user whether or not the numbers were typed in correctly in the first instance.

Functions

1. User prompt, 'Input two numbers'
2. Read X
3. Ready Y
4. Assign X to Temporary
5. Assign Y to X
6. Assign Temporary to Y
7. User prompt 'The numbers were in order'
8. Write to screen 'Numbers in ascending order', Numbers

Conditions

C1 If X is greater than Y select procedure Swap

C2 If X is not greater than Y select Noswap

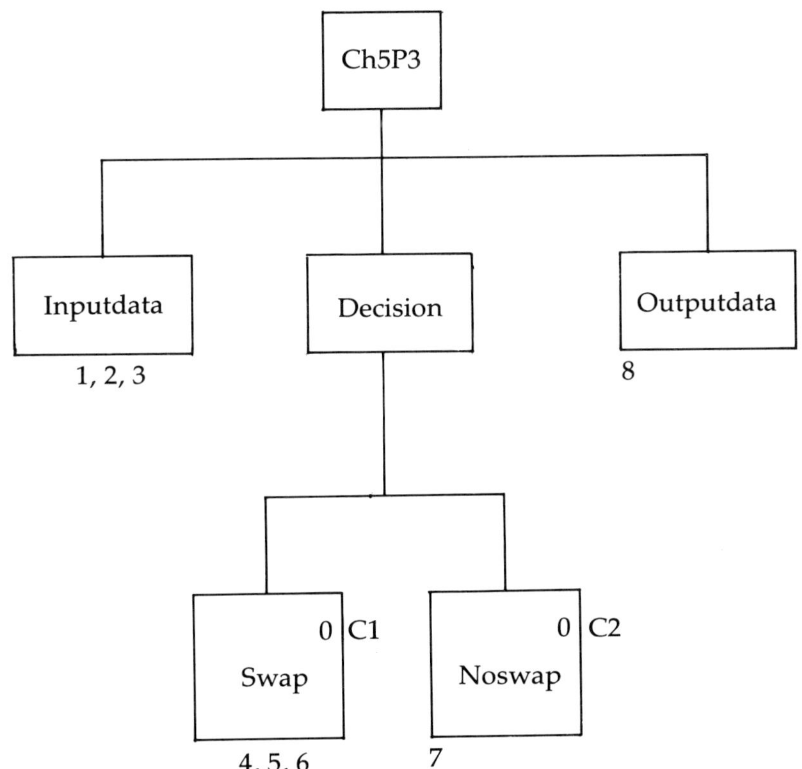


```
PROGRAM Ch5P3 (INPUT, OUTPUT);
(* Binary selection *)
VAR X, Y, Temporary: INTEGER;
```

```
PROCEDURE Inputdata;
BEGIN
        WRITELN('Input two numbers');
        READLN(X);
        READLN(Y)
END;
```

```
PROCEDURE Decision;

    PROCEDURE Swap;
    BEGIN
        WRITELN('The numbers were not in order');
        Temporary := X;
        X := Y;
        Y := Temporary
    END;

    PROCEDURE Noswap;
    BEGIN
        WRITELN('The numbers were in order')
    END;

BEGIN
    IF X > Y THEN
        Swap
    ELSE
        Noswap
END;

PROCEDURE Outputdata;
BEGIN
    WRITELN('Numbers in ascending order', X, Y)
END;

BEGIN
    Inputdata;
    Decision;
    Outputdata
END.
```

Again we can code in a more efficient manner:

```
PROGRAM Ch5P4 (INPUT, OUPUT);
(* Binary selection *)
VAR X, Y, Temporary: INTEGER;
```

```
BEGIN
    WRITELN('Input two numbers');
    READLN(X);
    READLN(Y)
    IF X > Y
    THEN
        BEGIN
            WRITELN('The numbers were not in order');
            Temporary := X;
            X := Y;
            Y := Temporary
        END
    ELSE
        WRITELN('The numbers were in order');
    WRITELN('Numbers in ascending order', X, Y)
END.
```

5.6 MULTIPLE SELECTION – The CASE Statement

While the IF statement allows for the conditional execution based on the two possible outcomes of a BOOLEAN expression, the CASE statement allows for multiple outcomes and multiple possible actions.

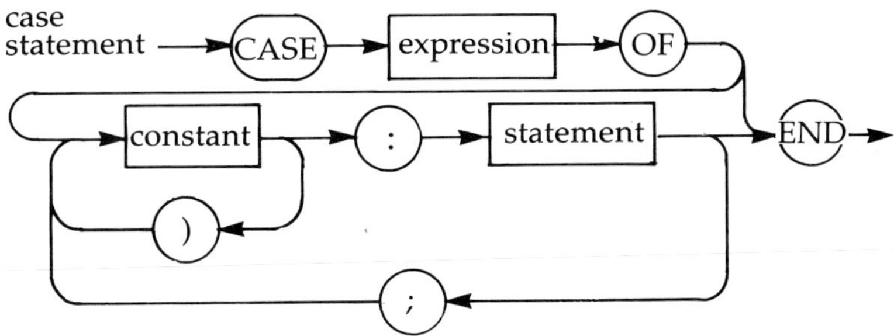

The CASE index is an expression which evaluates to an ordinal (non-REAL) value. The CASE constants must be of the same type as the CASE index. After its evaluation, the CASE index must be equal to one of the constants. The statement following that constant is then executed.

Usually the CASE index is a variable identifier. In the above example if the CASE index is not zero, one or two, then the entire CASE statement is undefined, its outcome will be unpredictable. Your program will almost certainly crash!

Upon completion of the selected statement, control is passed to END.

Consider the problem of the user typing a number 0 to 2 inclusive. The program will then convert the numeric character to the alphabetic equivalent, ie typing in 0 will produce the result 'zero'.

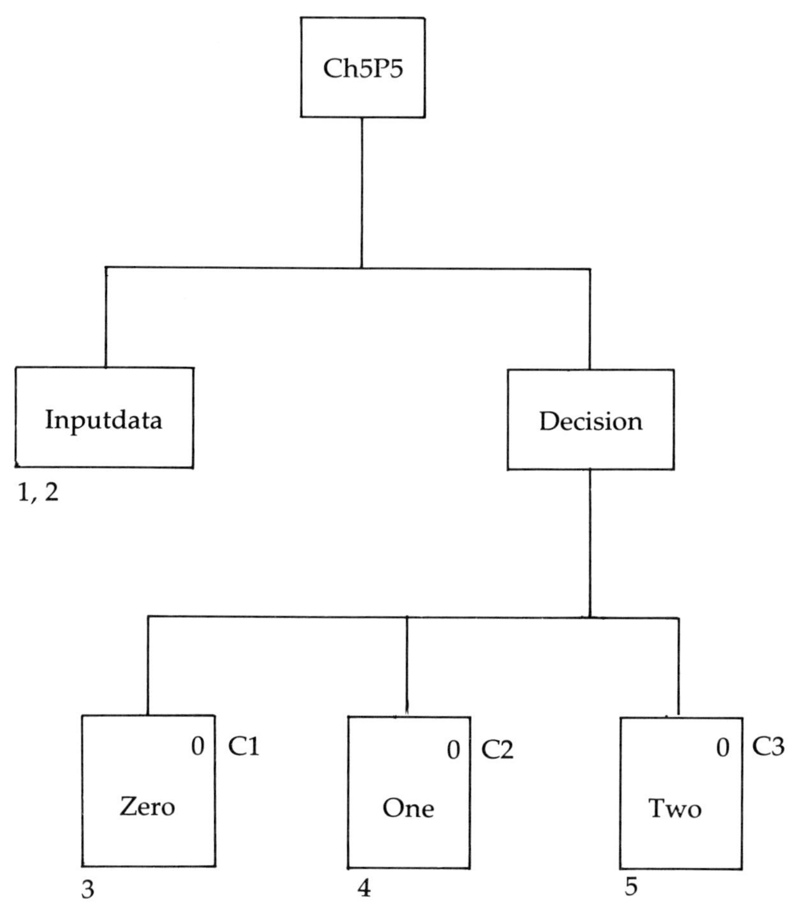

Functions	Conditions
1. User prompt 'Input a number'	C1 Number equals 0
2. Read number	C2 Number equals 1
3. Display 'Zero'	C3 Number equals 2
4. Display 'One'	
5. Display 'Two'	

```
PROGRAM Ch5P5 (INPUT, OUPUT);
(* Case selection *)
VAR Number : INTEGER;

    PROCEDURE Inputdata;
    BEGIN
        WRITELN('Input a number');
        READLN(Number)
    END;

    PROCEDURE Decision;
        PROCEDURE Zero;
        BEGIN
            WRITELN('Zero')
        END;

        PROCEDURE One;
        BEGIN
            WRITELN('One')
        END;

        PROCEDURE Two;
        BEGIN
            WRITELN('Two')
        END;

    BEGIN
        CASE Number OF
            0 : Zero;
            1 : One;
            2 : Two;
        END;
    END;
```

```
BEGIN
        Inputdata;
        Decision
END.
```

In a format that is not procedure based we have:

```
PROGRAM Ch5P6 (INPUT, OUTPUT);
(* Case selection *)
VAR Number : INTEGER;
BEGIN
        WRITELN ('Input a number');
        READLN(Number)
        CASE Number OF
                0 : WRITELN('Zero');
                1 : WRITELN('One');
                2 : WRITELN('Two');
END.
```

So far we have nested our procedures. Let's consider what we can do if the number and/or size of our procedure increases. Modifying the above program to include the digits 0 to 4 inclusive gives us the following SSI diagram:

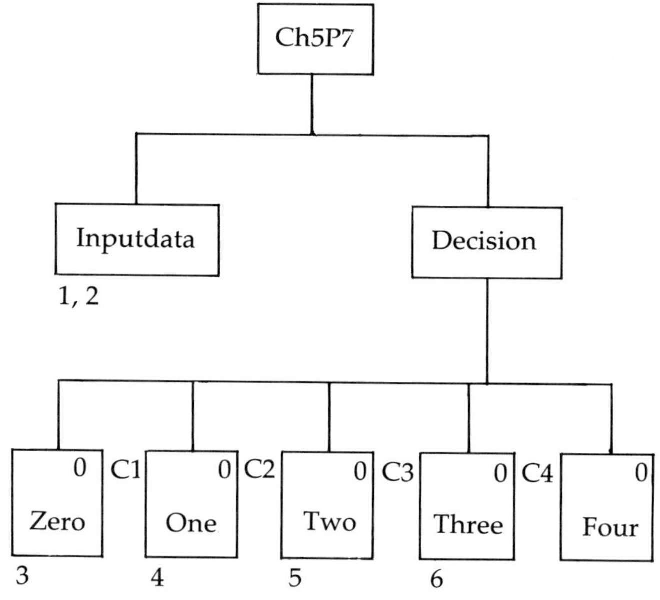

Functions	*Conditions*
1. User prompt 'Input a number'	C1 Number equals 0
2. Read Number	C2 Number equals 1
3. Display 'Zero'	C3 Number equals 2
4. Display 'One'	C4 Number equals 3
5. Display 'Two'	C5 Number equals 4
6. Display 'Three'	
7. Display 'Four'	

This can be implemented in two ways. Program Ch5P7 gives us a rather big procedure called Decision. Extrapolate further with even more digits with more instructions per procedure and we have a problem! We can overcome this by taking the procedures Zero, One, Two, Three and Four out of the procedure Decision as we have done in program Ch5P8. It is important to note that the structured diagram still applies. We can have our called procedures anywhere in the program with the proviso that we can only backward reference. It is possible to forward reference but this will be considered in Chapter 15.

```
PROGRAM Ch5P7 (INPUT, OUTPUT);
(* Case selection *)
VAR Number : INTEGER;


  PROCEDURE Inputdata; (* As before *)

PROCEDURE Decision;
            PROCEDURE Zero;
            BEGIN
               WRITELN('Zero)
            END;

            PROCEDURE One;
            BEGIN
               WRITELN('One')
            END;
```

```
        PROCEDURE Two;
        BEGIN
                WRITELN('Two')
        END;

        PROCEDURE Three;
        BEGIN
                WRITELN('Three')
        END;

        PROCEDURE Four;
        BEGIN
                WRITELN('Four')
        END;

BEGIN
        CASE Number OF
                0 : Zero;
                1 : One;
                2 : Two;
                3 : Three;
                4 : Four
        END;
END;

BEGIN
        Inputdata;
        Decision
END.
PROGRAM Ch5P8 (INPUT, OUTPUT);
(* Case selection *)
VAR Number : INTEGER;
PROCEDURE Inputdata; (* As before *)
```

```
PROCEDURE Zero;
BEGIN
    WRITELN('Zero')
END;
```

```
PROCEDURE One;
BEGIN
    WRITELN('One')
END;
```

```
PROCEDURE Two;
BEGIN
    WRITELN('Two')
END;
```

```
PROCEDURE Three;
BEGIN
    WRITELN('Three')
END;
```

```
PROCEDURE Four;
BEGIN
    WRITELN('Four')
END;
```

```
PROCEDURE Decision;
BEGIN
    CASE Number OF
        0 : Zero;
        1 : One;
        2 : Two;
        3 : Three;
        4 : Four
    END;
END;
```

```
BEGIN
        Inputdata;
        Decision
END.
```

5.7 SUMMARY

- 1. Selection statements allow the program to respond to different conditions.
- 2. The types of conditional statement are unary, binary and multiple.
- 3. Decisions are based on logical statements that can only be either TRUE or else FALSE, ie BOOLEAN expressions.
- 4. As well as relational operators BOOLEAN expressions can be written using the BOOLEAN operators AND, OR and NOT.
- 5. Conditionally selected procedures or code are diagrammatically represented with a superscript zero.
- 6. Procedures can be called from anywhere in the program as long as they are backward referenced. The structured diagrams still apply.

5.8 PROBLEMS

- 1. Program Ch5P1 allows the user to input two numbers and outputs them in order. Recall that relational operators can be applied to type CHAR. Modify this program to input two alphanumeric characters. Draw the associated structured diagram.
- 2. Similarly modify program Ch5p3 and draw the associated diagram. Do recall that the CASE index operates on ordinal (non-REAL) values. Produce the code from your diagram.
- 3. Modify the above diagram and program to allow the input to be a, b, c, d or e. Again the ouput being A, B, C, D or E accordingly.
- 4. Draw the structured diagram for a program that will prompt the user to enter lower case a or b or c. The output will be correspondingly A, B or C.

6 Iteration

6.1 INTRODUCTION

Repetitive statements specify repetition of an operation based on a certain condition or conditions. The repetitive statements are FOR, REPEAT and WHILE. The WITH statement will be considered in Chapter 10 on Records and Files. As we have seen before, structured statements can be classified:

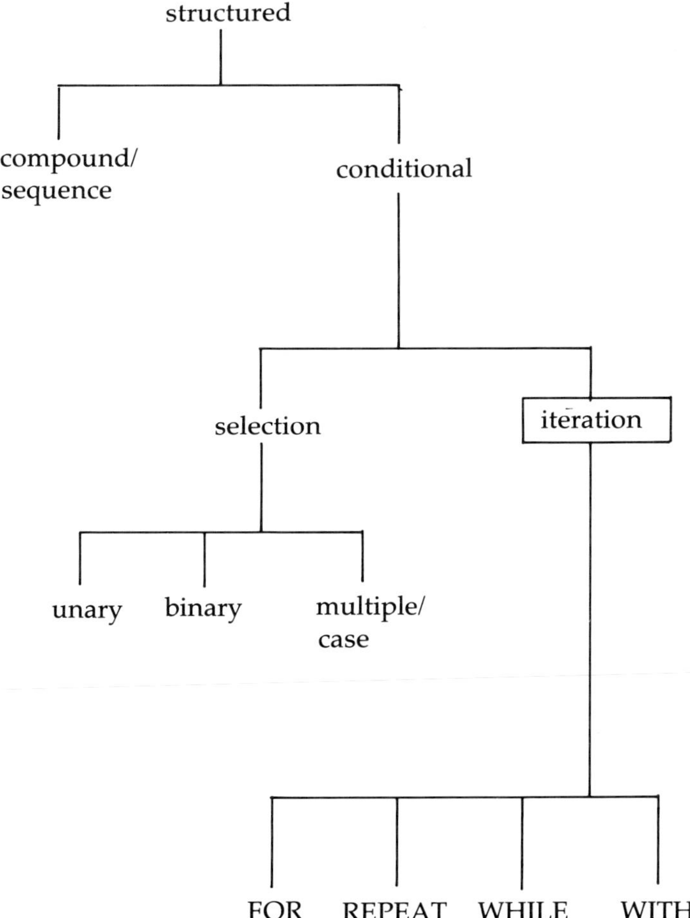

Consider now the problem of reading-in and adding three numbers. The output is then displayed on the screen. This can be done sequentially:

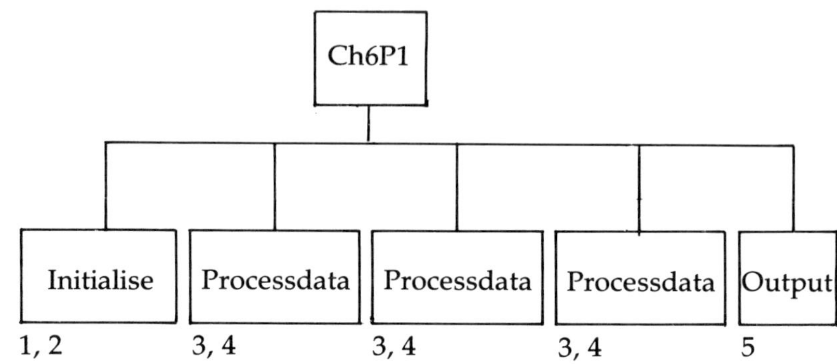

Functions

1. Initialise Sum to 0
2. User prompt 'Input three numbers'
3. Read Next
4. Sum := Sum + Next
5. Display Sum

Coding the structured diagram we could have:

```
PROGRAM Ch6P1 (INPUT, OUTPUT);

(* Iteration by multiple procedure calls *)

VAR Next, SUM : REAL;
```

```
PROCEDURE Initialise;
BEGIN
        Sum := 0;
        WRITELN('Input three numbers')
END;
```

```
PROCEDURE Add;
BEGIN
        READLN(Next);
        Sum := Sum + Next
END;
```

```
 PROCEDURE Outputdata;
 BEGIN
        WRITELN('Sum', Sum: 6 :2)
 END;
BEGIN
        Initialise;
        Add;
        Add;
        Add;
        Outputdata
END.
```

Our procedure Add is written once and called many times but what if there are a hundred numbers?

Referring again to our universal program, let us refine our model a little further. Typically our program will preset any conditions, process data and then output data whilst performing any terminating operations.

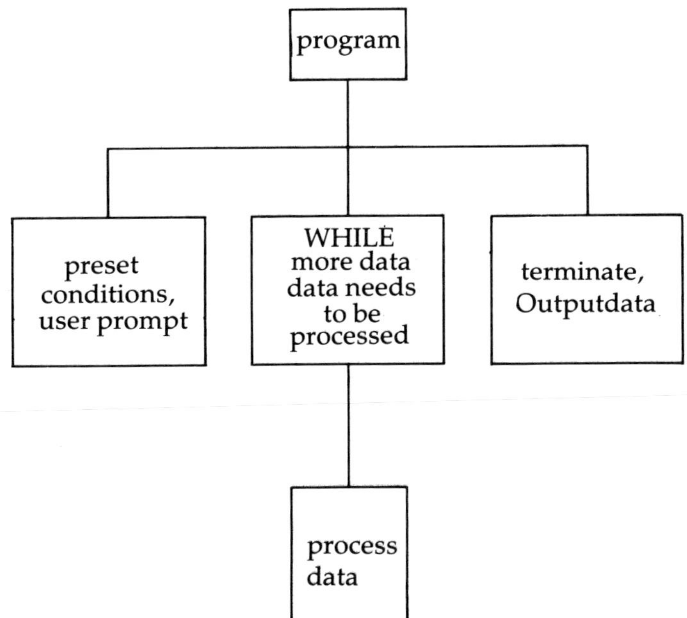

6.2 THE FOR STATEMENT

The FOR statement specifies repetitive execution of a section of code with the number of iterations determined by a control variable. The control variable is incremented or decremented by one step after each iteration. In the first format, the control variable is assigned the initial value and incremented to SUCC(control-variable) after each iteration of the block of code. The loop is exited when the control variable exceeds the final value. In the second format, the control variable is assigned the initial value and decremented to PRED(control-variable) after each iteration. The loop is exited when the control variable is less than the final value.

The control variable is a variable identifier and must be of the ordinal type eg INTEGER. Further it has to be declared as a local variable ie within the procedure that uses it.

FOR statement

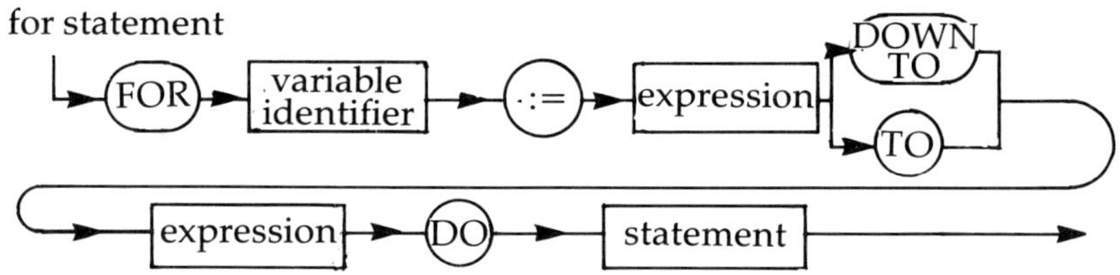

The FOR statement is used in situations where no programming exceptions occur – typically these would be mathematical problems.

Reconsidering our problem of adding three numbers we have:

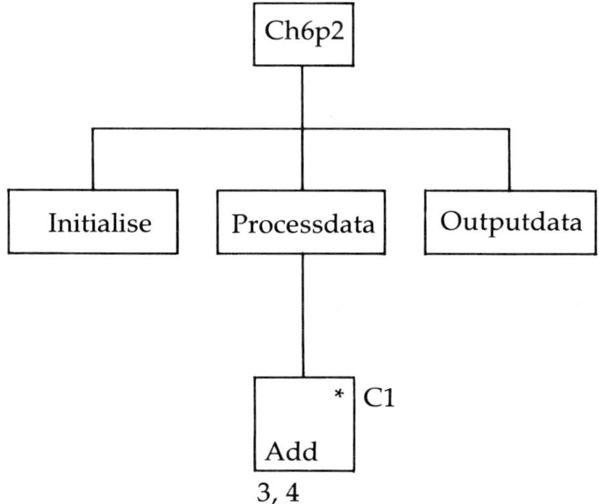

Functions	*Conditions*
1. Initialise Sum to 0	C1 For Count 1 To 3
2. User prompt 'Input three numbers'	
3. Read Next	
4. Sum := Sum + Next	
5. Display Sum	

The main program Ch6P2 sequentially calls Initialise, Processdata and then Outputdata. The procedure Processdata holds the iteration statement that controls the repeated use of the procedure Add. The iterated component, Add, is signified by an asterisk in conjunction with a condition flag. The iteration depends upon the condition specified. Again, note that control is not given to Outputdata until Processdata has been completed – GOTOs have not been used due to this intrinsic control. Do note, the functions list is exactly the same as that for program Ch6P1.

```
PROGRAM Ch6P2 (INPUT, OUTPUT);
(* The FOR statement, predefined iteration *)
VAR Next, Sum : REAL;

  PROCEDURE Initialise;
  BEGIN
        Sum := 0;
        WRITELN('Input three numbers')
  END;

  PROCEDURE Processdata;
  VAR Count : INTEGER;

        PROCEDURE Add ;
        BEGIN
              READ(Next);
              Sum := Sum + Next
        END;
```

```
BEGIN
        FOR Count := 1 TO 3 DO
              Add
END;
```

```
PROCEDURE Outputdata;
BEGIN
        WRITELN('Sum', Sum :6 :2)
END;
```

```
BEGIN
        Initialise;
        Processdata;
        Outputdata
END.
```

Do note the variable count has been declared as a local variable – local to the procedure Processdata that uses it.

This can be rewritten in a procedureless form as follows:

```
PROGRAM Ch6P3 (INPUT, OUTPUT);
(* The FOR statement, predefined iteration *)
VAR Next, Sum : REAL;
        Count     : INTEGER;
BEGIN
        Sum := 0;
        WRITELN('Input three numbers')
        FOR Count := 1 TO 3 DO
        BEGIN
                READ(Next);
                Sum := Sum + Next
        END;
        WRITELN('Sum', Sum :6 :2)
END.
```

As before, the emphasis is on the principles. Once these are fully understood it is appropriate to consider more complex problems.

From our syntax diagram we can see that it is possible to count down to an expression as well as up to an expression. The program remains the same except that the condition C1 will be For Count 3 to 1.

```
REPEAT PROGRAM Ch6P4 (INPUT, OUTPUT);

VAR Next, Sum : REAL;

(* The FOR statement, DOWN TO, predefined iteration *)
```

```
PROCEDURE Initialise;
BEGIN
        Sum := 0
        WRITELN('Input three numbers')
END;
```

```
PROCEDURE Processdata;
VAR Count : INTEGER;

                PROCEDURE Add;
                BEGIN
                        READ(Next);
                        Sum := Sum + Next
                END;
```

```
BEGIN
        FOR Count := 3 DOWN TO 1 DO
        Add
END;
```

```
PROCEDURE Outputdata;
BEGIN
        WRITELN('Sum', Sum :6 :2)
END;
```

```
BEGIN
        Initialise;
        Processdata;
        Outputdata
END.
```

In order to have some user interaction it is possible to modify the program to allow the user to specify how many numbers are to be added. This is done by changing the second iteration expression to a variable, number in this case. In the Initialisation procedure the user is prompted to specify how many iterations.

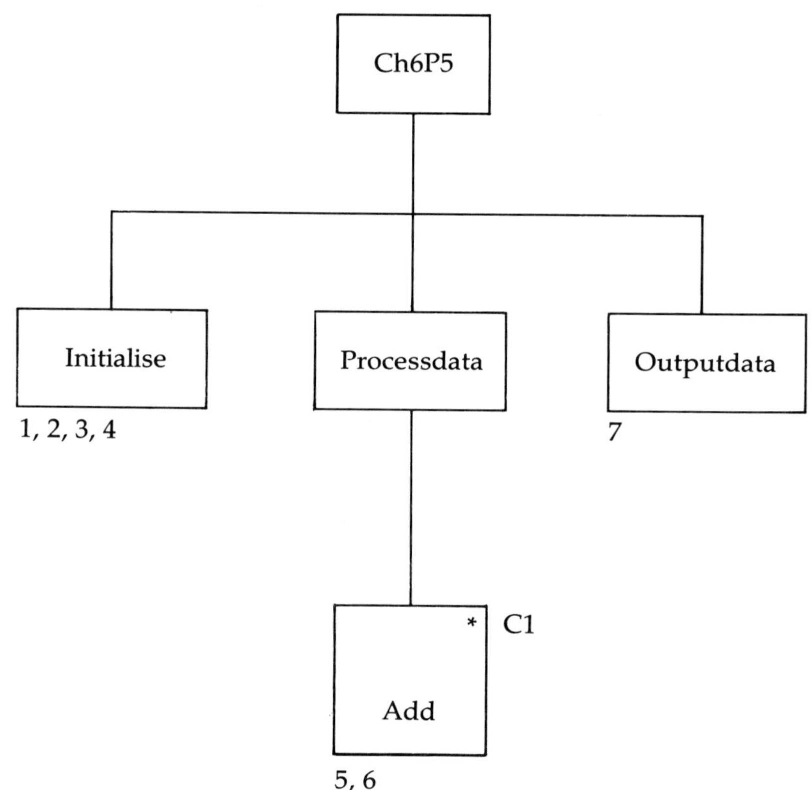

Functions

1. Initialise Sum to zero.
2. User prompt 'How many numbers ?'
3. Read Number

Conditions

C1 For Count
one to number

4. User prompt 'Input your numbers'
5. Read Next
6. Sum := Sum + Next
7. Display Sum

The code for the structured diagram is:

```
PROGRAM Ch6P5 (INPUT, OUTPUT);
(* The FOR statement, user defined iteration *)
VAR Next, Sum, Number : REAL;

PROCEDURE Initialise;
BEGIN
        SUM := 0
        WRITELN('How many numbers ?');
        READLN(Number);
        WRITELN('Input your numbers')
END;

PROCEDURE Processdata;
VAR Count : INTEGER;

        PROCEDURE Add;
        BEGIN
                READ(Next);
                Sum := Sum + Next
        END;

BEGIN
        FOR Count := 1 TO Number DO
        Add
END;

PROCEDURE Outputdata;
BEGIN
        WRITELN('Sum', Sum :6 :2)
END;
```

```
BEGIN
        Inputdata;
        Processdata;
        Outputdata;
END.
```

6.3 THE REPEAT STATEMENT

It may be that the user does not known how many numbers are to be counted. In this case the number of iterations cannot be specified in advance. In such a case the REPEAT statement provides this facility. The REPEAT statement specifies repetitive execution of a block of code until an expression becomes TRUE. The condition is evaluated after each iteration. Iteration will stop when the condition is TRUE. The REPEAT sequence is executed at least once.

The syntax diagram for the REPEAT statement is:

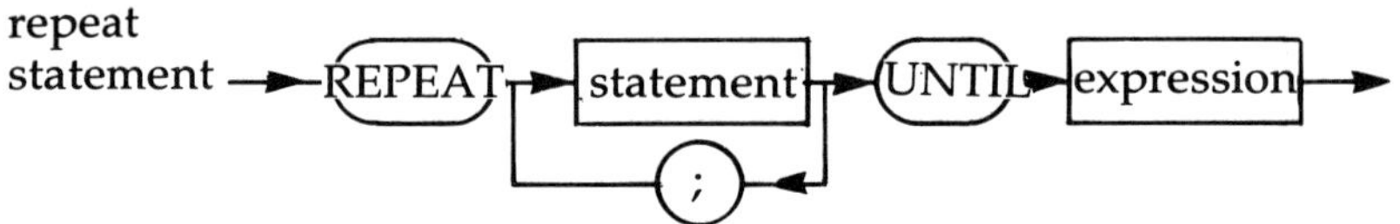

Reconsidering our problem of adding numbers we have the following design: The program will be terminated by data input of the negative value. Note, the variable Next must be initialised.

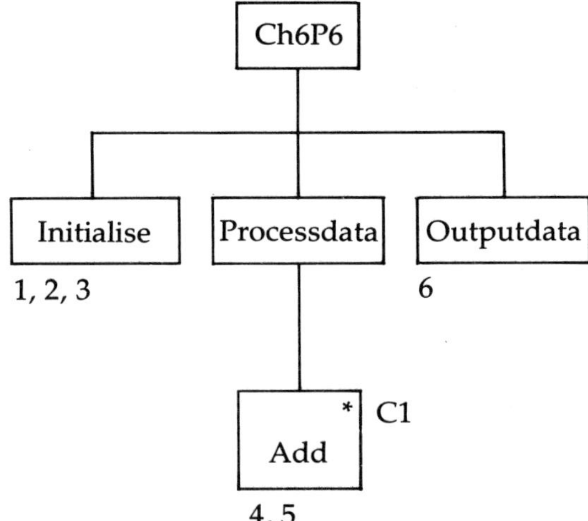

Functions	*Condition*
1. Initialise Sum to 0	C1 Repeat until Next zero
2. Initialise Next to 0	
3. User prompt 'Input your numbers, a negative number to terminate'	
4. Sum := Sum + Next	
5. Read Next	
6. Display Sum	

The code for the diagram is:

```
PROGRAM Ch6P6 (INPUT, OUTPUT);

(* The REPEAT statement *)

VAR Next, Sum, : REAL;
```

```
PROCEDURE Initialise;
BEGIN
        Sum := 0;
        Next := 0;
        WRITELN('Input your numbers')
END;
```

```
PROCEDURE Processdata;
        PROCEDURE Add;
        BEGIN
                Sum := Sum + Next;
                READ(Next)
        END;

BEGIN
        REPEAT Add UNTIL Next < 0
END;
```

```
PROCEDURE Outputdata;
BEGIN
        WRITELN('Sum', Sum :6 :2)
END;
```

```
BEGIN
        Inputdata;
        Processdata;
        Outputdata
END.
```

6.4 THE WHILE STATEMENT

The WHILE statement specifies iteration of a sequence while a condition is TRUE. It is important to note that, unlike REPEAT, the expression is evaluated before each iteration. If the expression is FALSE initially, the DO statement is not executed at all.

The syntax diagram for the WHILE statement is:

Employing the WHILE statement for our control structure means that we must modify our structured diagram slightly. The value of Next is not initialised, as such, but it is assigned a value by the user.

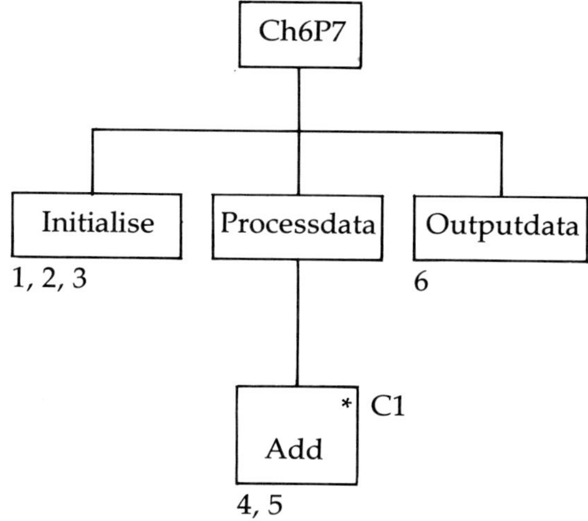

Functions

1. Initialise Sum to zero
2. Read Next
3. User prompt 'Input your numbers, a negative number to terminate'
4. Sum := Sum + Next
5. Read Next
6. Display Sum

Conditions

C1 While Next

zero

The associated code is:

```
PROGRAM Ch6P7 (INPUT, OUTPUT);

VAR Next, Sum, : REAL;

(* The WHILE statement *)
```

```
PROCEDURE Initialise;
BEGIN
        Sum := 0;
        READLN(Next)
        WRITELN('Input your numbers');
END;
```

```
PROCEDURE Processdata;
        PROCEDURE Add;
        BEGIN
                Sum := Sum + Next;
                READ(Next)
        END;

BEGIN
        WHILE NEXT ® O DO Add
END;
```

```
PROCEDURE Outputdata;
BEGIN
    WRITELN('Sum', Sum :6 :2)
END;
```

```
BEGIN
    Inputdata;
    Processdata;
    Outputdata
END.
```

6.5 THE READ AHEAD RULE

An important aspect of the iteration statements REPEAT and WHILE is the read ahead rule. Let's spend some time examining the importance of this rule, and the consequences of getting it wrong.

6.5.1 Simple Program Testing

One of the best ways to learn is from your mistakes. Things once taken for granted are not easily forgotton after the sting of failure.

A simple aid to either understanding a difficult program design or to find out why part of your program does not work is to perform a 'trace' or 'dry run'. This entails stepping through the code or design exactly as the computer would do so. In order to do this it is necessary to tabulate the variables and modify them as a consequence of the operation of the code. It is a laborious process and hence only performed on small sections of code.

We will be looking at program development and testing in some detail in Chapter 16.

The test data employed should be simple but efficient for the testing purpose. Selective use of good test data items is better than large quantities of poorly selected test data.

Test data 1	*Test data 2*
1	–1 to terminate
2	expected result 0
3	
–1 to terminate	
expected result 6	

6.5.2 The REPEAT Statement

Consider the REPEAT statement and the problem, as before, of adding a series of numbers with –1 to terminate. Using stripped-down structured diagrams we can perform a dry run.

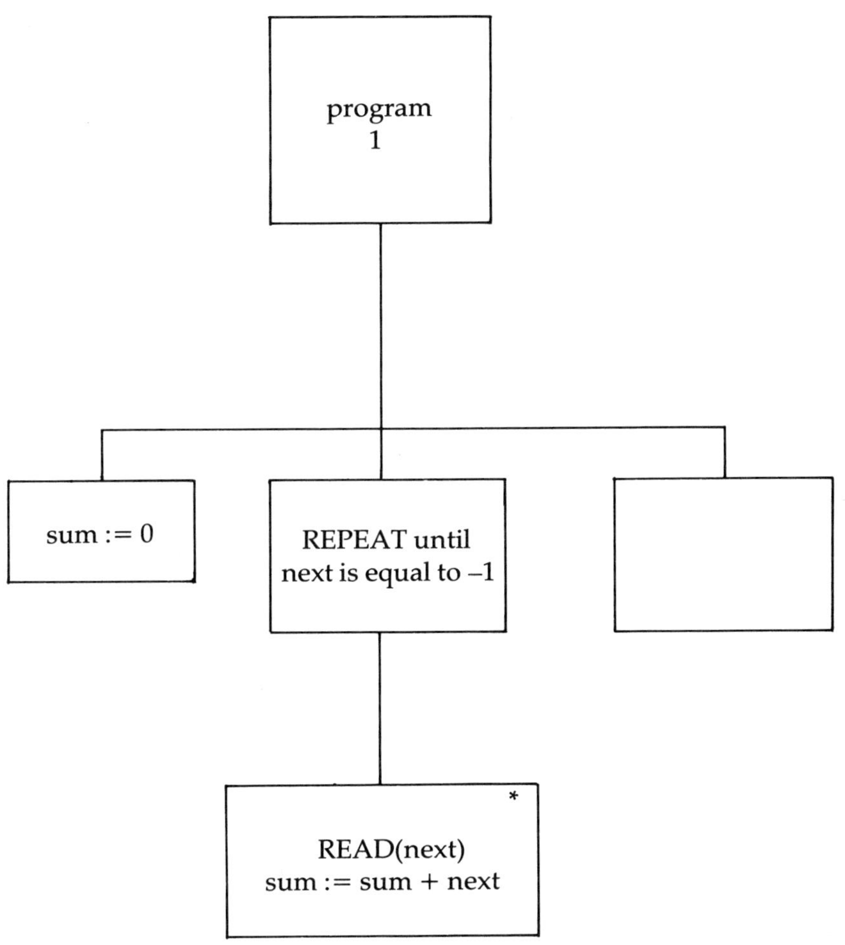

Test run 1

step	*statement*	*sum*	*next*	*comments*
1	sum := 0	0		initialise sum to 0

the first iteration is performed

step	*statement*	*sum*	*next*	*comments*
2	READ(next)	0	1	test item 1 is read
3	sum := sum + next	1	1	arithmetic operation

next is tested against the condition –1, iteration performed

4	READ(next)	1	2	test item 2 is read
5	sum := sum + next	3	2	arithmetic operation

next is tested against the condition –1, iteration performed

6	READ(next)	3	3	test item 2 is read
7	sum := sum + next	6	3	arithmetic operation

next is tested against the condition –1, iteration performed

8	READ(next)	6	–1	test item –1 is read
9	sum := sum + next	5	–1	arithmetic operation

next is tested against the condition –1, terminate iteration

We have a problem, the result is five when it should have been six. The last data item as well as terminating the iteration has been added to the sum. We need test the code no further. In order to overcome this problem let's reverse the order of the two statements READ(next) and sum := sum + next. This is shown in program 2. We can then desk-check it to observe how it works and see the result.

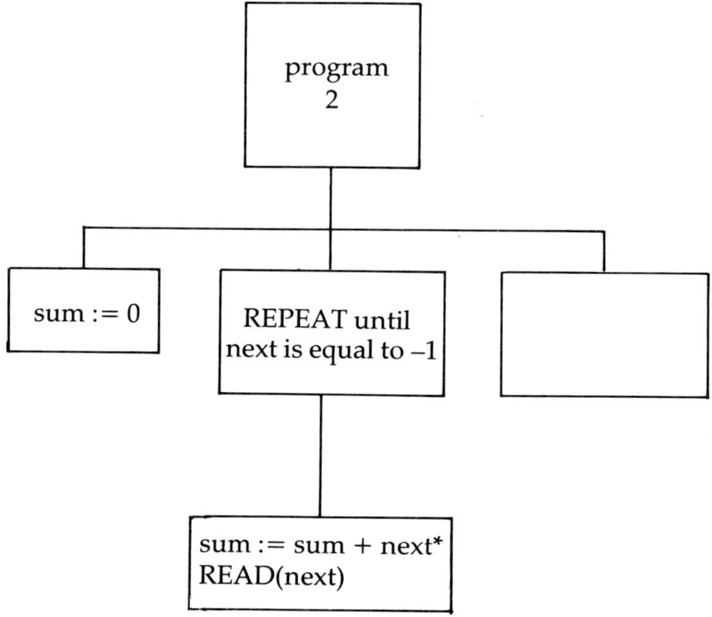

Test run 1

step	statement	sum	next	comments
1	sum := 0	0		initialise sum to 0

the first iteration is performed

2	sum := sum + next	0		

If the program were running it would give a run time error, next is not defined.

Perhaps the order of the two statements is still wrong. Let's revert to the original order, but include in the initialisation module the statement READ(next). This will ensure the variable next is defined.

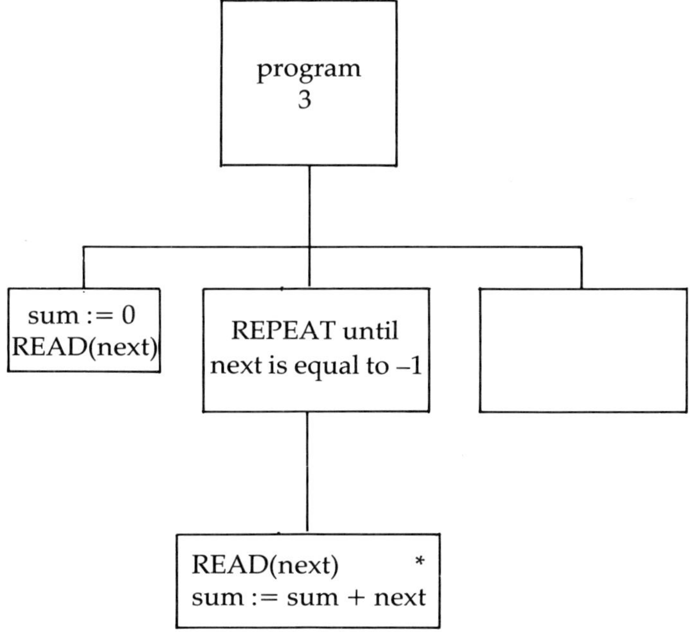

Test run 1

step	statement	sum	next	comments
1	sum := 0	0		initialise sum to 0
2	READ(next)	0	1	test item 1 is read

the first iteration is performed

3	READ(next)	0	2	test item 2 is read
4	sum := sum + next	2	2	arithmetic operation

next is tested against the condition –1, iteration performed

5	READ(next)	1	3	test item 2 is read
6	sum := sum + next	4	3	arithmetic operation

next is tested against the condition –1, iteration performed

7	READ(next)	4	–1	test item 2 is read
8	sum := sum + next	4	–1	arithmetic operation

next is tested against the condition –1, terminate iteration

Again, a problem. We have overwritten the variable next. Therefore let's again reverse the order of the statements sum := sum + next and READ(next).

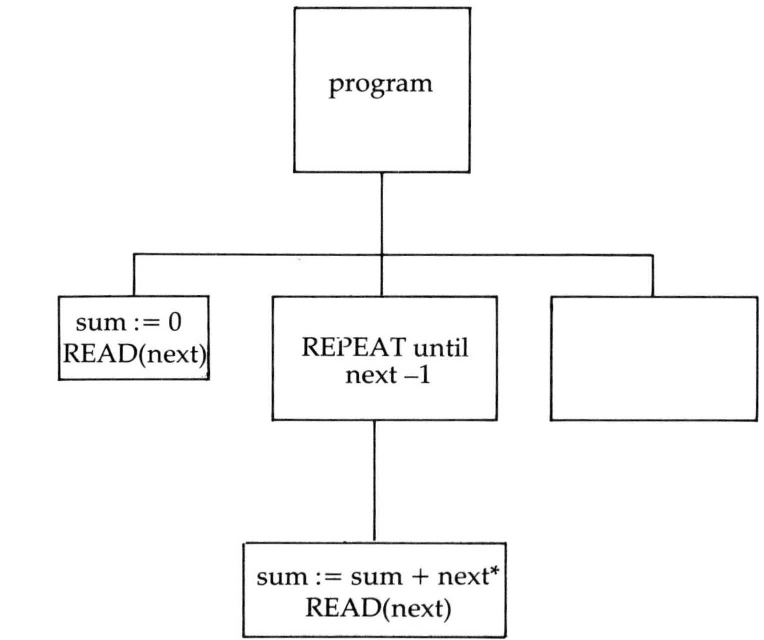

Test run 1

step	*statement*	*sum*	*next*	*comments*
1	sum := 0	0		initialise sum to 0
2	READ(next)	0	1	test item 1 is read
the first iteration is performed				
3	sum := sum + next	1	1	arithmetic operation
4	READ(next)	1	2	test item 2 is read
next is tested against the condition –1, iteration performed				
5	sum := sum + next	3	2	arithmetic operation
6	READ(next)	3	3	test item 3 is read
next is tested against the condition −1, iteration performed				
7	sum := sum + next	6	3	arithmetic operation
8	READ(next)	6	–1	test item 4 is read

next is tested against the condition –1, terminate iteration

At last, the correct answer. The variable next has been read ahead of its use in the control structure. This is sometimes called the 'READ AHEAD RULE'.

Alternatively we could initialise next to zero.

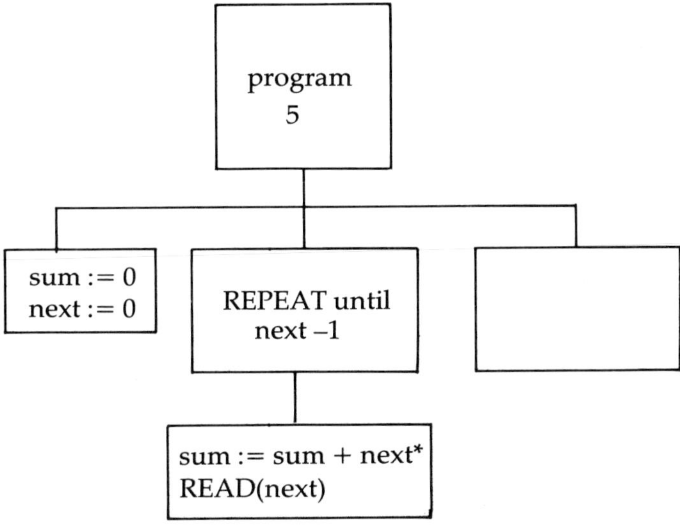

Test run 1

step	*statement*	*sum*	*next*	*comments*
1	sum := 0	0		initialise sum to 0
2	next := 0	0	0	initialise next to 0
the first iteration is performed				
3	sum := sum + next	0	0	arithmetic operation
4	READ(next)	0	1	test item 1 is read
next is tested against the condition –1, iteration performed				
5	sum := sum + next	1	1	arithmetic operation
6	READ(next)	1	2	test item 2 is read
next is tested against the condition –1, iteration performed				
7	sum := sum + next	3	2	arithmetic operation
8	READ(next)	3	3	test item 3 is read
next is tested against the condition –1, iteration performed				
9	sum := sum + next	6	3	arithmetic operation
10	READ(next)	6	–1	test item 4 is read

next is tested against the condition –1, terminate iteration

As an exercise perhaps you wish to perform dry runs using Test data 2. Also perform dry runs using the WHILE control statement. It is well worth the effort.

As a final point, WHILE is generally preferred to REPEAT – it's safer.

6.6 SUMMARY

- 1. Iteration is the repetitive execution of a task or series of tasks dependent on certain conditions.
- 2. Iteration statements are FOR, REPEAT, WHILE and WITH.
- 3. Iterated procedures or sections of code are diagrammatically represented by superscript *.

- 4. The control variable used in the FOR statement must be local to the procedure that uses it.
- 5. The REPEAT and WHILE statements do not require the number of iterations to be known in advance. The REPEAT sequence is executed at least once. It is possible that the WHILE sequence may not be executed at all.
- 6. Both REPEAT and WHILE statements employ the 'read ahead rule'.
- 7. Small programs or segments of programs can be tested by a trace or dry run.

6.7 PROBLEMS

- 1. A simple problem to start with, modify program Ch6p2 to add ten numbers.
- 2. Write a program that will prompt the user to enter the number of orders in, say, a warehouse. The prompt must then be to enter the number of each item and the associated unit price for each order. The total value of goods sold must be calculated and displayed on the screen.
- 3. Modify the above program to accommodate the user not knowing in advance the number of orders.
- 4. It is often said that you learn from mistakes. As you get more confident and friendly with your compiler it can be instructive to introduce a deliberate mistake in order to become familiar with the error diagnostics of the compiler. Certainly a common mistake is to not make the iteration variable local. Change one of the programs accordingly and observe the effect.

7 Structured Diagrams

7.1 INTRODUCTION

In this chapter we will further consolidate our knowledge of structured programming. In order to do this it is necessary to look again at the building blocks that are used.

Recall that our objective is to design programs which are:

- 1. easy to read
- 2. easy to understand
- 3. easy to modify

As we have previously mentioned, it is often the case that unreliable and expensive programs are produced which are delivered behind schedule.

Structured programming is a general term encompassing the many different methods used to construct programs. They range from simple guidelines to rigorous methods. However all, to various degrees, stress the need for a disciplined approach.

Advocates of structured programming claim that it is possible to reduce the introduction of mistakes and therefore the propagation of errors in the design and associated code. It is obviously possible to design at-the-keyboard but this method is restricted to small system problems.

Depending on the method used, with a structured design methodology the initial design process will take longer. However the potential benefits are worth considering. An important point to note, and a common criticism of structured programming, is its lack of efficiency. It is however, possible to have efficient code in the context of a structured environment and the principles can still be applied.

7.2 SSI DIAGRAMS

As far as we are concerned, all programming problems (algorithms) can be solved using only three programming statement types:

- 1. Sequence
- 2. Selection
- 3. Iteration

These three statements are arranged so that the flow of control passes from the top of the design to the bottom and back again.

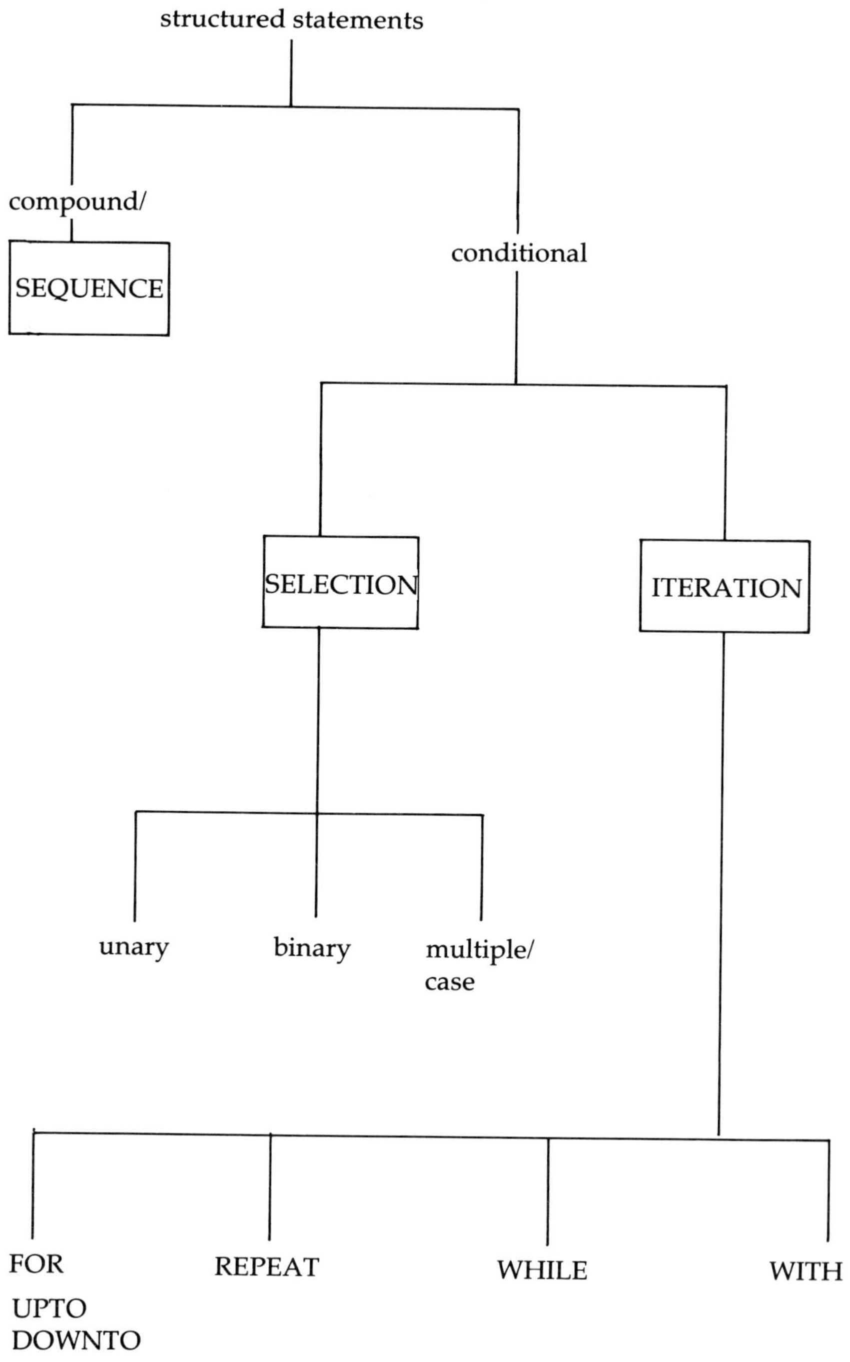

Unconditional jumps – GOTOs – can be avoided. Unconditional control constructs, if not strictly controlled, lead to complex code. Structured programming is sometimes called 'GOTOLESS' programming. The correct use of these control constructs ensures that return of the control is automatic thereby avoiding the explict use of GOTO. The use of GOTO should be restricted to the efficient recovery from an error. The aim is to have a method that will help us to produce logically correct designs that are independent of the target language. Coding then becomes the mechanical application of the target language programming rules. The vehicle for design should be the method not the keyboard. Consider now the constructs we are using.

7.3 SEQUENCE

The parent node consists of a sequence of child nodes.

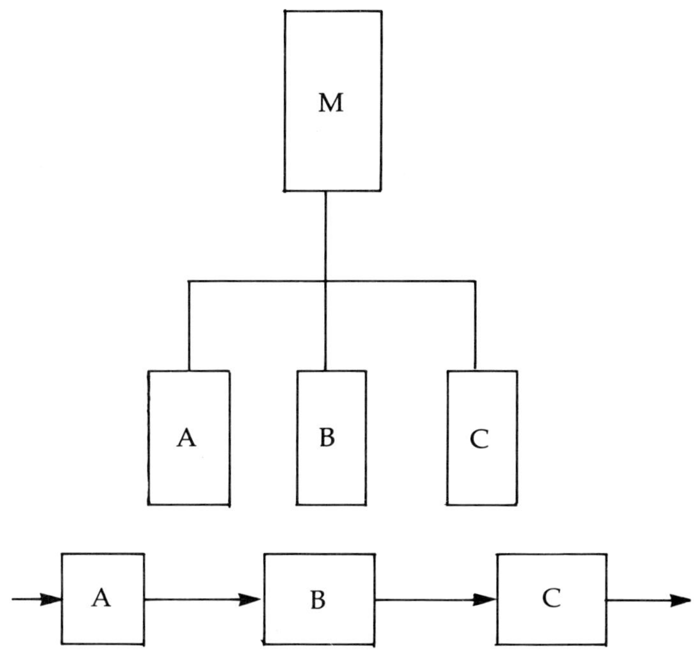

The unconditional sequential flow of control causes the statements to be executed in order from left to right. The control is passed from the root, M, to the first node A. When A has finished the execution of all its statements, it returns the control back to M. In this manner A, B and C are executed.

7.4 SELECTION

Selection allows a choice to be made between alternative courses of action. One of the choices may be to do nothing. However, regardless of which choice is made, program control should only pass to a single exit point, in this case the root node.

The parent node consists of a selection of child nodes. A is defined as a selection of A OR B OR C.

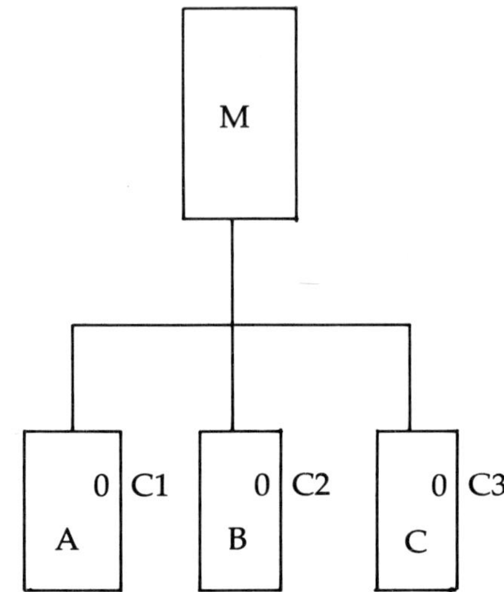

Conditional : condition (C1, C2, C3) TRUE to select the associated node.

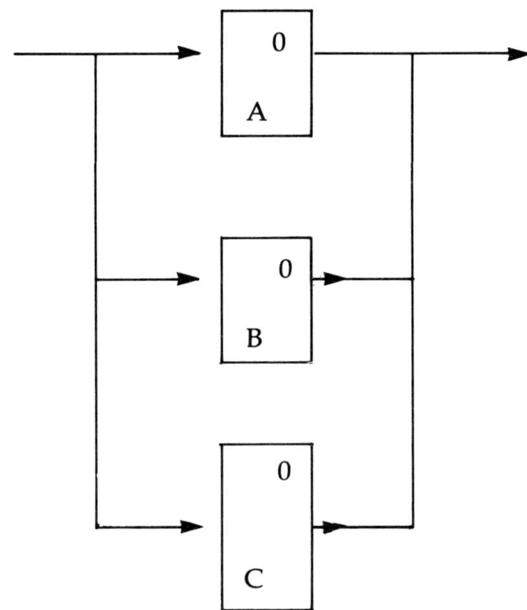

The control construct may be unary, binary or multiple selection (CASE).

7.5 ITERATION

The parent consists of a single child node. M is defined as an iteration of A, with zero or more occurrences.

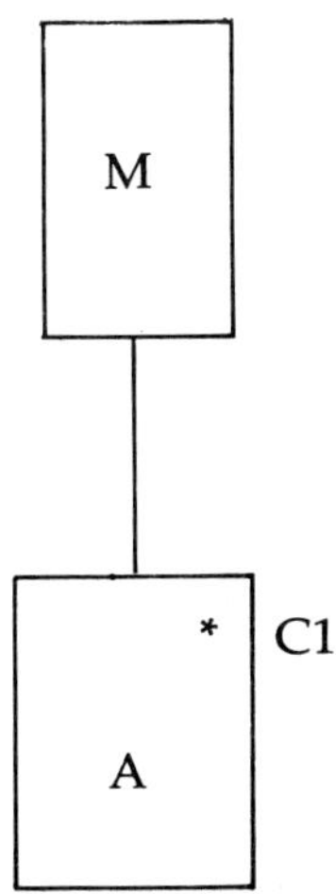

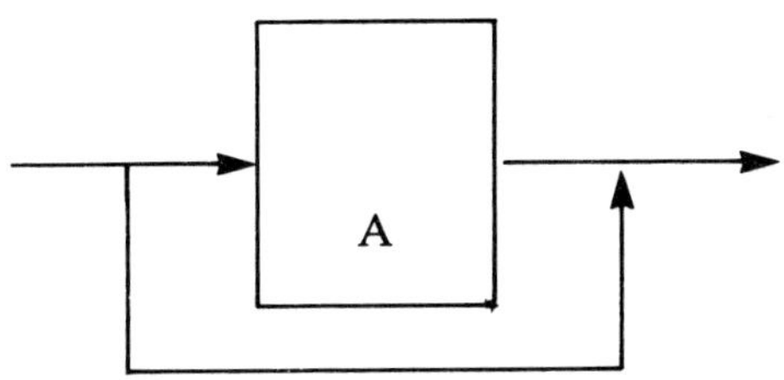

C1 determines the number of iterations.

The flow of control will depend on the actual iteration statement used.

The shape of the boxes will vary from author to author, also they are sometimes drawn sideways. It is not important. Try the different ways of representing your design.

7.6 SUMMARY

Let's have a look at the implementation of this.

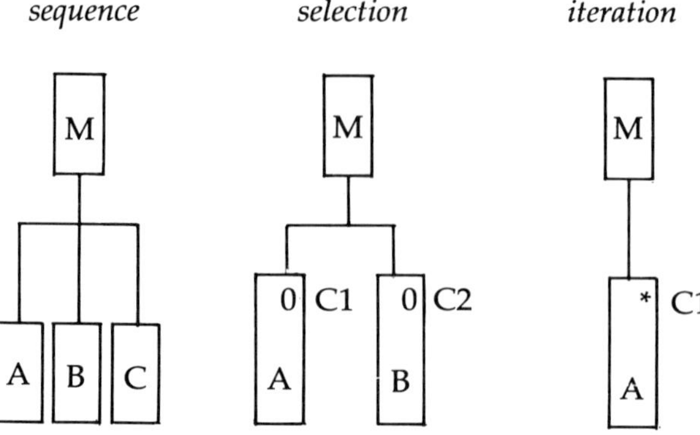

The relationship between the diagrams and code could be as follows :

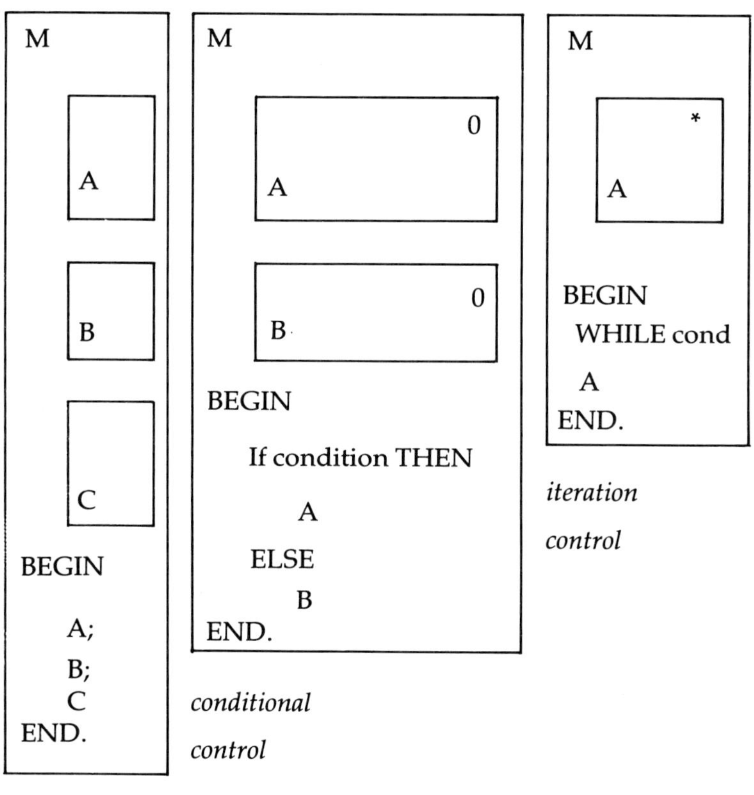

Do note that depending on the size of the modules A, B and C, they could be outside the main module M.

A

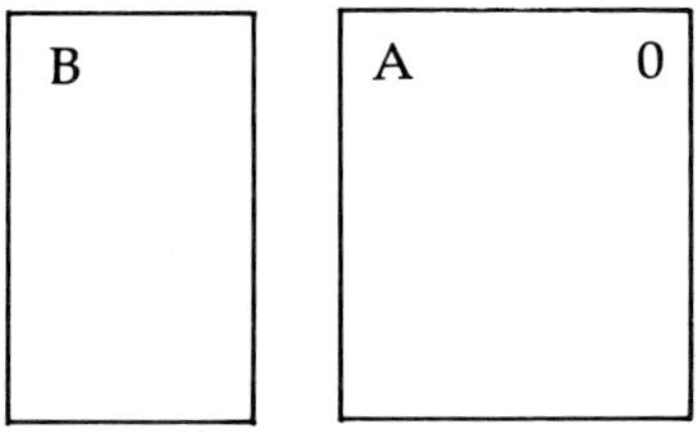

B

A 0

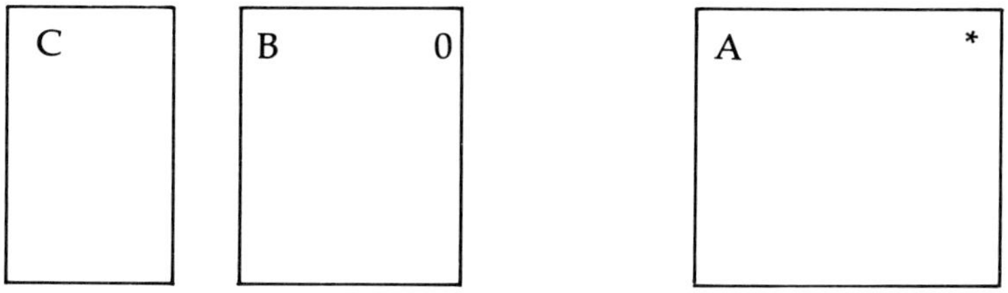

C

B 0

A *

```
M
BEGIN
      A;
      B;
      C
END.
```

```
M
  BEGIN
    IF condition THEN
       A
    ELSE
       B
  END.
```

```
M
 BEGIN
   WHILE cond
      A
 END.
```

7.7 RULES FOR DIAGRAM REPRESENTATION

There are three simple rules for constructing SSI diagrams:

– 1. A sequence component may only have other sequence components as siblings.

– 2. A selection component may only have other selection components as siblings.

– 3. An iterated component may have no siblings.

More simply the rules are:

– 1. No mixed siblings.

– 2. No iteration siblings.

Application of these simple rules will help to ensure good program design.

7.8 WORKED EXAMPLES

We will now put the rules into practice. It will at the moment seem a little abstract and mechanical. Chapter 8, on Structured Programs, will demonstrate the importance of what we learn here.

Example 1:

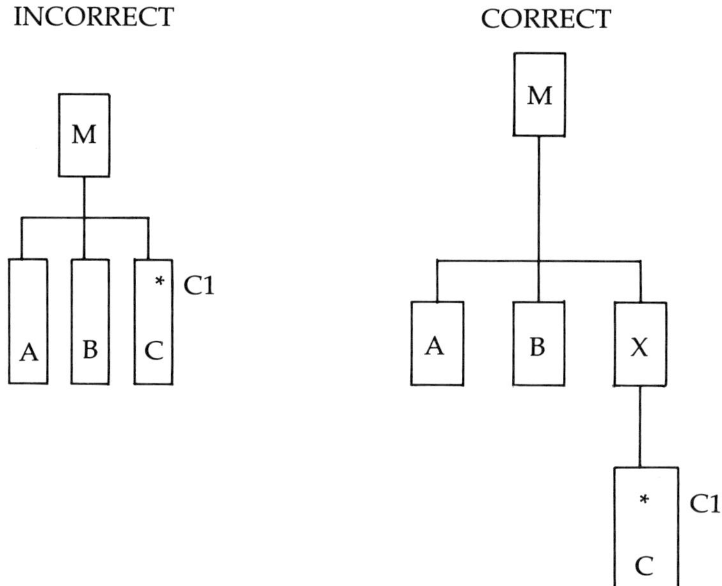

The rule 'no iteration siblings' has been broken. It is necessary to introduce another module, X, in order to offset the module C. In the correct design A, B and X represent a purely sequential control structure.

Example 2:

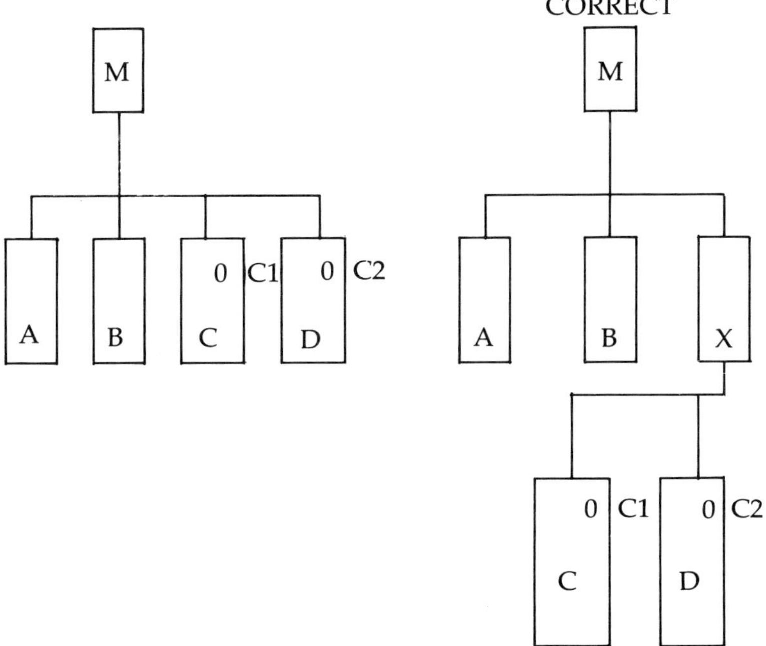

Here there are mixed siblings. The module X has to be introduced to ensure a purely sequential control structure.

Example 3:

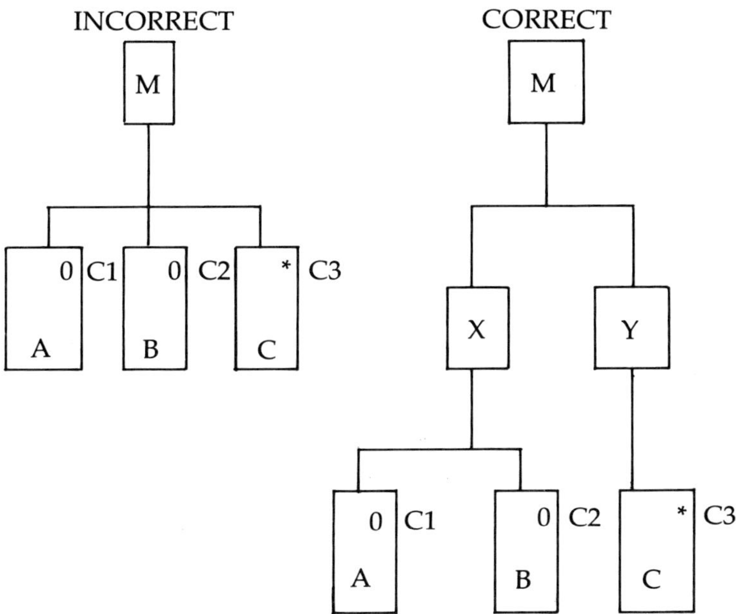

In the third example, the design is attempting to sequentially perform a selection between the modules A and B, and then perform an iteration of module C. Modules X and Y have to be introduced to give this sequential control.

Example 4:

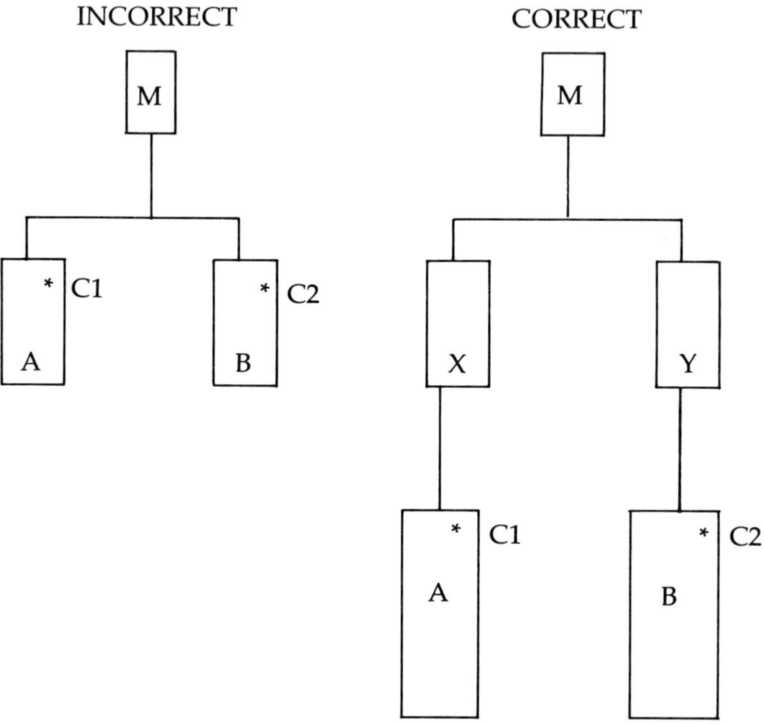

Sequentially we are performing two iterations. Modules X and Y explicitly define this sequence.

Example 5:

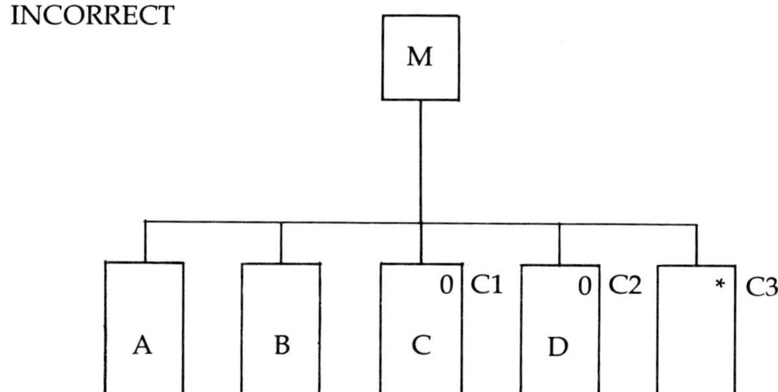

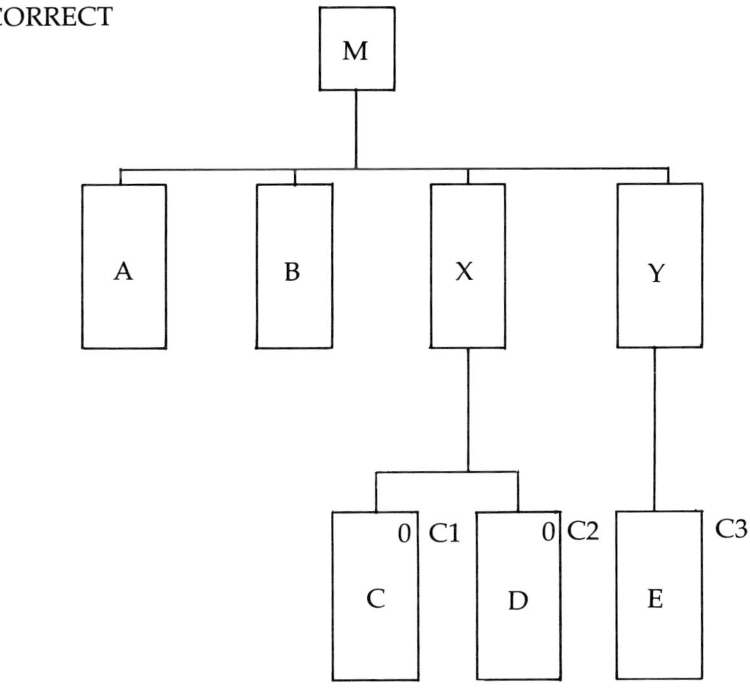

The same principles apply to even more complex examples. The design must be modified, by introducing other modules, to ensure the sequence is explicit.

7.9 SUMMARY

- 1. Only three programming statements are needed – sequence, selection and iteration.
- 2. The correct use of these constructs ensures that the return of control is automatic, hence 'GOTO' less programming.
- 3. The rules for diagram representation are, simply, no mixed siblings and no iteration siblings.

7.10 PROBLEMS

- 1. Investigate the control constructs available in other languages, eg FORTRAN, COBOL, ALGOL.
- 2. As a more extensive exercise you may like to produce a table that can be used to compare and contrast a selection of languages. Criteria you may like to include are:
  - layout and sequencing. As we know Pascal statements are

separated by semi-colons and enclosed by BEGIN and END. In FORTRAN only columns 7–72 can be used.

- simple data types. FORTRAN has INTEGER, REAL, DOUBLE PRECISON, COMPLEX, LOGICAL, LITERAL and CHARACTER.
- declarations. Explicit declarations are typical but not exclusively so, in APL no declarations for data are used.
- assignments.
- iteration. In FORTRAN we are limited to a DO statement in the beginning and a numbered executable statement at the end.
- selection.

8 Structured Programs

8.1 INTRODUCTION

We now have an appreciation of the basic control structures in Pascal – sequence, selection and iteration – and the associated structured diagrams. We have also considered the rules for the generation of more complex structures, though at this point I suspect they seem rather abstract. It is now essential to bring the two together in order to understand the relationship between diagram and code. We are gradually trying to make the transition from 'thinking in Pascal (or another language)', to 'thinking in Pascal and structured diagrams' and finally to 'thinking in structured diagrams'.

8.2 MORE COMPLEX STRUCTURED DIAGRAMS

We previously considered the problem of the user typing in a number from 0 to 2 inclusive, and the program then converting the numeric character to the alphabetic equivalent, ie typing in 0 will produce the result zero. This was solved using the CASE control structure in program Ch5P5.

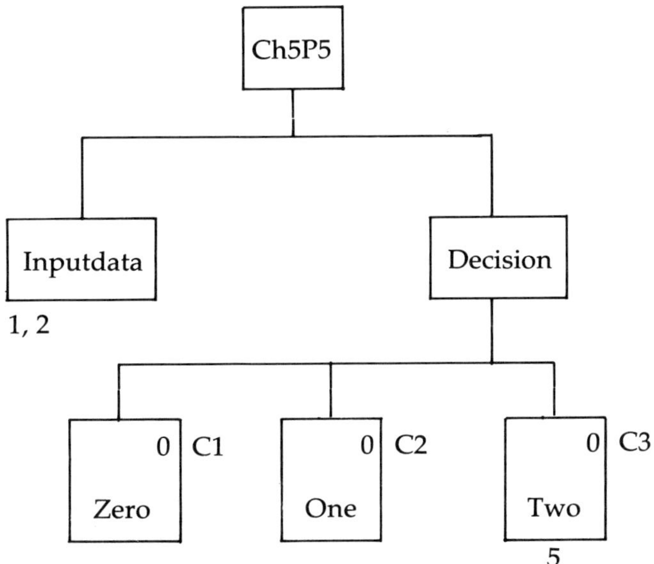

Functions	*Conditions*
1. User prompt 'Input a number'	C1 Number equals 0
2. Read Number	C2 Number equals 1
3. Display 'Zero'	C3 Number equals 2
4. Display 'One'	
5. Display 'Two'	

What if the number typed in is not within the permitted range? Our design must be modified to include a new procedure, which we can call Range, to hold the selection statement 'IF (Number > –1) AND (Number < 3) THEN Decision ELSE Error'. The procedure Error is a display to the user indicating the input number is out of range.

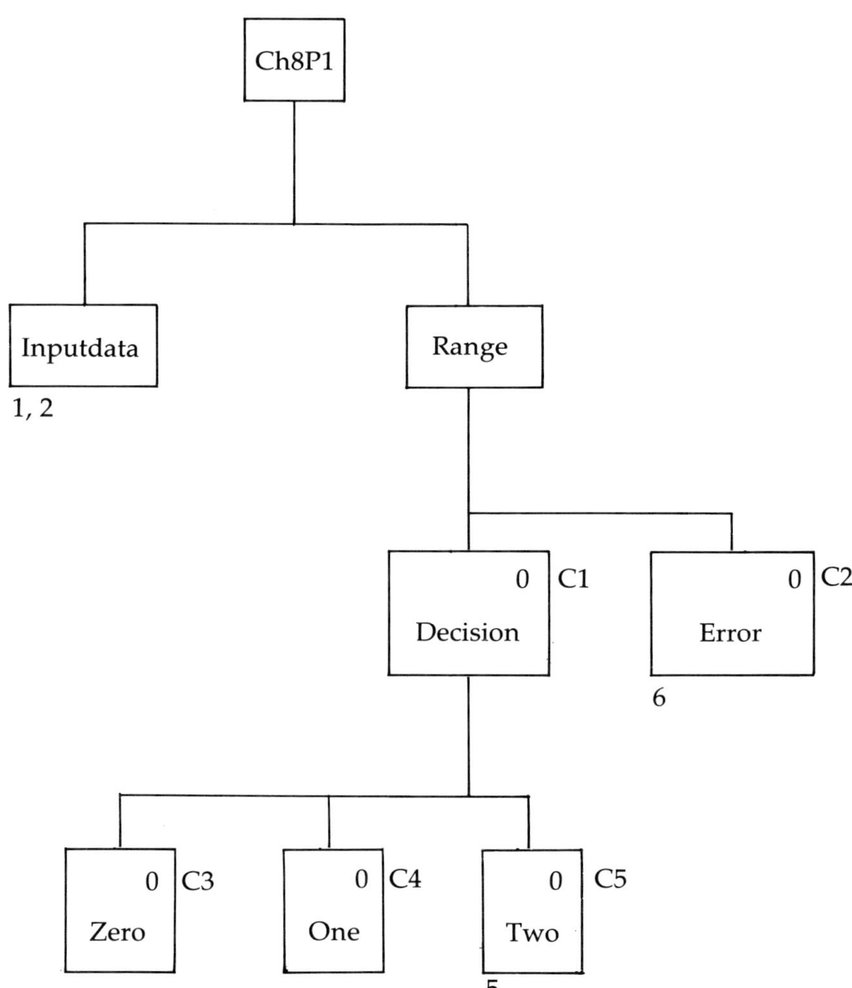

Functions	*Conditions*
1. User prompt 'Input a number'	C1 Number in range
2. Read Number	C2 Number out of range
3. Display 'Zero'	C3 Number equals 0
4. Display 'One'	C4 Number equals 1
5. Display 'Two'	C5 Number equals 2
6. User prompt	'number out of range'

```
PROGRAM Ch8P1 (INPUT, OUTPUT);

(* Simple range check for input data *)

VAR Number : INTEGER;

PROCEDURE Inputdata;
BEGIN
        WRITELN('Input a number');
        READLN(Number)
END;

PROCEDURE Range;
        PROCEDURE Decision;
                PROCEDURE Zero;
                BEGIN
                        WRITELN('Zero')
                END;

                PROCEDURE One;
                BEGIN
                        WRITELN('One')
                END;

                PROCEDURE Two;
                BEGIN
                        WRITELN('Two')
                END;
```

```
    BEGIN
        CASE Number OF
            0 : Zero;
            1 : One;
            2 : Two
        END;
    END;

    PROCEDURE Error:
    BEGIN
        WRITELN('Number out of range')
    END;

    BEGIN
        IF (Number < -1) AND (Number > 3) THEN
            Decision
        ELSE
            Error
    END;

BEGIN
    Inputdata;
    Range
END.
```

Important points to note are:

- 1. The procedures Decision, Zero, One and Two have not been altered.
- 2. The terminal functions have remained the same.
- 3. Because we have introduced another selection statement the conditions have been renumbered.
- 4. The indentation reflects the structure.
- 5. The modules or procedures represent cohesive functions.
- 6. The procedures are called by name. Hence we are employing the principle of abstraction.

– 7. Our structured diagram obeys the rules of structure ie no mixed siblings and no iteration siblings.

The program will run only once. Let us modify it to run an indeterminate number of times. The program is terminated by the user typing in 99.

Our structured diagram is now:

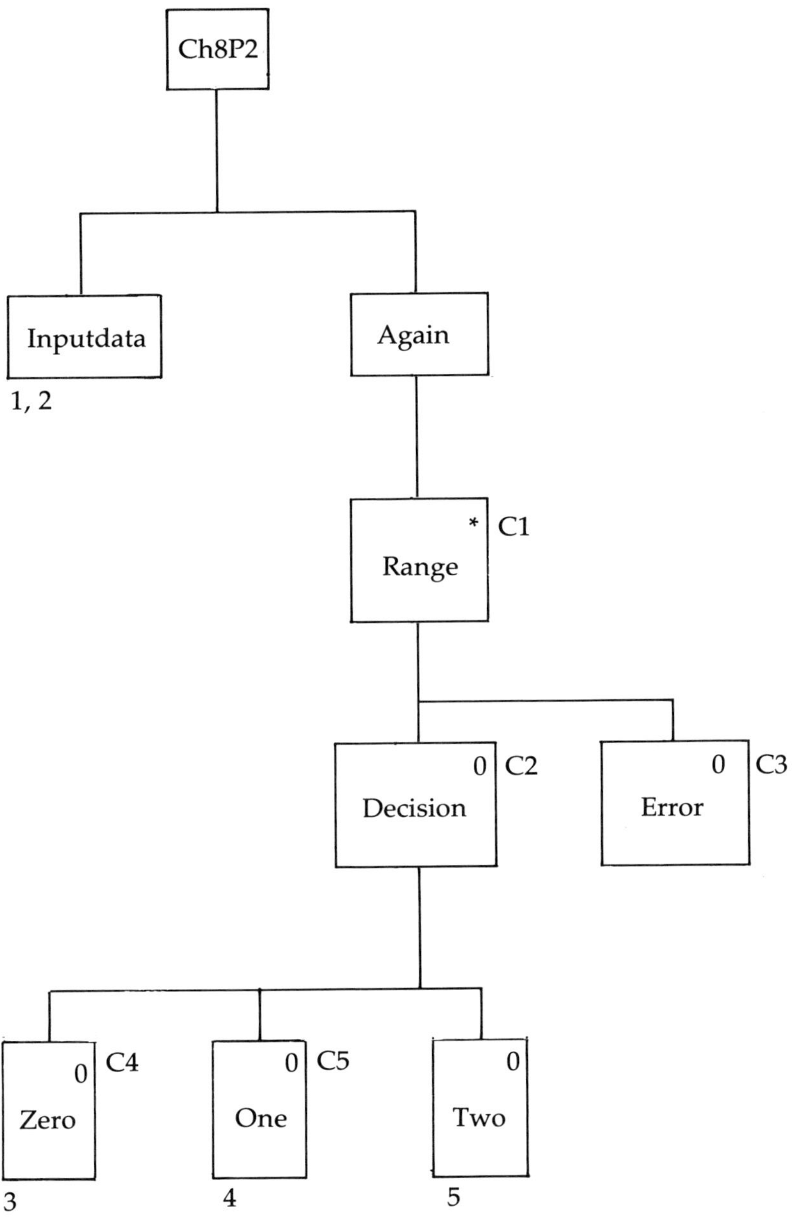

Functions	*Conditions*
1. User prompt 'Input a number'	C1 While number <> 99
2. Read Number	C2 Number in range
3. Display 'Zero'	C3 Number out of range
4. Display 'One'	C4 Number equals 0
5. Display 'Two'	C5 Number equals 1
6. User prompt 'number out of range'	C6 Number equals 2

```
PROGRAM Ch8P2 (INPUT, OUTPUT);

VAR Number : INTEGER;

PROCEDURE Inputdata;
BEGIN
        WRITELN('Input a number, 99 to terminate');
        READLN(Number)
END;

PROCEDURE Again;
    PROCEDURE Range;
        PROCEDURE Decision;
            PROCEDURE Zero;
            BEGIN
                    WRITELN('Zero');
                    WRITELN('Number ?');
                    READLN(Number)
            END;

            PROCEDURE One;
            BEGIN
                    WRITELN('One');
                    WRITELN('Number ?');
                    READLN(Number)
            END;
```

```
        PROCEDURE Two;
        BEGIN
            WRITELN('Two');
            WRITELN('Number ?');
            READLN(Number)
        END;
    BEGIN
        CASE Number OF
            0 : Zero;
            1 : One;
            2 : Two;
        END;
    END;

    PROCEDURE Error;
    BEGIN
        WRITELN('Number out of range')
        READLN (Number)
    END;
  BEGIN
    IF (Number > -1) AND (Number < 3) THEN
        Decision
    ELSE
        Error;
  END;
 BEGIN

 END;
BEGIN
    Inputdata;
    Again
END.
```

Once more the procedures previously written have not been changed. They are manipulated by a control structure at a higher hierarchical level. However the procedure Again is getting a little large. Recall this was a problem we met earlier in Chapter 5. Program Ch5P7 was modified to program Ch5P8 by moving subordinate procedures. The structured diagram still applies. Applying this principle to program Ch8P2 we have:

```
PROGRAM Ch8P3 (INPUT, OUPUT);

VAR Number : INTEGER;

PROCEDURE Inputdata;
BEGIN
        WRITELN('Input a number, 99 to terminate');
        READLN(Number)
END;

PROCEDURE Zero;
BEGIN
        WRITELN('Zero');
        WRITELN('Number ?')
        READLN(Number)
END;

PROCEDURE One;
BEGIN
        WRITELN('One');
        WRITELN('Number ?');
        READLN(Number)
END;

PROCEDURE Two;
BEGIN
        WRITELN('Two');
        WRITELN('Number ?');
        READLN(Number)
END;
```

```
PROCEDURE Decision;
BEGIN
        CASE Number OF
                0 : Zero;
                1 : One;
                2 : Two;
                3 : Three;
                4 : Four
        END;
END;
```

```
PROCEDURE Error;
BEGIN
        WRITELN('Number out of range')
        READLN (Number)
END;
```

```
PROCEDURE Range;
BEGIN
        IF (Number > -1) AND (Number < 3) THEN
                Decision
        ELSE
                Error;
END;
```

```
PROCEDURE Again;
BEGIN
        WHILE Number <> 99 DO Range
END;
```

```
BEGIN
        Inputdata;
        Again
END.
```

The location of the procedure, within certain restrictions considered later, is not important. We have been using our ability to free format to full advantage. The column indentation making the program more readable. We can do the same with the location of our procedures. It is important to stress that from the design we can produce a variety of forms in the target code. The final form depending on various other factors that we will consider as we proceed.

8.3 ANOTHER ANGLE

Without doubt this will be one of the most difficult chapters for most students. It is therefore worthwhile to spend some time on these topics and try to look at what we are trying to do from various angles.

Consider the Pascal code fragment:

```
PROGRAM Example1....

BEGIN

    statement1;

    statement2;

    WHILE condition

        BEGIN

            statement3;

            statement4;

            statement5;

        END;

    statement6;

    statement7
END.
```

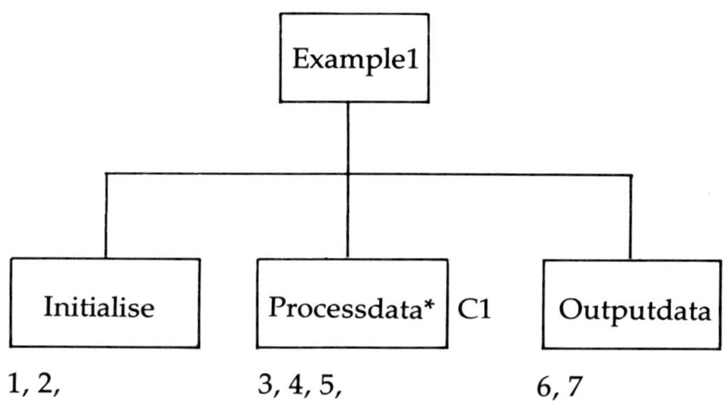

Certainly there is nothing wrong with the code. It would work. But we are trying to learn about structure. What if the number of statements in the iteration control structure is not three, but thirty? We can provide more structure by grouping together associated lines of code. As we have seen, if the groupings are done correctly we can give a name to the group that will define its function. We have greater cohesion through the use of abstraction.

The code for our diagram would be something like this:

```
PROGRAM Example1 ....

PROCEDURE Initialise;
BEGIN
        statement1;
        statement2
END;

PROCEDURE Processdata;
BEGIN
        WHILE condition
          BEGIN
              statement3;
              statement4;
              statement5
          END
END;

PROCEDURE Outputdata;
BEGIN
        statement6;
        statement7
END;

BEGIN
        Initialise;
        Processdata;
        Ouputdata
END.
```

Certainly this program would work, however the structure diagram is not quite right. The iteration statement has not been properly represented, there must be no iteration siblings. Statements 3, 4 and 5 are executed together in an iterative manner. Let us therefore group them together and call them procedure Processiteration.

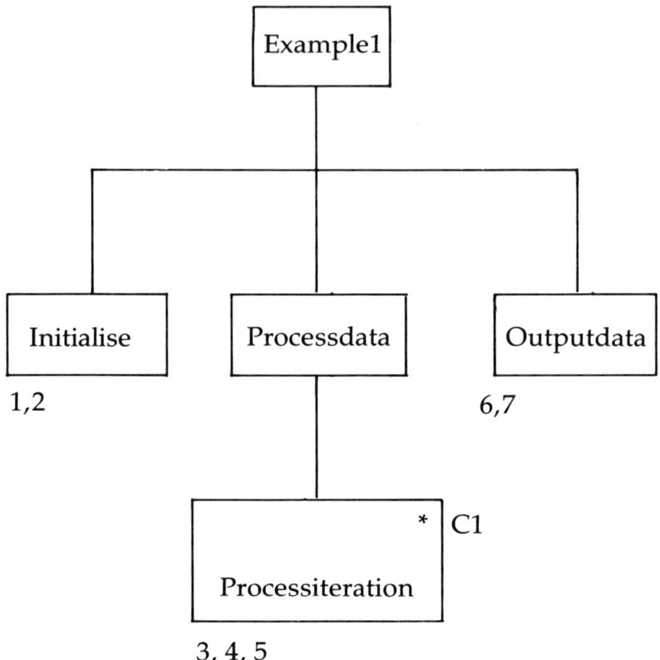

Hence we can isolate the iterated statements and more correctly represent them on our diagram. We have a sequential control structure – Initialise, Processdata and Outputdata. The procedure Processdata holds the iteration control statement that controls the iterated procedure Processiteration. Our diagram obeys the rules of structured diagrams. The associated code is:

```
PROGRAM Example1 ....
```

```
PROCEDURE Initialise;
BEGIN
    statement1;
    statement2
END;
```

```
PROCEDURE Processdata;

        PROCEDURE Processiteration;
        BEGIN
                statement3;
                statement4;
                statement5
        END;

BEGIN
        WHILE condition
            Processiteration
END;
```

```
PROCEDURE Outputdata;
BEGIN
        statement6;
        statement7
END;
BEGIN
        Initialise;
        Processdata;
        Outputdata
END.
```

Or, if the number of statements in the procedure Processiteration warrants it we could have:

```
PROGRAM Example1 ....
```

```
PROCEDURE Initialise;
BEGIN
        statement1;
        statement2
END;
```

```
PROCEDURE Processiteration;
BEGIN
        statement3;
        statement4;
        statement5;
        etc
END;
```

```
PROCEDURE Processdata;
BEGIN
        WHILE condition
                Processiteration
END;
```

```
PROCEDURE Outputdata;
BEGIN
        statementn;
        statementn + 1
END;
```

```
BEGIN
        Initialise;
        Processdata;
        Outputdata
END.
```

We can apply the same principles to the selection control structure. Starting with our Pascal code fragment:

```
Program Example2 . . . .
BEGIN
        statement1;
        statement2;
        IF condition THEN
            BEGIN
```

```
            statement3;
            statement4
        END
    ELSE
        BEGIN
            statement5;
            statement6
        END;
    statement7;
    statement8
END.
```

Grouping together associated statements would give us the following structure diagram:

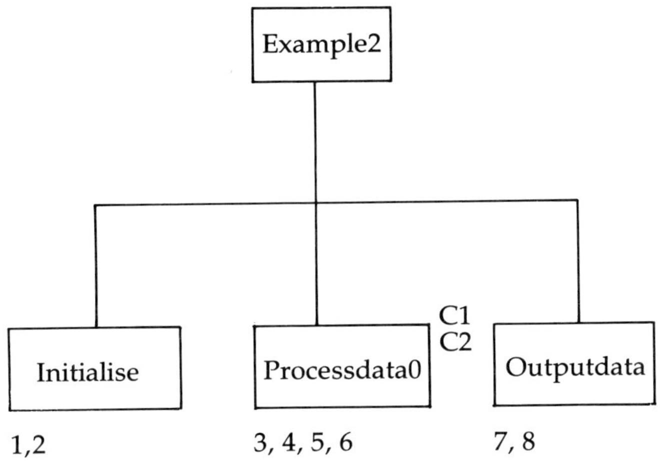

This can be converted to the target code as follows:

Program Example2 . . . .

```
PROCEDURE Initialise;
BEGIN
        statement1;
        statement2
END;
```

```
PROCEDURE Processdata;
BEGIN
        IF condition THEN
          BEGIN
               statement3;
               statement4
          END
        ELSE
          BEGIN
               statement5;
               statement6
          END;
END:
```

```
PROCEDURE Outputdata;
BEGIN
        statement7;
        statement8
END;
```

```
BEGIN
        Initialise;
        Processdata;
        Outputdata
END.
```

This program would work and as we will see there are many instances, such as complex algorithms, in which we would code like this. Again however we have not properly represented our selection structure. More correctly, this should be:

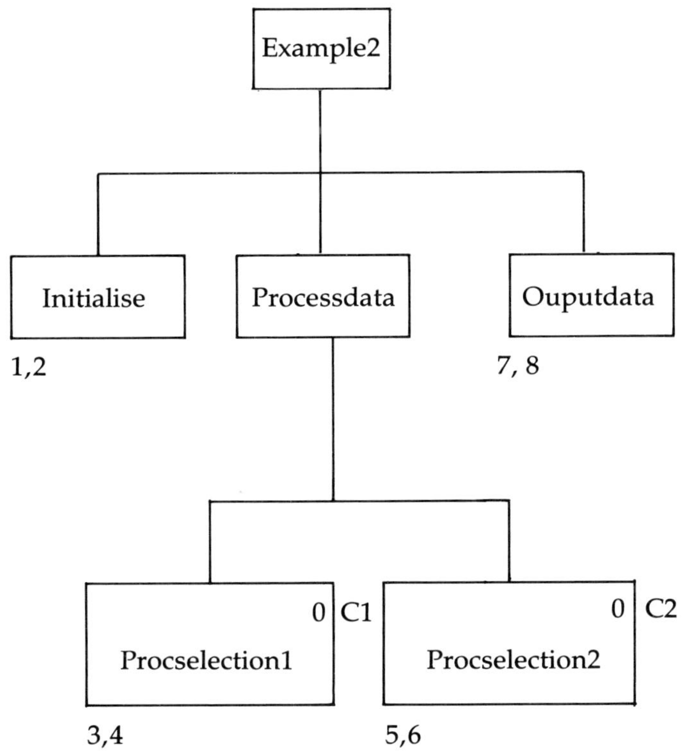

Program Example2....

```
PROCEDURE Initalise;
BEGIN
        statement1;
        statement2
END;
```

```
PROCEDURE Processdata;
        PROCEDURE Procselection1;
        BEGIN
                statement3;
                statement4
        END;
```

```
        PROCEDURE Procselection2;
        BEGIN
                statement5;
                statement6
        END;
    BEGIN
        IF condition THEN
            Procselection1
        ELSE
            Procselection2
    END:
PROCEDURE Outputdata;
BEGIN
        statement7;
        statement8
END;
BEGIN
        Initialise;
        Processdata;
        Outputdata
END.
```

The statements 3 to 6 have been encapsulated into procedures thus allowing us to easily move the code to our best advantage. If we had a large number of statements in our design the procedures Procselection1 and Procselection2 could easily be moved.

Program Example2 . . .

```
PROCEDURE Initialise;
BEGIN
        statement1;
        statement2
END;
```

```
PROCEDURE Procselection1;
BEGIN
        statement3;
        .
        .
        statementn
END;

PROCEDURE Procselection2;
BEGIN
        statementn + 1;
        .
        .
        statementn + n
END;

PROCEDURE Processdata;
BEGIN
        IF condition THEN
           Procselection1
        ELSE
           Procselection2
END:

PROCEDURE Outputdata;
BEGIN
        statement7;
        statement8
END;
BEGIN
        Initialise;
        Processdata;
        Outputdata
END
```

As we will see in Chapter 14, Modular Programming, what we are trying to do is group terminal functions into a module (procedure) such that they can be named with a closely related word that defines what the module will do. This is called cohesion. The advantage is that a highly cohesive module can be replaced by another module with minimum modifications to other modules.

8.4 SUMMARY

– 1. A good procedure can be written once but used many times; as such it must represent a set of cohesive (terminal) functions.

– 2. Procedures are called by name, hence we are using the principle of abstraction.

8.5 PROBLEMS

– 1. Modify program Ch8P1 to convert lower case letters to upper case letters as we saw in the problems in Chapter 5.

– 2. Similarly modify the rest of the programs in this chapter to lower/upper case conversion.

9 Arrays

9.1 INTRODUCTION

Information can be considered as data with a structure. Ultimately the computer can only hold data in a sequential binary store. This internal representation of data needs structure in the form of a set of rules to retain essential relationships. What one is trying to do is form a relationship between the complex data of the real-world and its storage and manipulation on a computer.

A data structure is a collection of elements with four aspects:

- 1. A description of the values that may be used and hence the storage requirements.
- 2. A description of the way the elements of the data structure are related.
- 3. A specification of the methods of access to the elements.
- 4. A specification of the permitted operations.

Careful and appropriate use of data structures help in the management of data. A list of objects, such as a parts list, can be viewed as a linear data structure. The list is sequential with the objects in the list being identified by their position in the list. Members can be selected by specifying their position or alternatively by searching the list.

9.2 ARRAYS

An array is a group of cells that can hold data of the same type. Here the emphasis is on group. Previously all variables have only been handled in a discrete manner. Let us consider a previously seen program, Ch5P7, and modify it slightly.

STRUCTURED DATA TYPES

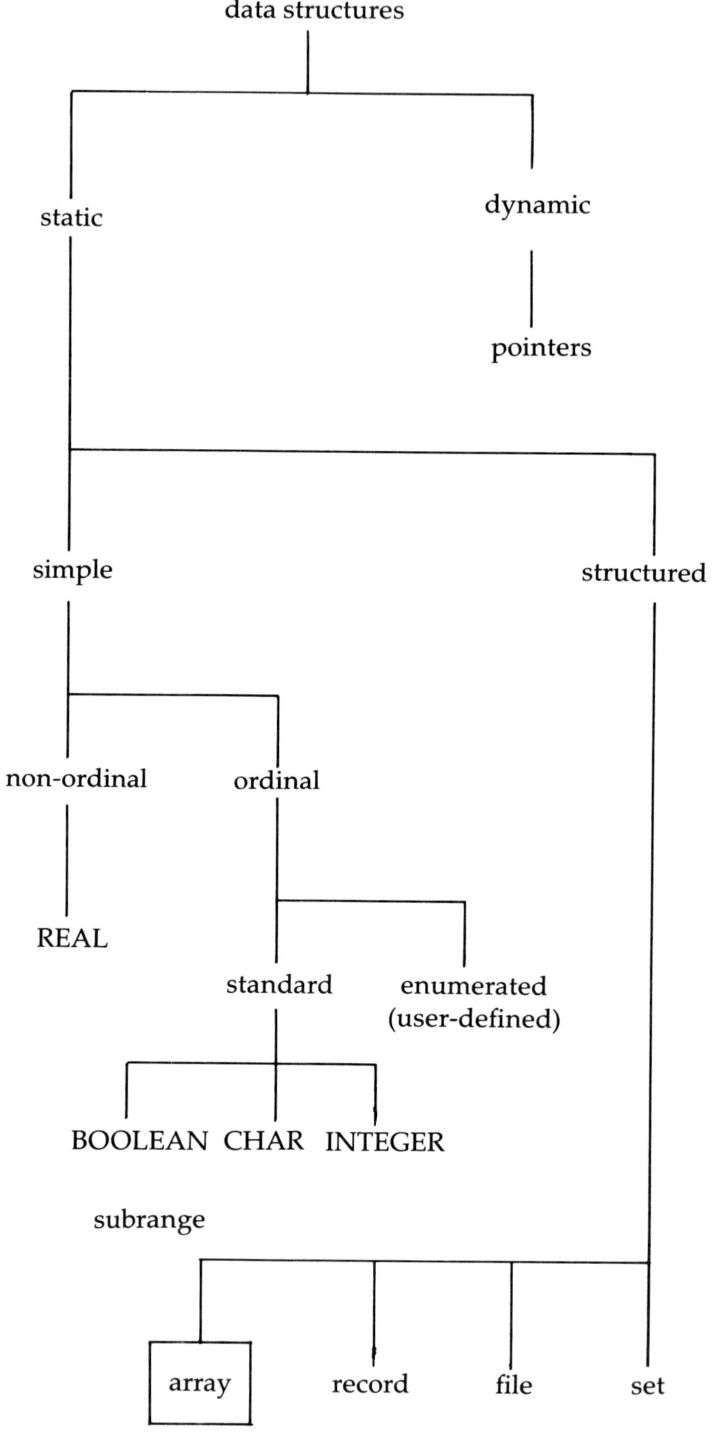

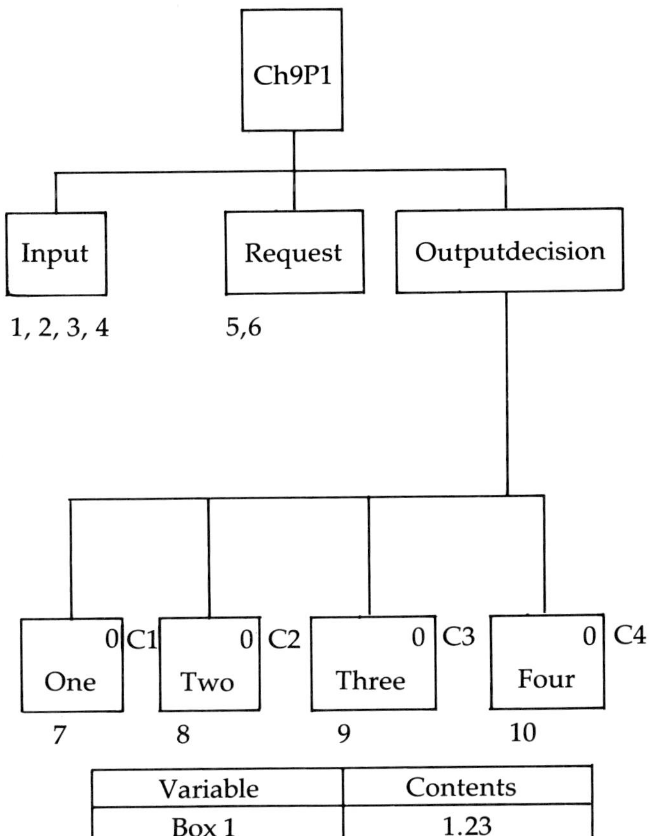

Variable	Contents
Box 1	1.23
Box 2	2.34
Box 3	3.45
Box 4	4.56

Functions

1. Box1 := 1.23
2. Box2 := 2.34
3. Box3 := 3.45
4. Box4 := 4.56
5. User prompt
6. Read Number
7. Display message and Box1 contents
8. Display message and Box2 contents
9. Display message and Box3 contents
10. Display message and Box4 contents

Conditions

C1 Number = 1

C2 Number = 2

C3 Number = 3

C4 Number = 4

```
PROGRAM Ch9P1 (INPUT, OUTPUT);
(* Linear data structure using CASE *)
VAR Box1, Box2, Box3, Box4 : REAL;
    Number : INTEGER;

PROCEDURE Initialise;

BEGIN
    Box1 := 1.23;
    Box2 := 2.34;
    Box3 := 3.45;
    Box4 := 4.56
END;

PROCEDURE Request;
BEGIN
    WRITELN('Input a number');
    READLN(Number)
END;

PROCEDURE Outputdecision;
    PROCEDURE One;
    BEGIN
        WRITELN('Contents of box 1', Box1 :6 :2)
    END;

    PROCEDURE Two;
    BEGIN
        WRITELN('Contents of box 2', Box2 :6 :2)
    END;
```

```
        PROCEDURE Three;
        BEGIN
            WRITELN('Contents of box 3', Box3 :6 :2)
        END;

        PROCEDURE Four;
        BEGIN
            WRITELN('Contents of box 4', Box4 :6 :2)
        END;

    BEGIN
        CASE Number OF
            1 : One;
            2 : Two;
            3 : Three;
            4 : Four
        END;
    END;

BEGIN
    Initialise;
    Request;
    Outputdecision
END.
```

What if there are a hundred data items? Now let's handle all four boxes as a single unit. This is done as follows:

- 1. Choose the array name, eg Boxes
- 2. Decide on the maximum number of elements, eg 1 . . . 4
- 3. Use a type INTEGER, eg Selector for access to individual elements.
- 4. Define the type of the contents, eg REAL

```
Boxes : ARRAY[ 1..4 ] OF REAL
```

A single identifier, in this case Boxes, refers to the array and array cells are identified by their array positions. A selector or index variable (ordinal) is used for selection.

A simplified version of our type declaration for an array is:

type

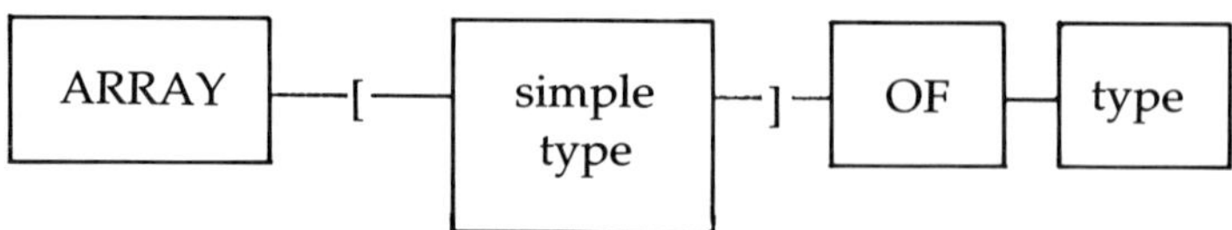

The consequence of this is that the CASE control structure can be taken care of by the data structure itself. As we know data structures have a specification of the methods of access to the elements and the permitted operations.

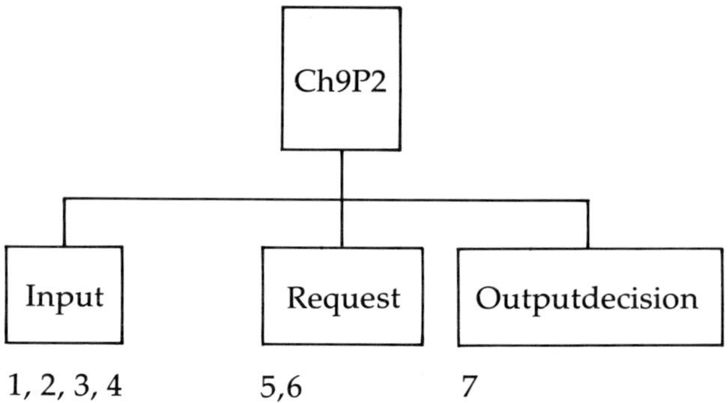

Functions

1. Box1 := 1.23
2. Box2 := 2.34
3. Box3 := 3.45
4. Box4 := 4.56
5. User prompt
6. Read Selector
7. Display message and Box[Selector] contents

Without doubt, we can see that appropriate use of a data structure simplifies our design and hence the associated code.

```
PROGRAM Ch9P2 (INPUT, OUTPUT);

(* Reading one data item from an array *)
```

```
VAR Selector :INTEGER;
    Boxes : ARRAY [ 1..4 ] OF REAL;

PROCEDURE Initialise;
BEGIN
    Box [ 1 ]:= 1.23;
    Box [ 2 ]:= 2.34;
    Box [ 3 ]:= 3.45;
    Box [ 4 ]:= 4.56
END;

PROCEDURE Request;
BEGIN
    WRITELN('Input selector number');
    READLN(Selector)
END;

PROCEDURE Outputdecision;
BEGIN
    WRITELN('Contents are', Boxes[ Selector ] :6 :2)
END;

BEGIN
    Initialise;
    Request;
    Outputdecision
END.
```

The data is stored in a structure with a single variable name, instead of four individual variables. Individual data items are selected and hence distinguished from each other by their position in the structure.

BOXES	
Position	Contents
1	1.23
2	2.34
3	3.45
4	4.56

9.3 ARRAY MANIPULATION

By a simple modification we can iteratively process our array. In Ch9P3, the procedure Boxesoutput can be controlled by the FOR – TO control structure.

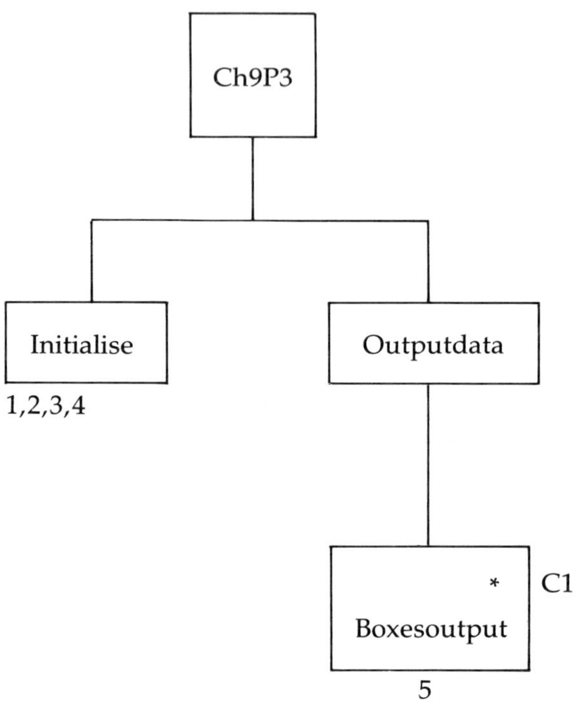

Functions

1. Box1 := 1.23
2. Box2 := 2.34
3. Box3 := 3.45
4. Box4 := 4.56
5. Display message and Box[Selector] contents

Conditions

C1 For Selector =
1 to 4

The corresponding Pascal code is :

```
PROGRAM Ch9P3 (INPUT, OUTPUT);

(* Reading all data items from an array *)

VAR Boxes : ARRAY [ 1..4 ] OF REAL;
```

```
PROCEDURE Initialise;
BEGIN
        Box [1] := 1.23;
        Box [2] := 2.34;
        Box [3] := 3.45;
        Box [4] := 4.56
END;
```

```
PROCEDURE Outputdata;
VAR Selector : INTEGER;
        PROCEDURE Boxesoutput;
        BEGIN
                WRITELN('Contents are', Boxes[Selector]:6 :2)
        END;

BEGIN
        FOR Selector := 1 TO 4 DO
        Boxesoutput
END;
```

```
BEGIN
        Initialise;
        Outputdata
END.
```

Here the control variable, selector, is used also as the variable to access each individual array element.

So far the user has not been able to define the contents of the array. Again this can be done iteratively with the procedure Boxesinput being controlled in the same manner as Boxesoutput.

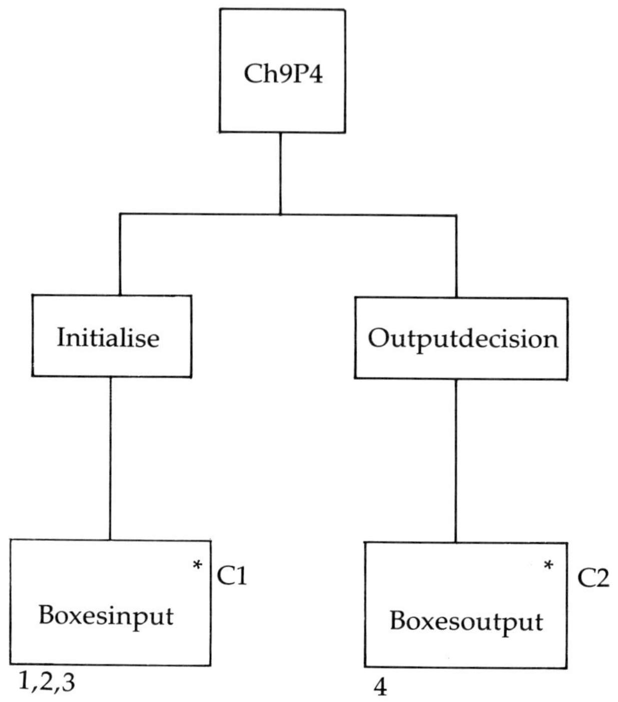

Functions	*Conditions*
1. User prompt	C1 For Selector1 =
2. Read Contents	1 to 4
3. Boxes[Selector] := Contents	C2 For Selector2 =
4. Display message and Box[Selector] contents	1 to 4

```
PROGRAM Ch9P4 (INPUT, OUTPUT);
(* Writing and Reading all data items in an array *)
VAR Contents : REAL;
     Boxes : ARRAY [ 1..4 ] OF REAL;
```

```
PROCEDURE Initialise;
VAR Selector1 : INTEGER;
```

```
        PROCEDURE Boxesinput;
        BEGIN
                WRITELN('Input data');
                READLN(Contents);
                Boxes[Selector]:= Contents
        END;

BEGIN
        FOR Selector1 := 1 to 4 DO
          Boxesinput
END;
```

```
PROCEDURE Outputdecision;
VAR Selector2 : INTEGER;
        PROCEDURE Boxesoutput;
        BEGIN
                WRITELN ('Contents are', Boxes
                                 [Selector]:6 :2)
        END;

BEGIN
        FOR Selector2 := 1 To 4 Do
          Boxesoutput
END;
```

```
BEGIN
        Inputdata;
        Outputdata
END.
```

Here two variables, Selector1 and Selector2, are used to control both the iteration and the selection of array elements.

Let us now allow the user to determine the contents of the array and also to select an array element to determine its contents.

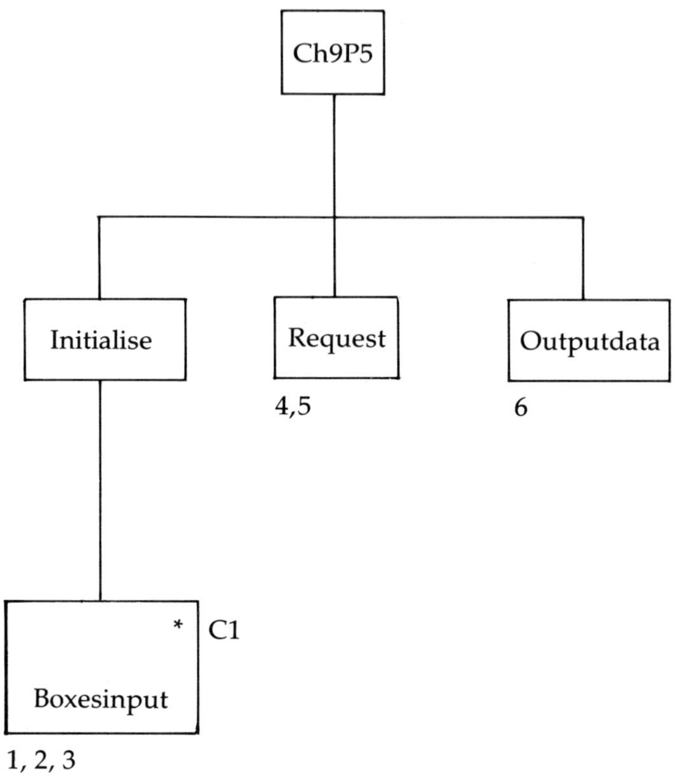

Functions	*Conditions*
1. User prompt 'Input data'	C1 For Selector
2. Read Contents	1 to 4
3. Boxes[Selector] := Contents	
4. User prompt 'Input box number'	
5. Read User choice	
6. Display 'Contents are', Boxes[Choice]	

```
PROGRAM Ch9P5 (INPUT, OUTPUT);
(* Writing all data items to an array, reading one data item *)
VAR Contents : REAL;
      Boxes : ARRAY [ 1..4 ] OF REAL;
      Choice : INTEGER;
```

```
PROCEDURE Inputdata;
VAR Selector : INTEGER;
    PROCEDURE Boxesinput;
    BEGIN
        WRITELN('Input data');
        READLN(Contents);
        Boxes[Selector]:= Contents
    END;
BEGIN
    FOR Selector := 1 TO 4 DO
      Boxesinput
END;

PROCEDURE Request;
BEGIN
    WRITELN('Input box number');
    READLN(Choice)
END;

PROCEDURE Outputdata;
BEGIN
    WRITELN('Contents are', Boxes[Choice]:6 :2)
END;

BEGIN
    Inputdata;
    Request;
    Outputdata
END.
```

After allowing the user to fill the array with data, the user can then select an array element.

9.4 CONVENIENT STYLE – BREAKING THE RULES

Finally, let us allow the user to define the contents of the array and repeatedly interrogate the array to determine the contents. Inputting 99 will terminate the program.

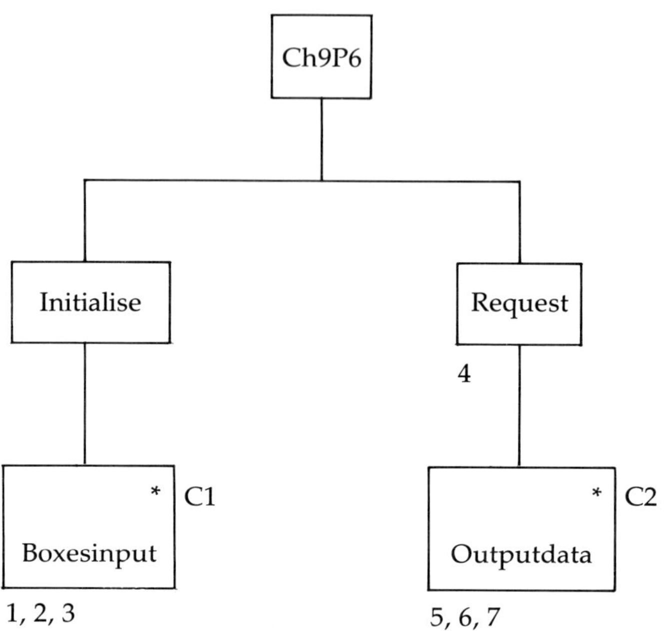

Functions	*Conditions*
1. User prompt 'Input data'	C1 For Selector1
2. Read Contents	1 to 4
3. Boxes[Selector] := Contents	C2 While Selector2
4. Prime Selector	<> 99
5. User prompt 'Input box number' 99 to end	
6. Read Selector2	
7. Display 'Contents are', Boxes[Selector2]	

An important point to note here is that one of the rules of structured diagrams has been broken. The procedure Request is a sequence of two statements, but one of them is an iteration statement. Recall, iteration statements must not have any siblings. This introduces the concept of convenient style. In order to correctly design the above problem the single statement, Selector2 := 1, would have to be in a procedure by itself.

```
PROGRAM Ch9P6 (INPUT, OUTPUT);

(* Writing all data items to an array, iterative selection of array
contents *)

VAR Contents : REAL;

      Boxes : ARRAY [ 1..4 ] OF REAL;

      Choice : INTEGER;

  PROCEDURE Inputdata;

  VAR Selector1 : Integer;

        PROCEDURE Boxesinput;

        BEGIN

              WRITELN('Input data');

              READLN(Contents);

              Boxes[Selector ] := Contents

        END;

  BEGIN

        FOR Selector1 := 1 TO 4 DO

           Boxesinput

  END;

  PROCEDURE Outputdata;

  VAR Selector2 : INTEGER:

        PROCEDURE Outputdata;

        BEGIN

              WRITELN('Input a number, 99 to end');

              READLN(Selector2)

              WRITELN('Contents are', Boxes[Selector ]:6 :2)

        END:

  BEGIN

        Selector2 := 1;

        While Selector2 <> 99 DO

           Outputdata

  END;
```

```
BEGIN
        Inputdata;
        REQUEST;
        Outputdata
END.
```

9.5 SUMMARY

- 1. An array is a named structured data type that allows random access to data of the same type.
- 2. Array contents are identified by their array position with a selector or index variable (ordinal) being used for selection.
- 3. Arrays are static data structures – the array size must be declared in advance.

9.6 PROBLEMS

This chapter is only a brief introduction to arrays – just sufficient for our purposes as we will see later. It is, for example, possible to perform arithmetic with array selector variables.

program fragment

```
VAR
        Numbers : ARRAY[ 1..100 ] OF INTEGER;
BEGIN
        .
        .
        WRITELN(Numbers[ 5 * Selector ];
```

where selector is the variable used to access array elements. Similarly array elements may be compared using, of course, relational operators.

```
IF Numbers[ Selector ] > Numbers[ Selector + 1 ] THEN
```

And finally it is possible to have multidimensional arrays of rows and columns.

column

row	1	2	3	4
1				
2				
3				
4				

The work recommended here is to further investigate the potential offered by arrays. Certainly if you are likely to do a lot of 'number crunching' arrays will be indispensable.

10 Records and Files

10.1 INTRODUCTION

What better introduction to records is there than to quote Niklaus Wirth, the father of Pascal:

'In an array all elements are of the same type. In contrast to the array, the record structure offers the possibility to declare a collection of elements as a unit even if the elements are of different types.'

With record types we have a collection of different pieces of information that are logically related. Hence a record can be handled as a single unit or the individual elements processed as appropriate. This makes files ideal for handling large data volumes.

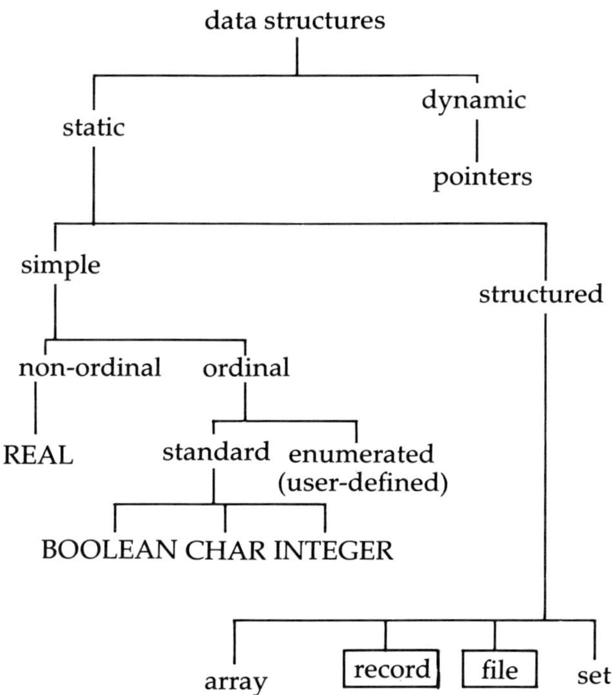

10.2 RECORDS

If you are new to files the easiest analogy is a card index. The card index box can be considered as the file with the individual cards representing the records.

Using a pay-slip as a example let us consider what one of these index cards may look like (see Figures 10.1 and 10.2):

Works number	:
Name	:
Taxable pay	:
NIERC contribution	:
etc	

Figure 10.1 Card Index Record

There can be many record fields such as:

Works number:

Name:

Taxable pay:

Pensionable pay:

NIERC contribution:

Superannuation:

Tax paid:

Each record has fields which may be different data types – typically numeric or alphanumeric. However the field layout is the same for each record (index card). Records can be considered as a collection of related items of data treated as a unit for the purposes of assessing and processing.

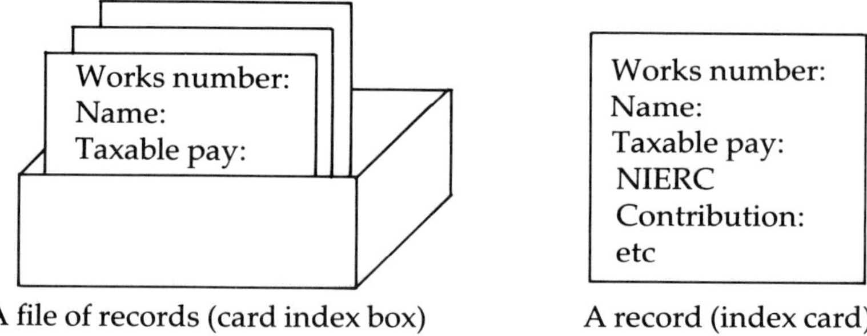

A file of records (card index box)   A record (index card)

Figure 10.2 A file of records

The data fields can be classified:

- 1. Control data. Each record must have a unique identifier, sometimes called a primary key. Using this key it is possible to access only one record. This is to avoid the obvious problem of two people with the same name.
- 2. Static data. These fields hold data that rarely changes, eg PAYE contributions. It is sometimes said that these fields are processed by amendment.
- 3. Dynamic data. These fields hold data that changes regularly eg taxable pay. These fields can be said to be processed by update.

We will grossly simplify our record in order to demonstrate the basic principles of record and file manipulation. Remember we are interested in the principles rather than the detail. Having established the basic theory we can then expand our view to take into account more complex and real-life systems.

Our new record is now simplified to have only three fields with simple data types:
Works number : 1234 (*INTEGER*)

Name : A (*CHAR*)

Taxcode : 7 (*INTEGER*)

Using our Pascal type declaration and field list determines how this is converted to Pascal.

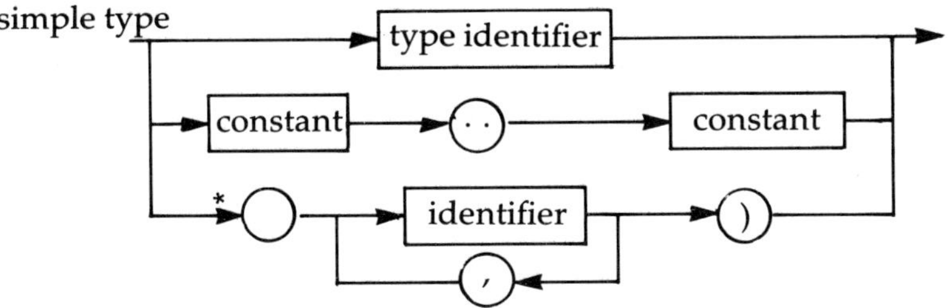

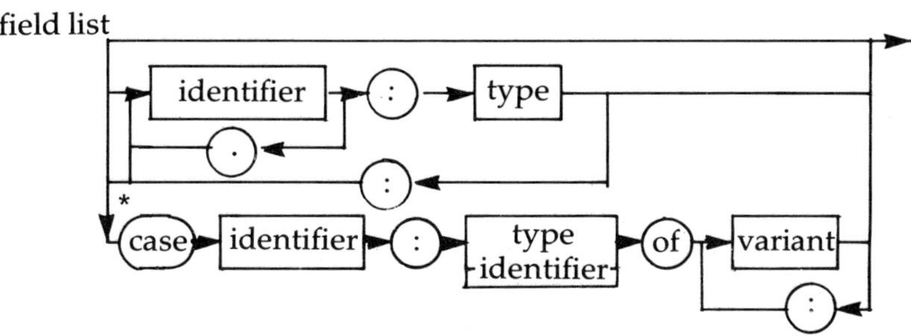

In our case the record would look like this:

```
TYPE Employee = RECORD
Worksnumber :  INTEGER;
Name        :  CHAR;
Taxcode     :  INTEGER;
END;
VAR Employeerecord : Employee;
```

This corresponds to having a variable of type employee where we have defined what type employee will look like.

Employee

Worknumber (INTEGER)

Name (CHAR)

Taxcode (INTEGER)

Figure 10.3 Variable of type Employee

Type declaration often causes problems, especially to those new to programming. We have met this before but perhaps did not realise it at the time.

```
(Type INTEGER)
VAR Number : INTEGER;
```

In this program fragment Number is a variable the contents of which can be changed. However the contents must be of type INTEGER – a signed or unsigned whole number. Type INTEGER has been put in parenthess to show that the type has been defined for you. Even though you cannot see it directly, it has been done for you.

```
TYPE Employee = RECORD
Worksnumber :  INTEGER;
Name        :  CHAR;
Taxcode     :  INTEGER;
END;
VAR Employeerecord : Employee;
```

tells us that Employeerecord is a variable the contents of which can be changed. However the contents must be of type Employee – a record with the fields we have defined. This gives the programmer considerable power. We could if we wish have any reasonable field definition.

```
TYPE Permanentemployee = Record
        Worksnumber :  INTEGER;
        Name        :  CHAR;
        Taxcode     :  INTEGER;
END;
TYPE Temporaryemployee = Record
        Worksnumber :  INTEGER;
        Name        :  CHAR;
        Taxcode     :  INTEGER;
        Contract-   :  INTEGER;
        period
        END;
```

Having defined the type we can then declare the variable types.

```
VAR Permanentstaff: Permanentemployee;
        Temporarystaff: Temporaryemployee;
```

10.3 FILES

There are many different types of files, reference, report, dump, historical, etc. Two common types are Master files that hold relatively permanent records and Transaction files that are made from source documents and are used to modify Master files.

Processes for a given file include:

- 1. Amend. The static (or control) data is altered.
- 2. Update. The dynamic data fields are altered to reflect the current position.
- 3. Addition/Insertion. Records can be added (appended) to a file or inserted according to some sequence.
- 4. Reference. Records can be displayed or sent to a printer for a hard copy.
- 5. Delete. Selected records can be removed.

The efficiency of file processing depends on the nature of the given application in conjunction with the processing system design.

Processing criteria include:

- 1. File size: the total number of records.

- 2. Activity: in a given processing period the number of records that need processing.
- 3. Response time: the elapsed period between the demand for processing and fulfilment of that demand.
- 4. Volatility: the proportion of records added to or deleted from a file over a given processing period.
- 5. Integration: the extent to which files are interdependent. Highly integrated files can be updated in one process run.
- 6. Security: back-ups and recovery.

We will only be considering file manipulation and not processing criteria.

10.4 FILE ORGANISATION

Primary storage media, ie RAM, is both volatile and expensive. Turn the power off and your data will be lost. Primary storage is complemented by secondary memory, disc and tape, which are cheaper and non-volatile. Different file organisation methods, when coupled with the operating characteristics of tape and disc storage, result in different efficiencies for different applications.

In magnetic tape storage media, individual storage locations cannot easily be accessed. To find a particular record the search must pass all preceding records – serial access. Do note that serial means in any order and sequential means ordered by key. With direct access storage devices, such as magnetic disc, storage locations are addressable. To find a particular record the search will either go directly to the storage location (random access) or go via an index (index sequential). Index sequential allows selective access, via an index, to a block or records that can then be searched sequentially, thus reducing the processing period. Direct access is via application of an algorithm to convert the key field to a disc address. Certainly the direct access and index sequential access times for disc are several orders of magnitude better than for magnetic tape; however the sequential access times for both media are comparable, the conclusion being that sequential file processing time on disc offers no significant advantage over tape.

10.5 SEQUENTIAL FILES

It is important to have an appreciation of magnetic tape and its operation. Sequential files can then better be understood in this context. The physical characteristics of magnetic tape vary in width, length, number of tracks, number of bits per inch etc. Regardless of these differences the operational characteristics are the same. In our tape assembly, Figure 10.4, the tape passes over two capstans rotating in opposite directions at constant speed. To transfer tape one of the pinch rollers makes contact. When enough tape has been drawn from the reservoir, say on the right, the top photoelectric cell is activated. Hence the right hand reel unwinds tape into the reservoir. The reservoir is filled until the bottom photoelectric cell is de-activated. When enough tape has been fed into reservoir on the left to activate the lower photelectic cell, the associated motor operates to wind tape onto the left

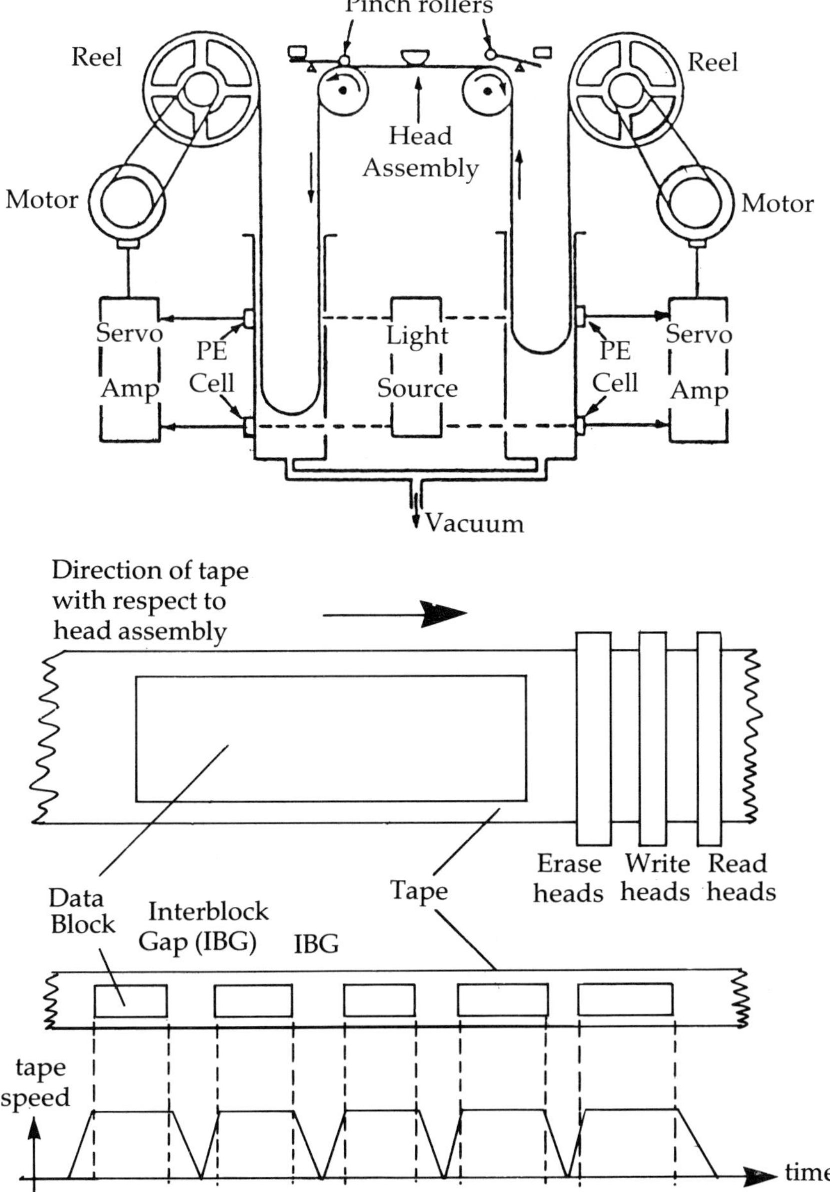

Figure 10.4 Magnetic Tape Storage – Mechanism and Tape Organisation

hand reel. Application of a partial vacuum to the bottom of the reservoirs forces the tape loops down in order to create spooling tension – the tape must make contact with the head assembly. With this system we have decoupled the two reels thus allowing very fast acceleration and deceleration of the tape. The tape is accelerated to a constant speed for correct reading/writing and then decelerated. Blocks of data are therefore separated by Interblock Gaps (IBG's). It is in these gaps that the tape is brought up to the correct speed and then brought to a halt. In magnetic tape storage media, the individual storage locations cannot be directly accessed. To find a particular record in a block, the search must pass all preceding records – serial access. One further important point to note is that it is not possible to write records back to the same position on the tape from which they have been read. The method of updating therefore is to form a new master file each time the updating process is carried out.

The sequence of events is therefore:

- Accelerate tape to constant speed
- Read or write data
- Decelerate tape

10.6 FILES IN PASCAL

In standard Pascal, input and output is performed through external files identified as program parameters in the program heading. Two standard files provided for input and output are INPUT and OUTPUT. Additional or alternative files may also be listed in the program heading. All files listed in the heading, with the exception of INPUT and OUTPUT, must be declared as file variables.

```
PROGRAM Programname (INPUT, OUTPUT, File1, File2);
VAR File1, File2 : TYPE;
```

The standard procedures available for use on files are READ, READLN, WRITE and WRITELN.

Standard Pascal supports only serial/sequential file organisation. In a serial file our records are therefore in any order in the blocks on the tape. The relative position of records has no significance. To access a given record each record key has to be matched to the desired key.

Our program heading now looks like this:

```
PROGRAM Simple1 (INPUT, OUTPUT, MASTER);
TYPE Employee = RECORD

                    Worksnumber :  INTEGER;

                    Name        :  CHAR;
```

```
                    Taxcode          : INTEGER;
            END;
        Personnel : FILE of Employee;
VAR Employeerecord : Employee;
        Master : Personnel;
```

Worksnumber (INTEGER)

Name (CHAR)

Taxcode (INTEGER)

Figure 10.5 Variable Employeerecord of type Employee

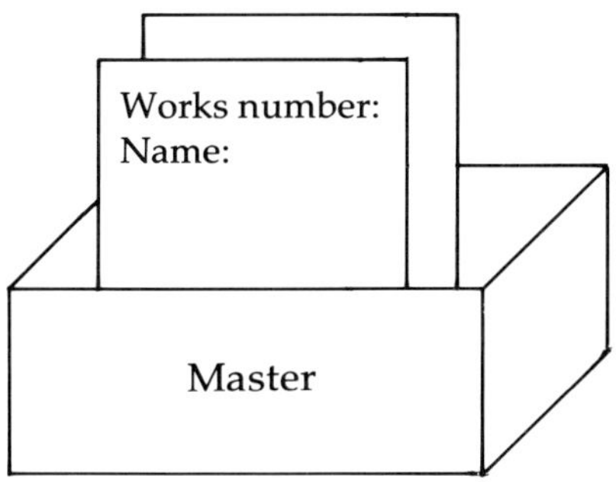

Figure 10.6 Variable Master of type Personnel

Do note that what we are defining here is a file, called Master, that holds records of type Employee.

10.7 FILE PROCESSING IN PASCAL

Opening a file

Prior to use a file must be opened. REWRITE(filename) opens a file for writing; the file pointer is positioned at the beginning of the file. In our example this would be REWRITE(Master). We can now write records to the file. Using our card index analogy, we have just emptied out any index cards and the box is empty. RESET(filename) opens a file for reading, the file pointer is again positioned at the beginning of the file but this time we have access to the first record. (See Figures 10.7 and 10.8.)

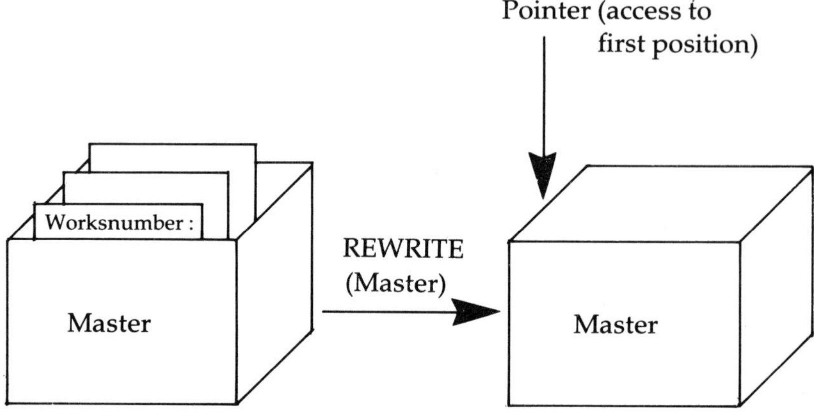

Figure 10.7 REWRITE

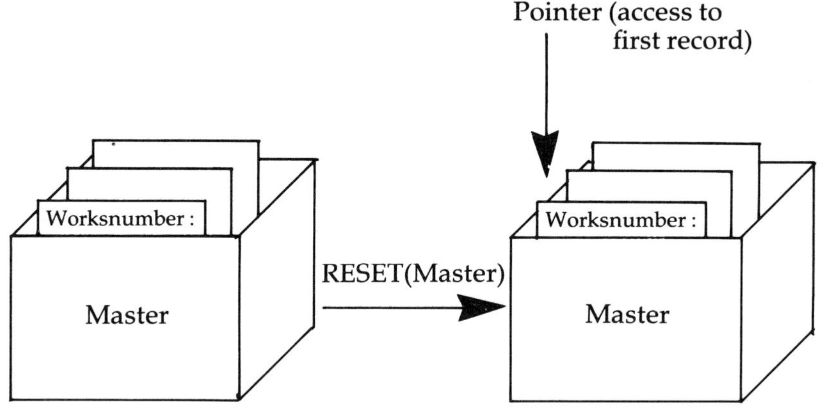

Figure 10.8 RESET

Writing records to a file

Records can be written to a file by using the modified WRITE procedure. WRITE(Filename, Recordname) places the record into the file and increments the file pointer. (See Figures 10.9 and 10.10.)

Before execution of WRITE(Master, Employeerecord)

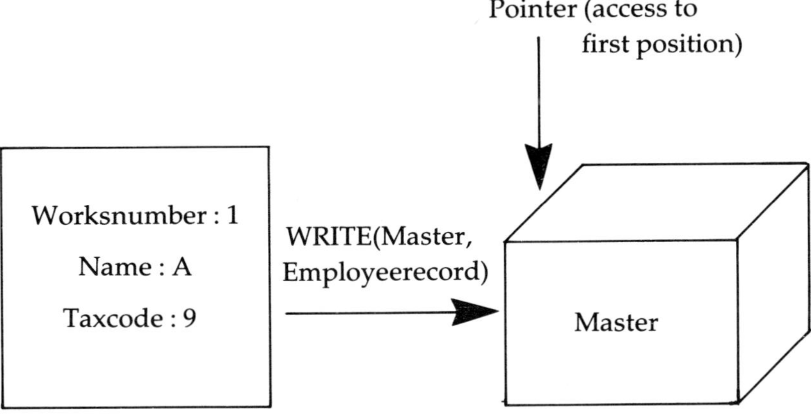

After execution of WRITE (Master, Employeerecord)

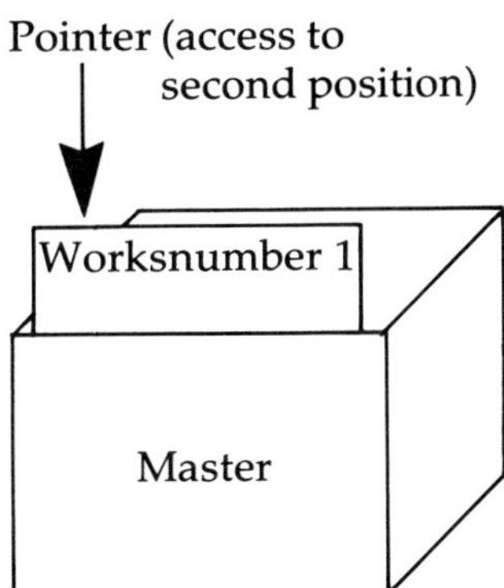

10.9 WRITE (Filename, Recordname) – First record

If the file is empty, the file pointer will have been set to zero. The first instruction to WRITE(Filename, Recordname) will therefore place the first record in the file.

All subsequent instructions to WRITE(Filename, Recordname) will place the records in the file sequentially, incrementing the file pointer each time.

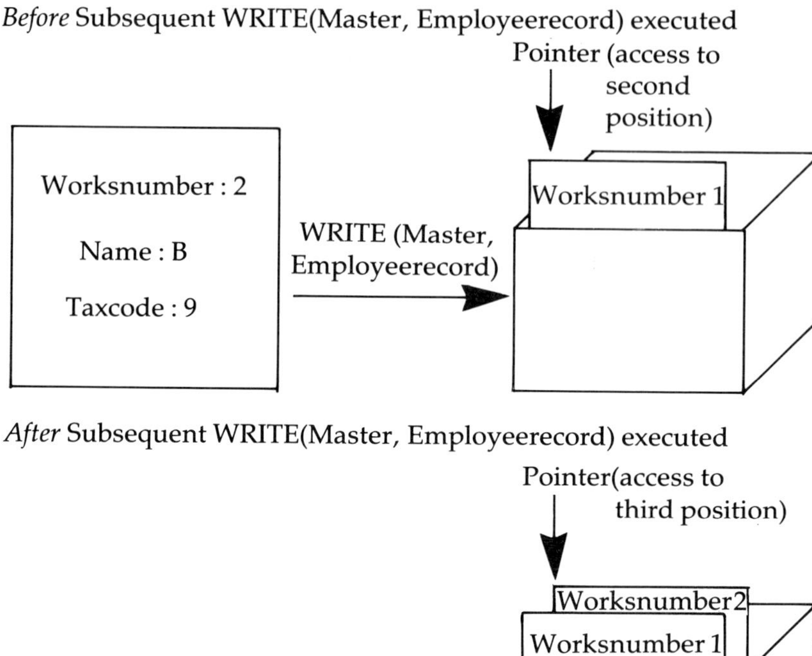

Figure 10.10 WRITE (Filename, Recordname) – Subsequent record

Reading records from a file

This is quite simple. The modified procedure READ(Filename, Recordname) stores the record that is currently being pointed to by the file pointer into the variable name Recordname. The file pointer is then incremented thus giving access to the next record.

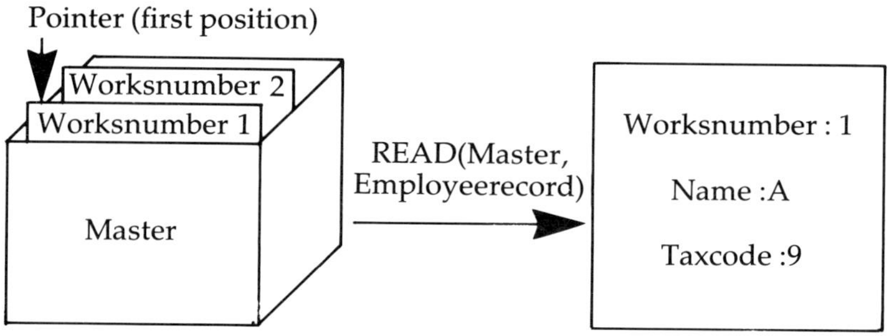

Figure 10.11 Reading the first record

It is only possible to read from a file that has records in it. Assuming therefore that our file contains records and we have not previously read from the file, then the pointer is at the first record after we have RESET (Filename).

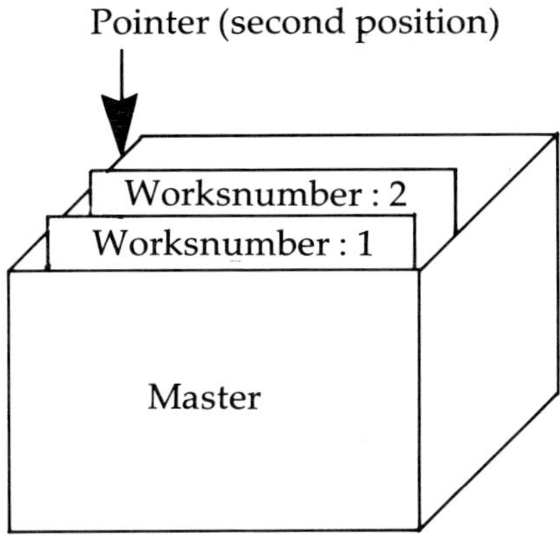

Figure 10.12 After reading the first record

After the execution of the first READ(Filename, Recordname) the pointer will automatically be incremented to give access to the next record in sequence.

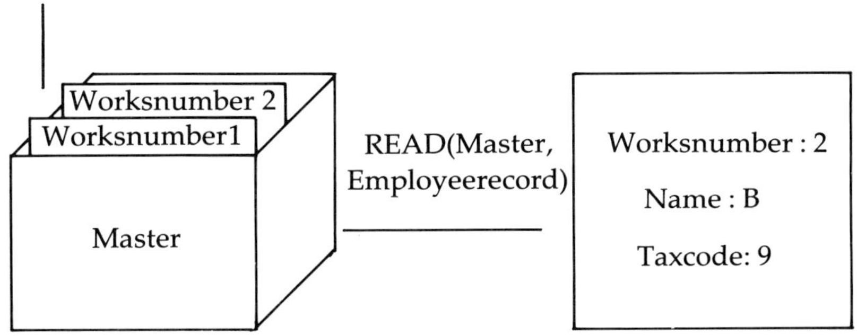

Figure 10.13 Reading subsequent records

This operation is a Non Destructive Read Out (NDRO). The contents can be read again and again – only after file initialisation.

Detecting the end-of-file

There are two methods. The BOOLEAN function EOF will automatically become TRUE when, after successive READ(Filename, Recordname), the file pointer has gone past the last record in the file. The method we will be using is to place a sentinel or dummy record at the end of the file. The presence of this indicates the end of the file. (See Figure 10.14.)

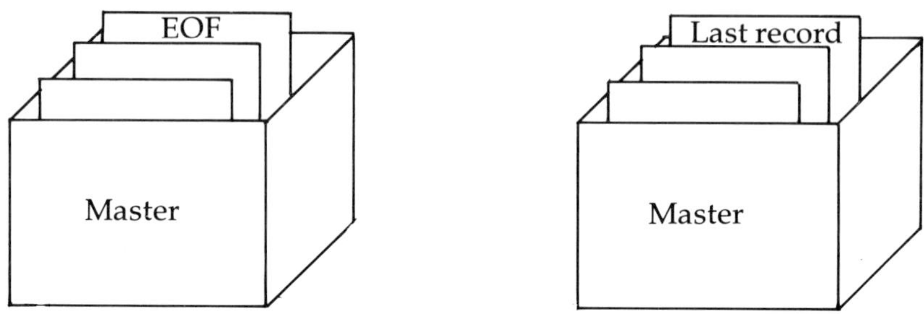

Figure 10.14 End-of-file markers

Closing a file

This is done for you in Pascal! This however is not the case with some other languages. Without due care this can be a problem with our language independent design, as we will see. (See Figure 10.15.)

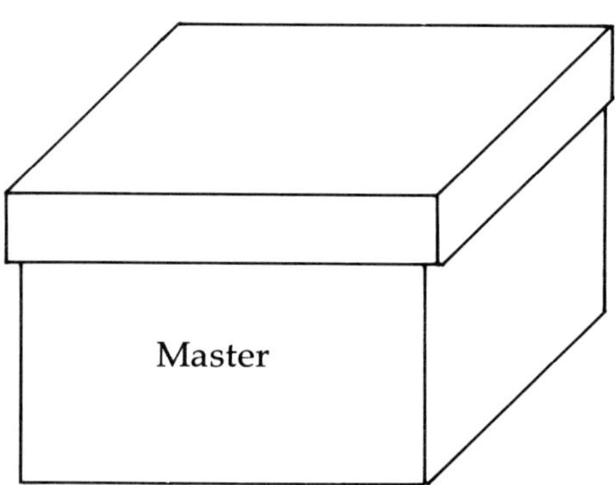

Figure 10.15 Closing a file

Record manipulation

It is possible to access individual fields with the READ and WRITE commands.

```
READ(Recordname.fieldname)

WRITE(Recordname.fieldname)
```

In our case we could have READ(Employeerecord.Worksnumber). This would allow us to read the Worksnumber. To read the next field another statement is needed, READ(Employeerecord.Name) and so on. The sampe applies to the WRITE(Recordname.Fieldname) statement. (See Figures 10.16, 10.17 and 10.18.)

WRITE (Employeerecord.Worknumber)

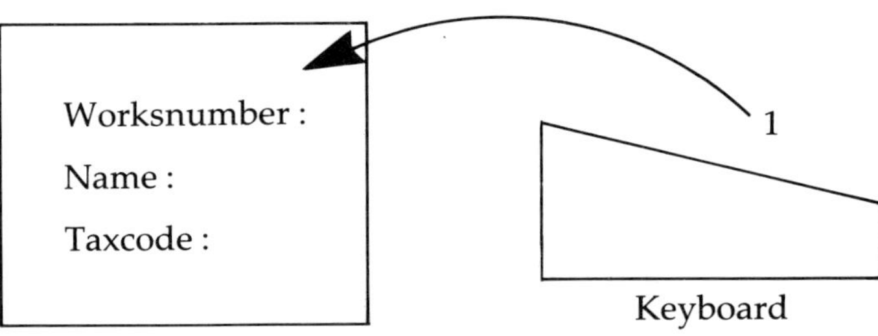

Figure 10.16 WRITE(Employeerecord.Worksnumber)

WRITE(Employeerecord.Name)

Worksnumber : 1
Name :
Taxcode :
A
Keyboard

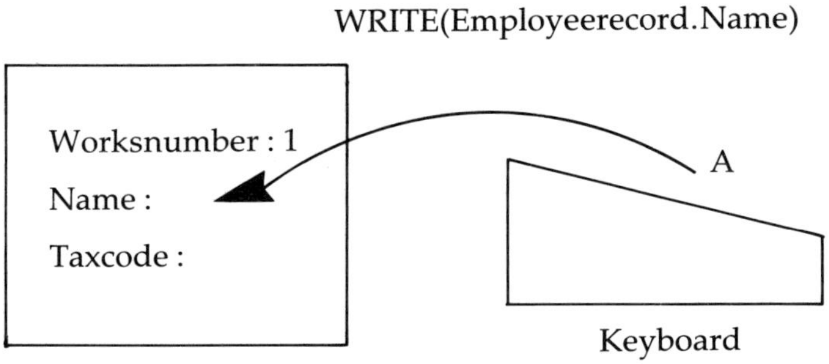

Figure 10.17 WRITE(Employeerecord.Name)

WRITE(Employeerecord.Taxcode)

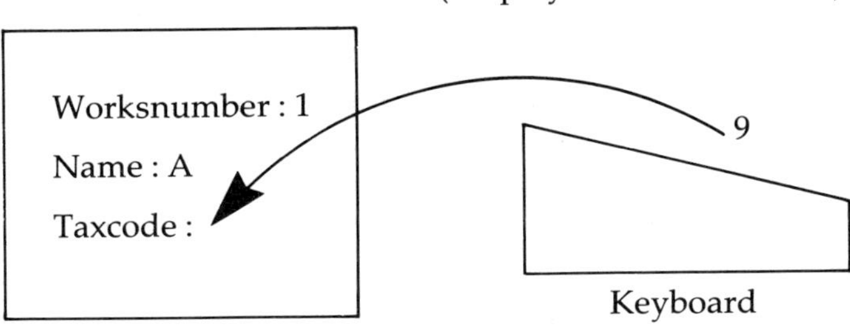

Figure 10.18 WRITE(Employeerecord.Taxcode)

In the case of records with large numbers of fields, or just for convenience, it is possible to use the WITH statement. (See Figure 10.19.)

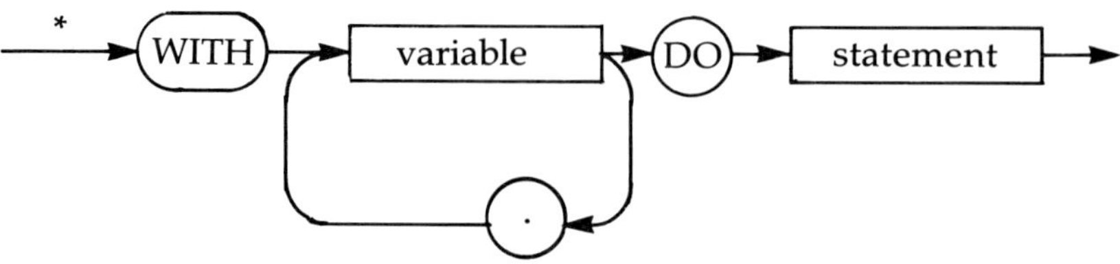

In our case we have Employeerecord for our variable.

```
WITH Employeerecord DO
        BEGIN
                READLN(Worksnumber);
                READLN(Name);
                READLN(Taxcode)
        END;
```

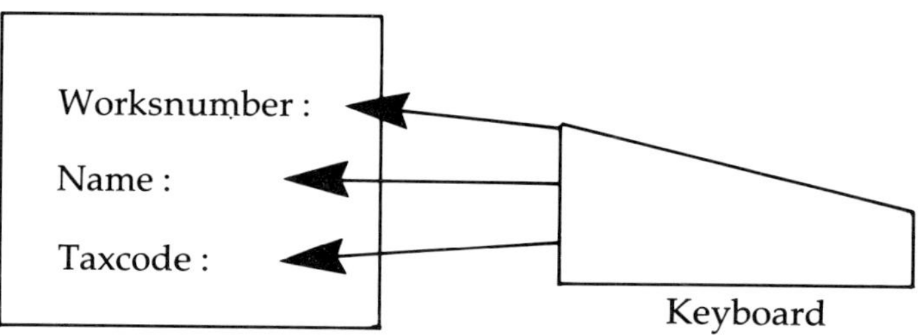

Figure 10.19 The WITH command

10.8 CREATING A NEW FILE

Sequentially we have to

- 1. Open the file for writing and initialise the variables.
- 2. While there are more records to be entered, read in the record details and write them to the file.
- 3. Do procedure termination which consists of placing the last or Sentinel record at the end of the file.

This is very much like the universal program we have seen before. (See Figure 10.20.)

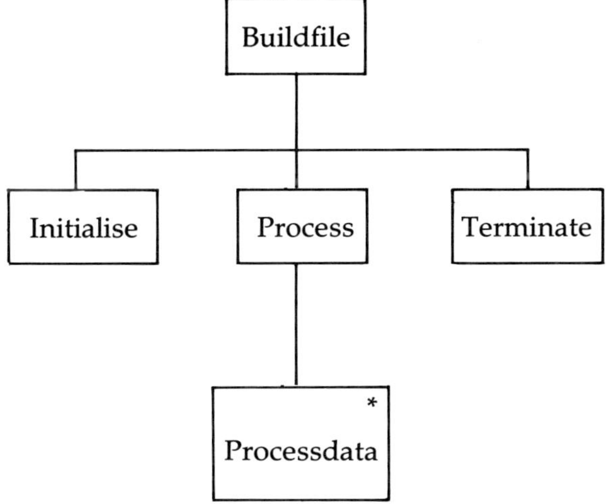

This can be represented diagrammatically:

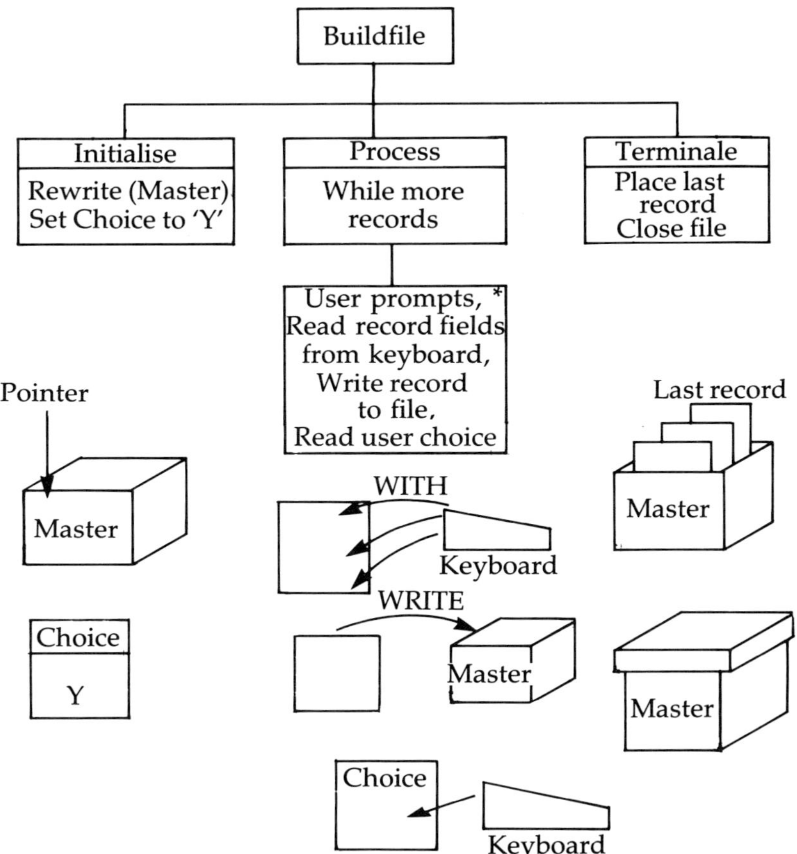

Figure 10.20 Operations to generate a file

This is more conveniently represented using our SSI diagrams:

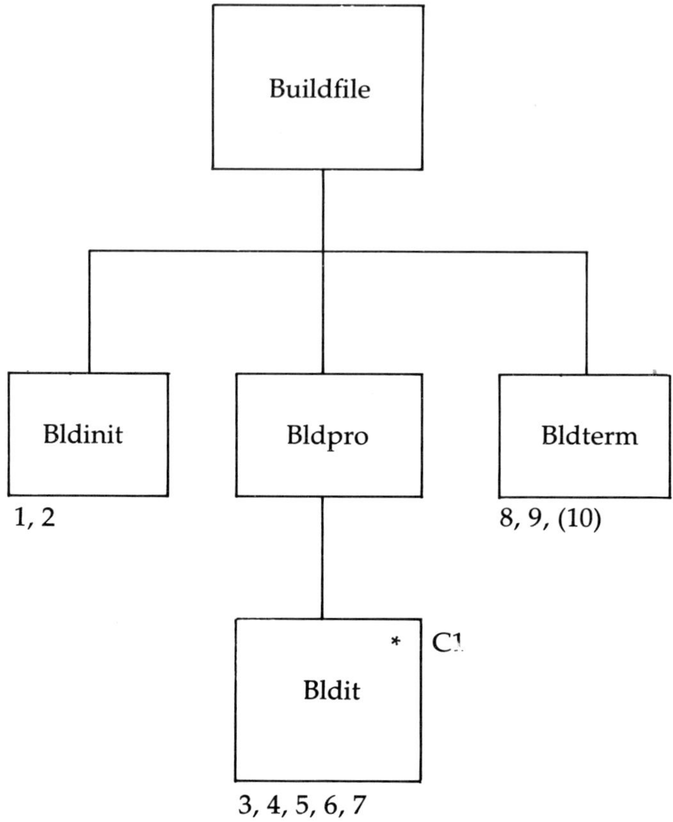

Functions	*Conditions*
1. Open file Master for Writing	C1 While choice = 'Y'
2. Initialise Choice to 'Y'	
3. User prompt for all record fields } ie WITH	
4. Read record fields	
5. Write record to file Master	
6. User prompt	
7. Read user choice	
8. Lastrecord	
9. Write Lastrecord to file Master	
(10. Close file – done for you in Pascal)	

```
PROCEDURE Buildfile;
(* This procedure allows records to be entered into the file Master. *)
VAR Choice : CHAR;

PROCEDURE Bldinit;
BEGIN
        REWRITE(Master);
        Choice := 'Y'
END;

PROCEDURE Bldpro;
        PROCEDURE Bldit;
        BEGIN
                WITH Employeerecord DO
                        BEGIN
                                WRITELN('Worksnumber ?');
                                READLN(Worksnumber);
                                WRITELN('Name ?');
                                READLN(Name);
                                WRITELN('Taxcode ?');
                                READLN(Taxcode)
                        END;
                WRITELN(Master, Employeerecord);
                WRITELN('More records, type Y or N');
                READLN(Choice)
        END;

BEGIN
        WHILE Choice = 'Y' DO
        Bldit
END;
```

```
PROCEDURE Bldterm;
BEGIN
        Lastrecord;
        WRITE(Master, Employeerecord)
        (* Close file *)
END;
```

```
BEGIN
        Bldinit;
        Bldpro;
        Bldterm
END;
```

The actions needed for Lastrecord could be incorporated into Buildfile either as lines of code or an internal procedure. The actions can be considered as an independent routine. This procedure, when called will assign a Sentinel value to the Worksnumber field, and dummy values to the other fields. We will therefore write it as a standalone procedure. Do note that Procedure Lastrecord must precede the Procedure Buildfile.

```
PROCEDURE Lastrecord;
BEGIN
        WITH Employeerecord DO
        BEGIN
                Worksnumber := 99;
                Name := 'X';
                Taxcode := 99
        END;
END;
```

10.9 DISPLAYING A FILE ON SCREEN

Functions	*Conditions*
1. Open file Master for reading	C1 While not Sentinel
2. Read record (first) from Master	
3. Write all record fields to screen	
4. Read record (next) from Master	

(5. Close file, no need in Pascal)

The second terminal function is an example of the 'Read Ahead Rule'.

The SSI diagram is as follows:

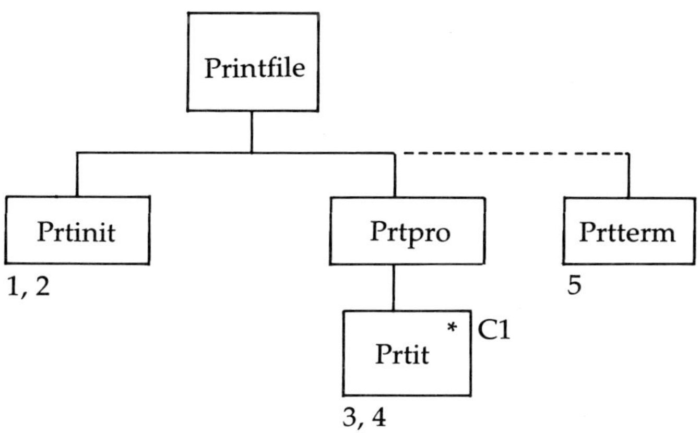


```
PROCEDURE Printfile;

(* This procedure displays all of the records in the file Master on the
screen. Note the Lastrecord with the sentinel is not displayed *)

PROCEDURE Prtinit;
BEGIN
        RESET(Master);
        READ(Master, Employeerecord)
END;

PROCEDURE Prtpro;
        PROCEDURE Prtit;
        BEGIN
                WITH Employeerecord DO
                        BEGIN
                                WRITELN(Worksnumber);
                                WRITELN(Name);
                                WRITELN(Taxcode)
                        END;
                READ(Master, Employeerecord)
        END;
```

```
BEGIN
        WHILE Employeerecord.worksnumber <> 99
        DO Prtit
END;
```

```
BEGIN
        Prtinit;
        Prtpro
END;
```

10.10 BRINGING IT ALL TOGETHER

We now have two main procedures, Buildfile and Printfile. These can be manipulated as follows :

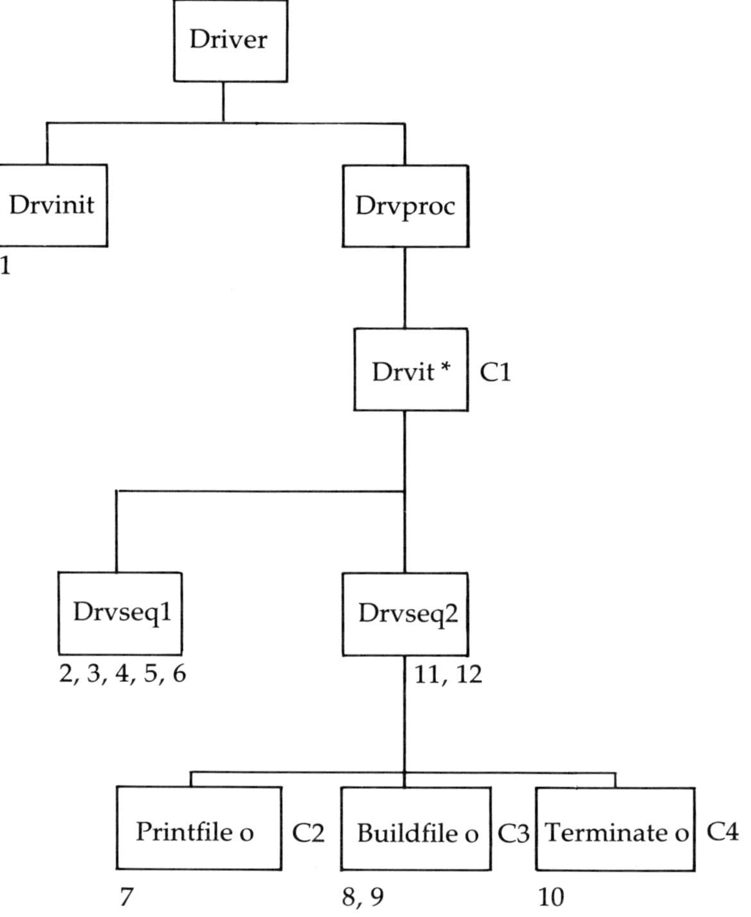

Functions	*Conditions*
1. Initialise Mainchoice to 'Y'	C1 While Mainchoice = 'Y'
2 to 5. User prompts	C2 Option = 1
6. Read user Option	C3 Option = 2
7. Printfile	C4 Option = 3
8. Buildfile	
9. Printfile	
10. Mainchoice := 'N'	
11. User prompt	
12. Read(Mainchoice)	

Do note the use of convenient style. Terminal functions 11 and 12 should, strictly be in a procedure by themselves. Due to textual layout restrictions, the procedure names are in abbreviated form.

```
PROCEDURE Driver;
(* This is the control procedure that displays the menu to the user *)
VAR Mainchoice : CHAR;
        Option : INTEGER

PROCEDURE Drvinit;
BEGIN
        Mainchoice := 'Y'
END;

PROCEDURE Drvproc;
        PROCEDURE Drvit;
            PROCEDURE Drvseql;
            BEGIN
                    WRITELN('Choose one option :');
                    WRITELN('1 : Display all records');
                    WRITELN('2 : New file of records');
                    WRITELN('3 : End session');
                    READLN(Option);
            END;
```

```
PROCEDURE Drvseq2;
BEGIN
        CASE Option OF
                1 : Printfile;
                2 : BEGIN
                        Buildfile;
                        Printfile
                END;
                3 : Mainchoice := 'N'
                END;
                WRITELN('Again Y or N');
                READLN(Mainchoice)
END;

BEGIN
        Drvseq1;
        Drvse2
END;

BEGIN
        WHILE Mainchoice = 'Y' DO
            Drvit
END;

BEGIN
        Drvinit;
        Drvproc
END;

BEGIN
        Driver
END.
```

10.11 SUMMARY

Let us now have a look at the 'big picture'. A module is defined by its name, with the name being self explanatory. The module can be decomposed into other modules again referenced by name. This top down decomposition process continues down to the terminal function level, ie where no further decomposition is possible. We can then convert to the target language.

We are therefore in the very strong position of being able to work at any level within the hierarchy. If we are designing at the highest level we can manipulate the modules Printfile and Buildfile. At this level there is no need to define all the detail of these levels – unless that is our wish. Therefore the lines of code and complexity are hidden from us. We are working in the abstract.

– 1. A record is a collection of different pieces of information that are logically related and hence can be handled as a single unit and the individual elements or fields, accessed accordingly. A record is a structured data type.

– 2. There are three principle types of record field – control, static and dynamic.

– 3. A file is a collection of records. File organisational methods differ. In standard Pascal we only consider sequential file organisation. A file is a structured data type.

– 4. The different types of file processing include amendment, updating, addition/insertion, referencing and deleting.

– 5. The standard procedures for file manipulation are REWRITE(Filename), RESET(Filename), WRITE(Filename, Recordname), READ(Filename, Recordname).

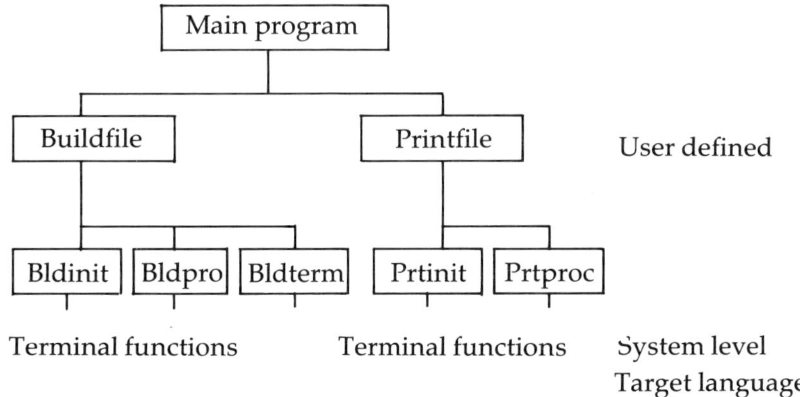

Figure 10.21 Abstraction

– 6. End of file can be detected by the BOOLEAN function EOF or a sentinel record.

– 7. Files are closed automatically in Pascal.

– 8. Individual record fields can be manipulated by READ/WRITE(Filename. Fieldname). Alternatively the WITH statement may be employed.

10.12 PROBLEMS

We have now completed the basic format for file manipulation. What you may like to do is:

– 1. Design your own record. Start with a simple one similar to the one above. Do note that string handling will come in the next chapter.

– 2. Convert the above program to handle your record type.

– 3. Records may be nested. Investigate how this is done.

11 String Manipulation in Files

11.1 INTRODUCTION

The program so far can only handle type INTEGER and CHAR – something of a limitation! How character strings are manipulated depends on the compiler and hence the version of Pascal you are using. First let's have a look at standard Pascal and then consider how other versions work.

11.2 FIELDS SO FAR

Consider our declarations so far:

```
PROGRAM Simple1 (INPUT, OUTPUT, MASTER);
TYPE Employee = RECORD
                   Worksnumber : INTEGER;
                   Name        : CHAR;
                   Taxcode     : INTEGER;
              END;
      Personnel = FILE of Employee;
VAR Employeerecord: Employee;
      Master: Personnel;
```

* Worksnumber and Taxcode are of TYPE INTEGER.
Name is of TYPE CHAR.

11.3 STRINGS IN STANDARD PASCAL

The way to handle strings is to use arrays. Using arrays we can redefine our record as follows:

```
Employee = RECORD
                Worksnumber:  PACKED  ARRAY[1..4]  OF
                CHAR;
                Name:        PACKED ARRAY[1..10] OF CHAR;
                Taxcode:      INTEGER
        END;
```

Here we have defined the maximum length of the field Worksnumber to be four characters. Similarly the field Name is defined to be ten characters. The Taxcode field has been kept the same. We can, obviously within limitations, have any length of field we wish. We can further improve our declarations by defining further types.

```
    TYPE Namestring = PACKED ARRAY[1..10] OF CHAR;
         Keystring = PACKED ARRAY[1..4] OF CHAR;
         Employee = RECORD

         Worksnumber         : Keystring;
         Name                : Namestring;
         Taxcode             : INTEGER
    END;
```

Here Type Namestring and Keystring are declared as PACKED ARRAYS. This makes it easier for our record declaration.

Finally we can make a constant declaration as follows:

```
  CONST Namelength = 10;
        Keylength = 4;
   TYPE Namestring = PACKED   ARRAY[1..Namelength]   OF
                     CHAR;
        Keystring = PACKED ARRAY[1..Keylength] OF CHAR;
        Employee = Record

        Worksnumber        : Keystring;
        Name               : Namestring;
        Taxcode            : INTEGER;
```

But to what advantage? There are several reasons, again we are employing the principle of abstraction to aid readability and design. To declare Worksnumber to be of type Keystring is certainly a help. The details associated with Keystring are available but do not clutter up our code. There is appropriate detail to the level we are working in. If we wish to change either, or both, the Keylength and Namelength all we need to modify are the constants.

How do we handle these strings? For this, two more variables are needed which we are going to call Gname and Gkey.

```
VAR Employeerecord: Employee;
        Master: Personnel;
        Gname: Namestring;
        Gkey: Keystring;
```

Two procedures are employed here. Getnamestring will read characters from the keyboard; if the character string is less than the length of the array then spaces will be inserted. The predefined word EOLN is used to detect the end of the character string. The final READLN picks up the carriage return. The procedure Getkeystring works in a similar manner except for the length of the array.

```
PROCEDURE Getnamestring;
(* Procedure to read characters from the keyboard *)
(* EOLN to detect end of character string for namelength *)
VAR
        i : INTEGER;
BEGIN
        FOR i := 1 to Namelength DO
           IF EOLN THEN
                Gname[i] := ''
           ELSE
                READ(Gname[i]);
           READLN
END;
```

```
PROCEDURE Getkeystring;
(* Procedure to read characters from the keyboard *)
(* EOLN to detect end of character string for keylength *)
VAR
        i : INTEGER;
BEGIN
```

```
        FOR i:= 1 to Keylength DO
          IF EOLN THEN
              Gkey[i]:= ''
          ELSE
              READ(Gkey[i]);
          READLN
END;
```

The only other modification to our program is in the procedure Bldpro in Buildfile. Our procedures fill the arrays Gname and Gkey accordingly. The arrays can then be assigned to the record fields.

No other modifications are needed. The procedure Printfile remains the same.

```
PROCEDURE Bldit;

BEGIN
      WITH Employeerecord DO
            BEGIN
                  WRITELN('Worksnumber ?');
                  Getkeystring;
                  Worksnumber := Gkey;
                  WRITELN('Name ?');
                  Getnamestring;
                  Name := Gname;
                  WRITELN('Taxcode ?');
                  READLN(Taxcode)
            END;
            WRITE(Master, Employeerecord);
            WRITELN('More records, type Y or N');
            READLN(Choice)
END;
```

For clarification the complete program Ch11P1 is included.

```
PROGRAM Ch11P1 (INPUT, OUTPUT, MASTER);
(* Program to generate and read a file *)
```

```
(* Standard Pascal file handling with procedures to handle charac-
ter strings *)
CONST Namelength = 10;
       Keylength = 4;
       Sentinel = '9999';
       Dummy = ' ';
TYPE Namestring = PACKED ARRAY[1..Namelength] OF CHAR;
      Keystring = PACKED ARRAY[1..Keylength] OF CHAR;
      Employee = RECORD
                      Worksnumber     : Keystring;
                      Name            : Namestring;
                      Taxcode         : INTEGER;
                 END;
           Personnel = FILE of Employee;
VAR Employeerecord: Employee;
     Master: Personnel;
     Gname: Namestring;
     Gkey: Keystring;
```

```
PROCEDURE Getnamestring;
(* Procedure to read characters from the keyboard *)
(* EOLN to detect end of character string for Namelength *)
VAR
       i : INTEGER;
BEGIN
       FOR i := 1 to Namelength do
              IF EOLN THEN
                     Gname[i] := ' '
              ELSE
                     READ(Gname[i]);
              READLN
END;
```

```
PROCEDURE Getkeystring;
(* Procedure to read characters from the Keyboard *)
(* EOLN to detect end of character string for Keylength *)
VAR
        i : INTEGER
BEGIN
        FOR i := 1 to Keylength DO
                IF EOLN THEN
                        Gkey[i] := ' '
                ELSE
                        READ (Gkey[i];
                READLN
 END;
```

```
PROCEDURE Lastrecord;
BEGIN
        WITH Employeerecord DO
        BEGIN
                Worksnumber := Sentinel;
                Name := Dummy;
                Taxcode := 9
        END;
END;
```

```
PROCEDURE Printfile;
(* This procedure displays all the records in the file Master on the
screen. Note, the last record with the sentinel is not displayed *)

        PROCEDURE Prtinit;
        BEGIN
                RESET(Master);
                READ(Master, Employeerecord)
        END;
```

```
PROCEDURE Prtpro;
    PROCEDURE Prtit;
    BEGIN
        WITH Employeerecord DO
            BEGIN
                WRITELN(Worksnumber);
                WRITELN(Name);
                WRITELN(Taxcode)
            END;
        READ(Master, Employeerecord)
    END;
BEGIN
    WHILE Employeerecord. Worksnumber <> Sentinel
        DO Prtit
END;

BEGIN
    Prtinit;
    Prtpro
END;
```

```
PROCEDURE Buildfile;
(* This procedure allows records to be entered in the file Master *)
VAR Choice: CHAR;
```

```
PROCEDURE Bldinit;
BEGIN
    REWRITE(Master);
    Choice := 'Y'
END;
```

```
PROCEDURE Bldpro;
    PROCEDURE Bldit;
    BEGIN
        WITH Employeerecord DO
            BEGIN
                WRITELN('Worksnumber ?');
                Getkeystring;
                Worksnumber := Gkey;
                WRITELN('Name ?');
                Getnamestring;
                Name := Gname;
                WRITELN('Taxcode ?');
                READLN(Taxcode)
            END;
        WRITELN(Master, Employeerecord);
        WRITELN(Master, Employeerecord);
        READLN(Choice)
    END;
BEGIN
    WHILE Choice = 'Y' DO
        Bldit
END;
PROCEDURE Bldterm;
BEGIN
    Lastrecord;
    WRITE(Master, Employeerecord)
END;
BEGIN
    Bldinit;
    Bldpro;
    Bldterm
END;
```

```
PROCEDURE Driver;
(* This is the control procedure that displays the menu to the user *)
VAR Mainchoice: CHAR;
    Option: INTEGER;

    PROCEDURE Drvinit;
    BEGIN
        Mainchoice := 'Y'
    END;

    PROCEDURE Drvproc;

        PROCEDURE Drvit;

            PROCEDURE Drvseq1;
            BEGIN
                WRITELN('Choose one option :');
                WRITELN('1 : Display all records');
                WRITELN('2 : New file of records');
                WRITELN('3 : End session');
                READLN(Option);
            END;

            PROCEDURE Drvseq2;
            BEGIN
                CASE Option OF
                    1 : Printfile;
                    2 : BEGIN
                            Buildfile;
                            Printfile
                        END;
                    3 : Mainchoice := 'N'
                END;
                WRITELN('Again Y or N');
                READLN(Mainchoice)
            END;
```

```
            BEGIN
                Drvseq1;
                Drvseq2;
            END;

        BEGIN
            WHILE Mainchoice = 'Y' DO
                Drvit
        END;

    BEGIN
        Drvinit;
        Drvproc
    END;

BEGIN
    Driver
END.
```

11.4 SIMPLIFIED STRING HANDLING

One Pascal compiler I have been using handles character strings rather well. There is no need for Gname, Gkey, Getnamestring or Getkeystring. It handles the character strings implicitly. Do check how your compiler handles character strings.

```
PROGRAM Ch11P2 (INPUT, OUTPUT, MASTER)
(* Program to generate and read a file *)
(* Pascal compiler used has simplified string handling facilities *)
CONST Namelength = 10;
      Keylength = 4;
      Sentinel = '9999';
      Dummy = ' ';
TYPE Namestring = PACKED ARRAY[ 1..Namelength ] OF CHAR;
     Keystring = PACKED ARRAY[ 1..Keylength ] OF CHAR;
```

```
        Employee = RECORD
                        Worksnumber         : Keystring;
                        Name                : Namestring;
                        Taxcode             : INTEGER;
                     END;
        Personnel = FILE OF Employee;
  VAR Employeerecord: Employee;
       Master            : Personnel;
```

```
PROCEDURE Lastrecord;
BEGIN
        WITH Employeerecord DO
        BEGIN
                Worksnumber := Sentinel;
                Name := Dummy;
                Taxcode := 9
        END;
END;
```

```
PROCEDURE Buildfile;
(* This procedure allows records to be entered into the file Master *)
VAR Choice: CHAR;
```

```
PROCEDURE Bldinit;
BEGIN
        REWRITE(Master);
        Choice := 'Y'
END;
```

```
PROCEDURE Bldpro;
        PROCEDURE Bldit;
        BEGIN
                WITH Employeerecord DO
                BEGIN
```

```
                    WRITELN('Worksnumber ?');
                    READLN(Worksnumber);
                    WRITELN('Name ?');
                    READLN(Name);
                    WRITELN('Taxcode ?');
                    READLN(Taxcode)
                END;
                WRITE(Master, Employeerecord);
                WRITELN('More records, type Y or N');
                READLN(Choice)
            END;
BEGIN
        WHILE Choice = 'Y' DO
                Bldit
END;
```

```
PROCEDURE Bldterm;
BEGIN
        Lastrecord;
        WRITE(Master, Employeerecord)
        (* Close file *)
END;
```

```
BEGIN
        Bldinit;
        Bldpro;
        Bldterm
END;

PROCEDURE Printfile;
(* This procedure displays all of the records in the file Master on the
   screen. Note, the last record with the Sentinel is not displayed *)
```

```
PROCEDURE Prtinit;
BEGIN
    RESET(Master);
    READ(Master, Employeerecord)
END;

PROCEDURE Prtpro;

    PROCEDURE Prtit;
    BEGIN
        WITH Employeerecord DO
        BEGIN
            WRITELN(Worksnumber);
            WRITELN(Name);
            WRITELN(Taxcode)
        END;
        READ(Master, Employeerecord)
    END;

BEGIN
    WHILE Employeerecord.Worksnumber <> Sentinel
        DO Prtit
END;

BEGIN
    Prtinit;
    Prtpro
END;
PROCEDURE Driver;
(* As before *)
```

11.5 SUMMARY

– 1. String handling in standard Pascal is cumbersome. Strings are defined using arrays and manipulated by procedures that insert the correct number of spaces and use the pre-defined EOLN to detect the end of the character string.

- 2. Other compilers can greatly simplify string handling.

11.6 PROBLEMS

- 1. In the previous chapter, if you have been doing your homework, you will have designed your own record. Now that we are in a position to handle strings, design a more realistic record.
- 2. Modify the above program to handle your record design.
- 3. Investigate how your compiler handles strings. Typically Pascal compilers will allow you to select standard or non-standard Pascal. Modify your code accordingly.

12 Further File Manipulation

12.1 APPEND A RECORD INTO THE FILE

In this chapter we will look at other file processing. Let's first consider how to append a record into the file of records previously generated. Recall that logically we are using only sequential files. It is therefore not possible to write records back to the same position on the tape from which they have been read. We need two files. We will read from our Master file and write each record to another file, Copy.

```
PROGRAM XXXXX (INPUT, OUTPUT, Master, Copy);

CONST as before

TYPE as before

VAR as before but also

        Copy: Personnel;
```

Here we have declared Copy to be a file of the same type as Master. For our initialisation we need to RESET(Master) as we are reading from it, prime the iteration variable and read the first record. Note the user choice variable, Appendchoice, could be the same as that used in Buildfile, Choice. They are local variables and this would work. Where possible however keep the names of local variables different. The compiler will not get confused but you might when you get your error diagnostics from a run-time or compilation error! Because we need two files we also have to REWRITE(Copy). Copy is now empty and ready to be written to. This is done using procedure Apdseq1.

It is now necessary to sequentially copy all the records, except the Sentinel record, from the file Master to the file Copy, ie Apdseq2.

Using the procedure Apdproc new records can be written to the file Copy. Note that this procedure is functionally identical to Bldproc in Buildfile.

In the procedure Adpterm, the functions are the same as Bldterm. The problem is now that our records are in Copy and not Master. Copy needs updating. We could include the code for the update functions in the procedure for append. However, as we will see, we will use update again. It is better to have update as a separate, self contained procedure.

A simpler way would be to kill the file Master and rename Copy as Master. However the way we are doing it does serve as a useful exercise. Recall that we are not at the moment interested in efficiency but rather the basic principles.

The layout restrictions here mean that the procedure names have to be rather short. Do note, however, that where possible sibling procedure names are partially derived from the parent procedure. Depending on the quality of the compiler you are using, this can be an invaluable aid in error location and diagnostics.

Append a record structured diagram

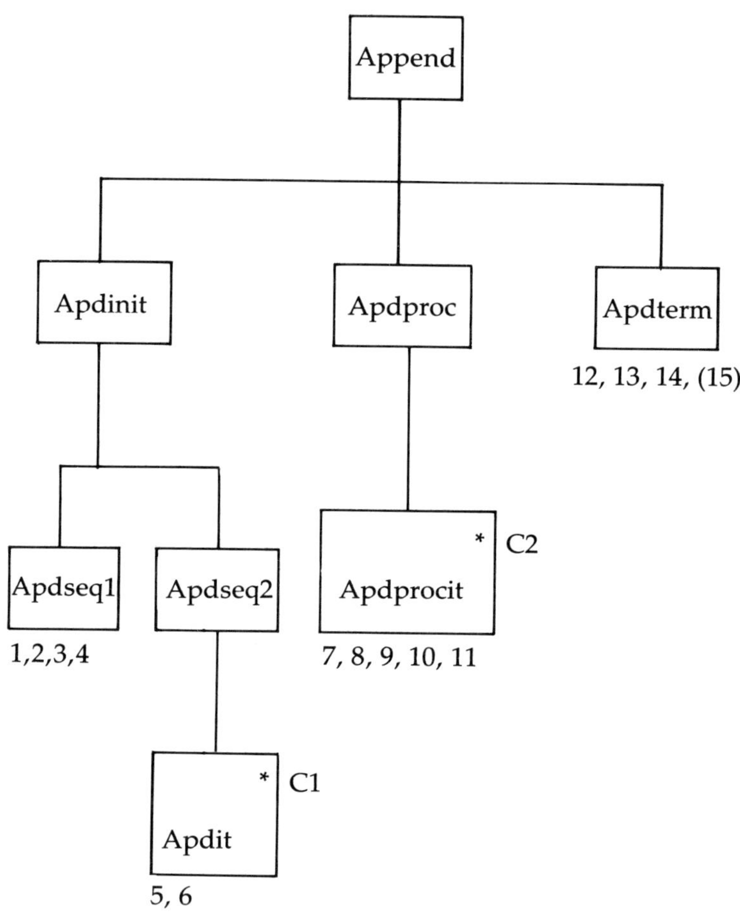

Functions

1. Open file Master for reading
2. Open file Copy for writing
3. Initialise Appendchoice to 'Y'

Conditions

C1 While not Sentinel

C2 While Appendchoice is 'Y'

4. Read record (first) from Master
5. Write record (current) to file Copy
6. Read record (next) from Master
7. User prompts
8. Read fields
9. Write record to file Copy
10. User prompt
11. Read user option Appendchoice
12. Lastrecord
13. Write record (last) to file Copy
14. Updatefile

(15. Close files)

```
PROCEDURE Append;
(* Procedure to append a record on the end of a file *)
(* All the records from the Master file are copied to *)
(* the Copy file except for the Lastrecord. *)
(* The new record is then written to the file Copy. *)
(* After the Lastrecord has been added to file Copy *)
(* the records are written back to Master file using *)
(* the procedure Update *)
VAR Appendchoice: CHAR;

PROCEDURE Apdinit;
    PROCEDURE Apdseq1;
    BEGIN
        RESET(Master);
        REWRITE(Copy);
        Appendchoice := 'Y';
        READ(Master, Employeerecord)
    END;
```

```
        PROCEDURE Apdseq2;

                PROCEDURE Apdit;
                BEGIN
                        WRITE(Copy, Employeerecord);
                        READ(Master, Employeerecord)
                END;

        BEGIN
                WHILE Employeerecord.Worksnumber <> Sentinel
                    DO Apdit
        END;

BEGIN
        Apdseq1;
        Apdseq2
END;
```

```
PROCEDURE Apdproc;
        PROCEDURE Apdprocit;
        BEGIN
                WITH Employeerecord DO
                        BEGIN
                                WRITELN('Worksnumber ?');
                                READLN(Worksnumber);
                                WRITELN('Name ?');
                                READLN(Name);
                                WRITELN('Taxcode ?');
                                READLN(Taxcode)
                        END;
                        WRITE(Copy, Employeerecord);
                        WRITELN('More ?, Y or N');
                        READLN(Appendchoice);
        END;
```

```
BEGIN
        WHILE Appendchoice = 'Y' DO
        Apdprocit
END;
```

```
PROCEDURE Apdterm;
BEGIN
        Lastrecord;
        WRITE(Copy, Employeerecord);
        Updatefile
END;
```

```
BEGIN
        Apdinit;
        Apdproc;
        Apdterm
 END;
```

With practice, you should easily see the relationship between the design and the code. The module names should be chosen to allow ease of use – abstraction – with rapid module identification. This is useful in the case of compilation of run-time error detection and the localisation of the errors. The indentation allowed to us by free formatting is visually very powerful and further enhances module identification and realisation of the relationships.

The functions to close files are included in the design even though this is not needed in Pascal. Our design is going to be used with other target languages where it is essential to close all files after use.

Procedure Apdinit is the initialisation procedure that also copies all the records, except the last record, to the file Copy. The user is then prompted to complete the fields of a record that is then written to the file Copy. This is an iterative process controlled by the user. Finally, in procedure Apdterm, the last record is written to the file Copy and the Master file is updated.

12.2 UPDATE A FILE

Here we have a self contained module of code which will copy across all the records from the file Copy to the file Master. The last record (Sentinel) is also written to the Master file.

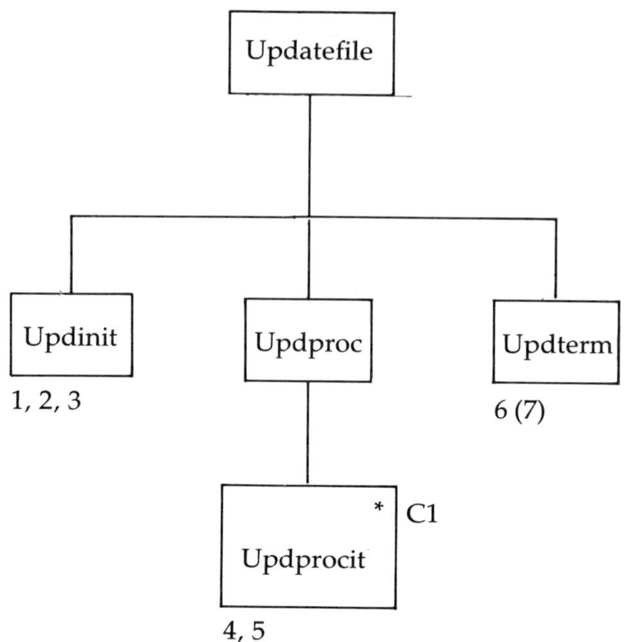

Functions

1. Open file Copy for reading
2. Open file Master for writing
3. Read record (first) from Copy
4. Write record to file Master
5. Read record from Copy
6. Write record (last) to file Master

(7. Close files)

Conditions

C1 While not Sentinel

```
PROCEDURE Updatefile;
(* This procedure copies all the records from file Copy to file Master *)

  PROCEDURE Updinit;
  BEGIN
          RESET(Copy);
          REWRITE(Master);
          READ(Copy, Employeerecord)
  END;
```

```
PROCEDURE Updproc;

    PROCEDURE Updprocit;
    BEGIN
        WRITE(Master, Employeerecord);
        READ(Copy, Employeerecord);
    END;

BEGIN
    WHILE Employeerecord.Worksnumber <> Sentinel
  DO Updprocit
END;

PROCEDURE Updterm;
BEGIN
    WRITE(Master, Employeerecord)
END;

BEGIN
    Updinit;
    Updproc;
    Updterm
END;
```

12.3 DELETE A RECORD

In order to delete a given record we must sequentially search the file, copying each record to our temporary file Copy, until we find the record we are looking for. This record is not copied across to the temporary file but we continue to copy across any remaining records. Updatefile will then return all the records to the Master file.

If you are still having difficulty with the relationship between code and design, try placing the designs on the side. This will more accurately reflect the levels of indentation. Similarly, in conjunction with typing in this code, design your own record with its fields and modify this code accordingly. The design will still be the same. As a further exercise, modify the design to allow the user to make repeated deletions. Certainly experimentation with the designs and code is to be encouraged. Make your mistakes here and not when it is critical.

Procedure Delinit is our initialisation procedure and includes a user prompt for the number of the record to be deleted. Procedure Delpro is our iteration procedure that ensures all records in file Master are processed. Delproit is the iterated selection procedure. If the current record is not the selected record, it is written to the file Copy and the next record is read from file Master, ie Delprocsel1. However, if the current record is the one to be deleted, it is not written to the file Copy, and the next record is read from file Master, ie Delprocsel2. Finally, in Delterm, the last record is written to the file Copy and the Master file updated.

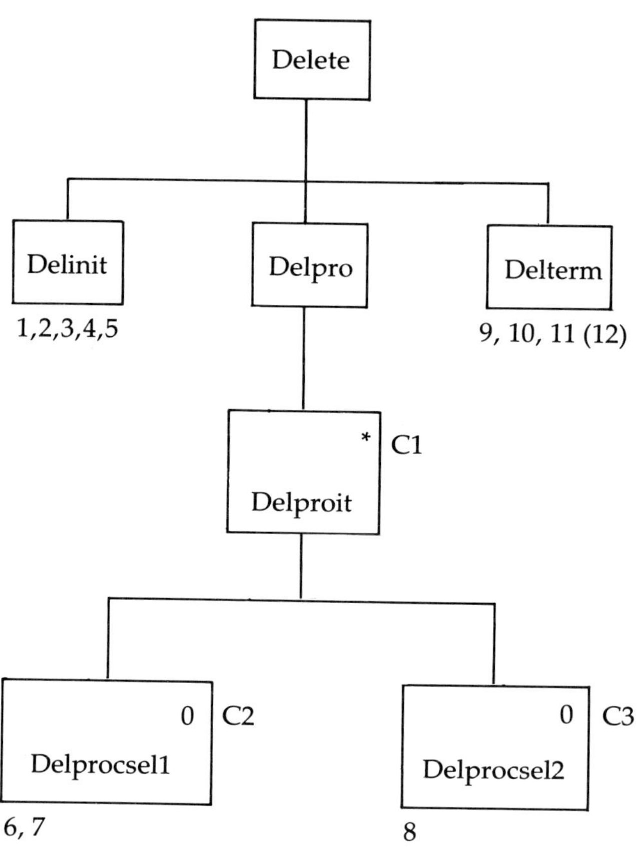

Functions

1. Open file Master for reading
2. Open file Copy for writing
3. Read record (first) from Master
4. User prompt
5. Read Cancel

Conditions

C1 While not Sentinel

C2 If Worksnumber <> Cancel

C3 If Worksnumber = Cancel

6. Write record (current) to file Copy
7. Read record (next) from file Master
8. Read record (next) from file Master
9. Lastrecord
10. Write record (last) to file Copy
11. Updatefile
(12. Close files)

```
PROCEDURE Delete;
(* This procedure allows the user to select a record *)
(* by Worksnumber for deletion *)
(* The selected record is not copied across to Copy file *)
(* Updatefile restores the status of Masterfile *)
VAR Cancel: INTEGER;
```

```
PROCEDURE Delinit;
BEGIN
        RESET(Master);
        REWRITE(Copy);
        READ(Master, Employeerecord);
        WRITELN('Number of the record be deleted');
        READLN(Cancel)
END;
```

```
PROCEDURE Delpro;

    PROCEDURE Delproit;

        PROCEDURE Delprocsell;
        BEGIN
                WRITE(Copy, Employeerecord);
                READ(Master, Employeerecord)
        END;
```

```
PROCEDURE Delprocsel2;
BEGIN
        READ(Master, Employeerecord);
END;

BEGIN
   IF Employeerecord.Worksnumber <> Cancel
   THEN
     Delprocsel1
   ELSE
     Delprocsel2
END;

BEGIN
        WHILE Employeerecord.Worksnumber <> Sentinel
          DO Delproit
END;

PROCEDURE Delterm;
BEGIN
        Lastrecord;
        WRITE(Copy, Employeerecord);
        Updatefile
END;

BEGIN
        Delinit;
        Delpro;
        Delterm
END;
```

12.4 EDIT A RECORD

Why have an Edit procedure? As we have previously discussed, operations on files must allow us to change the contents of the fields. The static or control data is amended while we say the dynamic data fields are updated. The module Edit will allow us to access a specified record and then change the Worksnumber. It is obviously possible to modify the other fields; this is left as an exercise to the reader. On completion of the exercise your design and code will allow the user to amend and update a file.

By this time you should be starting to be able to see the patterns in the structure. With experience you will find that the most convenient module size is about one page with three to four levels of indentation. A module smaller than this tends to be trivial. A module larger than this is difficult to grasp quickly and easily. You should be able to determine what a module does at one sitting; remember one of our aims is readability. Also with practice you will develop your own style within the bounds of, or slightly outside, the rules of structured design.

It is essential to develop the ability to think in terms of the design. This again can only come with practice.

The procedure Edinit is the initialisation procedure that includes a user prompt for the record to be changed. Procedure Edpro ensures that all the records in the file Master are processed. If the current record is the one to be changed, Procedure Editseq1 allows the user to modify the fields accordingly. Note that this is a unary selection. Irrespective of whether the record is to be changed or not, Procedure Editseq2 is performed, which writes all the records to the file Copy and reads the next record from file Master.

Functions	*Conditions*
1. Open file Master for reading	C1 While not Sentinel
2. Open file Copy for writing	C2 If Worksnumber = Change
3. Read record (first) from Master	
4. User prompt	
5. Read Change	
6. User prompt	
7. Read new Worksnumber	
8. Write record to file Copy	
9. Read record from Master	
10. Write record (last) to file Copy file Copy	
11. Updatefile	
(12. Close files)	

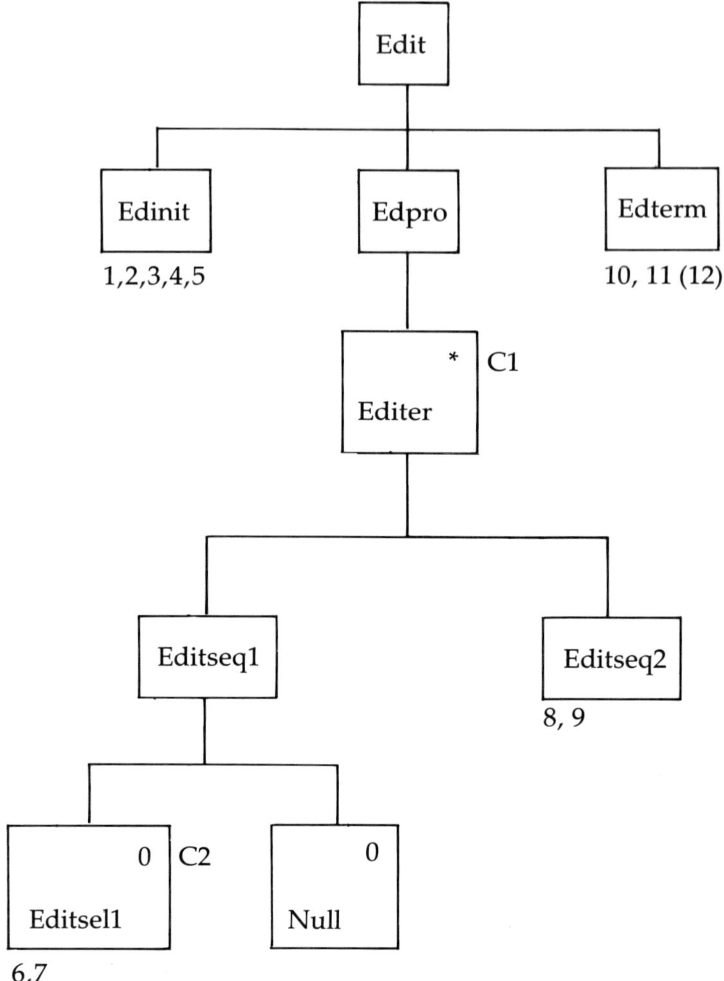


```
PROCEDURE Edit;
(* This procedure allows the user to edit a specified *)
(* record. The record is selected by Worksnumber and *)
(* the Worksnumber field contents may be changed *)
(* All records are copied across to Copy file *)
(* and the status of Master file is restored *)
(* using Updatefile *)
VAR Change: INTEGER;
```

```
PROCEDURE Edinit;
BEGIN
        RESET(Master);
        REWRITE(Copy);
        READ(Master, Employeerecord);
        WRITELN('Record to be changed?');
        READLN(Change)
END;

PROCEDURE Edpro;
        PROCEDURE Editer;
                PROCEDURE Editseq1
                        PROCEDURE Editsel1;
                          BEGIN
                               WRITE('New number of the ');
                               WRITELN('record?');
                               READLN (Employeerecord.
                                              Worksnumber);
                          END;
                BEGIN
                        IF Employeerecord.Worksnumber
                                 = change
                        THEN Editsel1
                END;
                PROCEDURE Editseq2;
                BEGIN
                        WRITE(Copy, Employeerecord);
                        READ(Master, Employeerecord)
                END;
        BEGIN
                Editseq1;
                Editseq2
        END;
```

```
BEGIN
        WHILE Employeerecord.Worksnumber <> Sentinel
        DO Editer
END;
```

```
PROCEDURE Edterm;
BEGIN
        WRITE(Copy, Employeerecord);
        Updatefile
END;
```

```
BEGIN
        Edinit;
        Edpro;
        Edterm;
END;
```

12.5 SORT

There are two ways to sort a file:

- 1. *Internal sort;* in this technique a complete copy of the file is transferred from the secondary memory storage area to the main memory. The file is then sorted according to the algorithm used. The sorted file is then written back to secondary memory. This assumes either the file is small or the main memory is very large.

- 2. *External sort;* in this method only a segment of the file to be sorted is brought into main memory, sorted and then saved in a temporary file. Then a new segment is brought into main memory, sorted and then appended to the end of the temporary file. This is repeated until all the segments of the original file have been sorted and appended to the temporary file. If the file is very large segments can be paged in and out of the main memory as appropriate.

The type of algorithm employed here is the bubble sort, sometimes known as the exchange sort. Whilst this sort technique has little claim to efficiency it is relatively easy to understand.

Examination of the design reveals very quickly that it is very complex. We are trying to produce a design for an algorithm with a comparatively large number of control structures. There are eight terminal functions and four control conditions. This can be contrasted to the other algorithms with two or three control conditions and ten or twelve terminal functions, the consequence being that the sort design has a larger number of levels than recommended. Throughout the text reference has been made to convenient or appropriate style. As it stands we are in danger of having too much structure. We have perhaps lost the goals of readability, maintainability and portability. It must ultimately be a compromise and it is left for the reader to decide on!

Our bubble sort design uses an internal sort. The algorithm manipulates an array of records. Our file of records must therefore be an array of records. To do this we need another procedure that we will call Order.

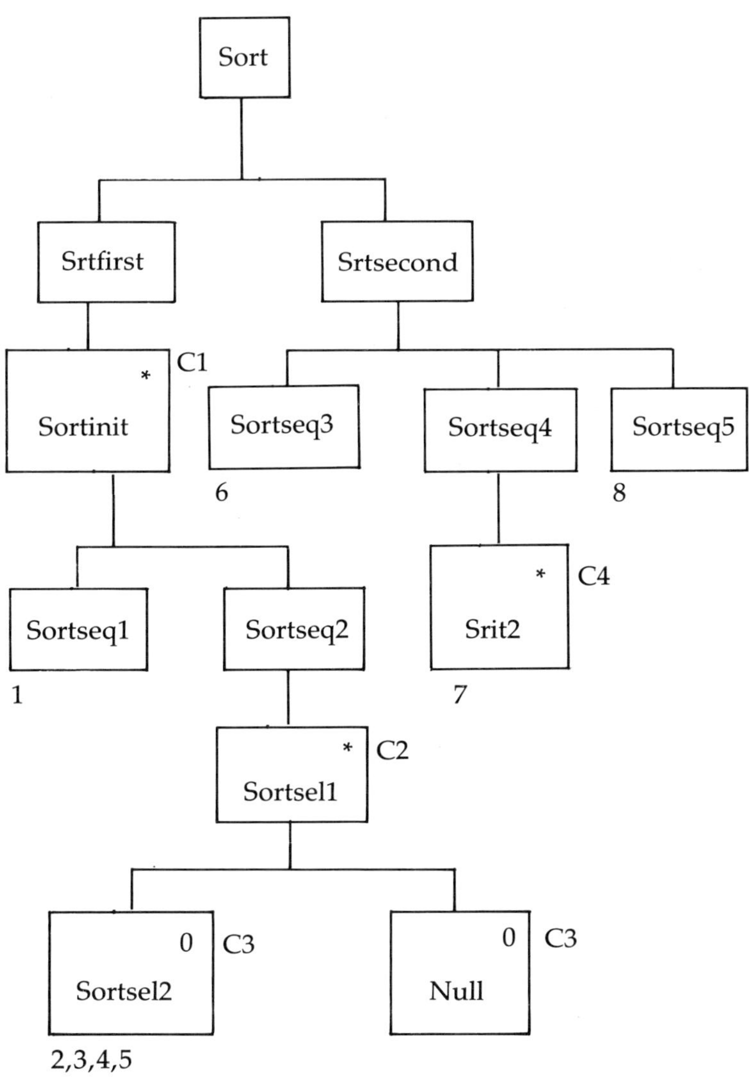

Functions

1. Sorted := TRUE
2. Sorted := FALSE
3. Temp := Sortarray[Index2]
4. Sortarray[Index2] := Sortarray[Index2 + 1]
5. Sortarray[Index2 +1] := Temp
6. Open file Master for writing
7. Write Sortarray[Index1] to file Master

(8. Close files)

Conditions

C1 Repeat until Sorted TRUE

C2 For Index2 := 1 to Recordcount −1

C3 If Sortarray[Index2].Worksnumber > Sortarray[Index 2 +1].Worksnumb

C4 For Index1 := 1 to Recordcount +1

```
PROCEDURE Sort;
(* This sort procedure uses the Bubble sort algorithm. *)
(* It is an internal sort with the records having been placed in
Sortarray by the procedure Order *)
VAR Sorted: BOOLEAN;
      Temp: Employee;
PROCEDURE Srtfirst;
      PROCEDURE Sortinit;
            PROCEDURE Sortseq1;
            BEGIN
                  Sorted := TRUE
            END;
            PROCEDURE Sortseq2;
            VAR Index2 : INTEGER;
            PROCEDURE Sortsel1;
                  PROCEDURE Sortsel2;
                  BEGIN
                   Sorted := FALSE;
                   Temp := Sortarray[ Index2 ];
                   Sortarray[ Index2 ] := Sortarray[ Index2 + 1 ];
                   Sortarray[ Index2 + 1 ] := Temp
                END;
```

```
          BEGIN
                IF   Sortarray[Index2].Worksnumber >
                          Sortarray[Index2 + 1].Worksnumber
                THEN
                     Sortsel2
          END;
          BEGIN
                FOR Index2 := 1 TO Recordcount - 1 DO Sortsel1
          END;
     BEGIN
          Sortseq1;
          Sortseq2
     END;
BEGIN
     REPEAT Sortinit UNTIL Sorted
END;

PROCEDURE Srtsecond;
          PROCEDURE Sortseq3;
          BEGIN
                REWRITE(Master)
          END;
          PROCEDURE Sortseq4;
          VAR Index1 : INTEGER;
                PROCEDURE Srtit2;
                BEGIN
                     WRITE(Master, Sortarray[Index1])
                END;
          BEGIN
                FOR Index1 := 1 TO Recordcount + 1 DO Srtit2
          END;
```

```
            PROCEDURE Sortseq5
            BEGIN
                    (* Close files, not needed in Pascal *)
            END;
BEGIN
        Sortseq3;
        Sortseq4;
        (* Sortseq5 *)
END;
BEGIN
        Srtfirst;
        Srtsecond
END.
```

The procedure Order assigns each record in turn to an array element. In our variable declaration we therefore must have:

```
VAR Employeerecord: Employee;
        Master: Personnel;
        Copy: Personnel;
        Recordcount: INTEGER;
        Sortarray: ARRAY[ 1..100 ] OF Employee;
```

Recordcount is needed to keep track of the number of records. This is used in the Sort algorithm. Sortarray is an array of type Employee. Each array element can now hold a single record of type employee. Arbitrarily we have allowed for 100 records. An improvement on this would be to have:

```
CONST Max = 100;
        .
        .
VAR     .
        .
        Sortarray : ARRAY[1..Max] OF Employee;
```

Note that procedure Order must be called before the Sort procedure.

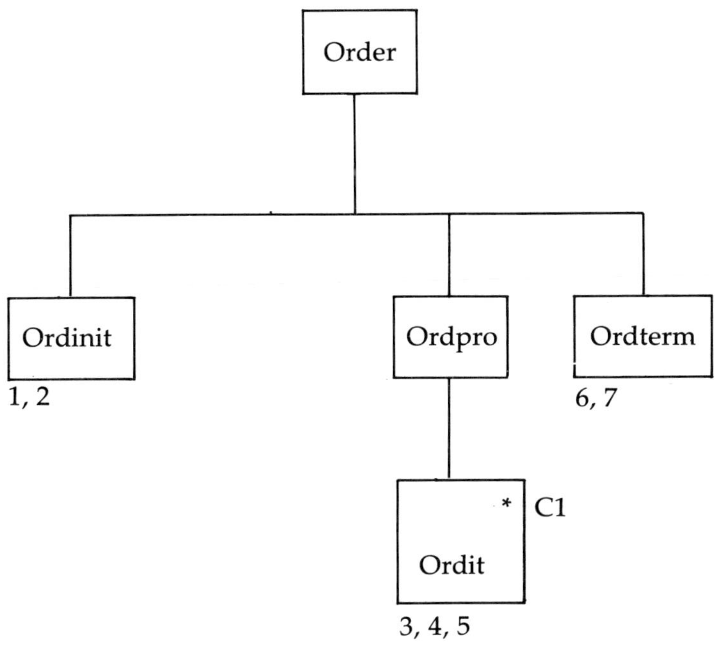

Functions

1. Open file Master for writing
2. Initialise Index to 0
3. Increment Index
4. Read record from file Master
5. Place record in array
6. Recordcount := Index

(7. Close files)

Conditions

C1 While not Sentinel

```
PROCEDURE Order;
(* This procedure places the records from file Master into Sortarray
prior to performing bubble sort *)
VAR Index : INTEGER;

 PROCEDURE Ordinit;
 BEGIN
        RESET(Master);
        INDEX := 0
 END;
```

```
PROCEDURE Ordpro;

    PROCEDURE Ordit;
    BEGIN
        Index := Index + 1;
        READ(Master, Employeerecord);
        Sortarray[Index] := Employeerecord
    END;

BEGIN
    REPEAT Ordit UNTIL
        Employeerecord.Worksnumber = Sentinel
END;

PROCEDURE Ordterm;
BEGIN
    Recordcount := Index
END;

BEGIN
    Ordinit;
    Ordpro;
    Ordterm
END;
```

12.6 BRINGING IT ALL TOGETHER – THE MENU

The menu is the top hierarchy in the design. This controls the manipulation of the previous procedures.

Functions	*Conditions*
1. Initialise Mainchoice to 'Y'	C1 While Mainchoice = 'Y'
2.. 5 User prompts	C2 Option = 1
6. Read user Option	C3 Option = 2
7. Printfile	C4 Option = 3
8. Buildfile	C5 Option = 4

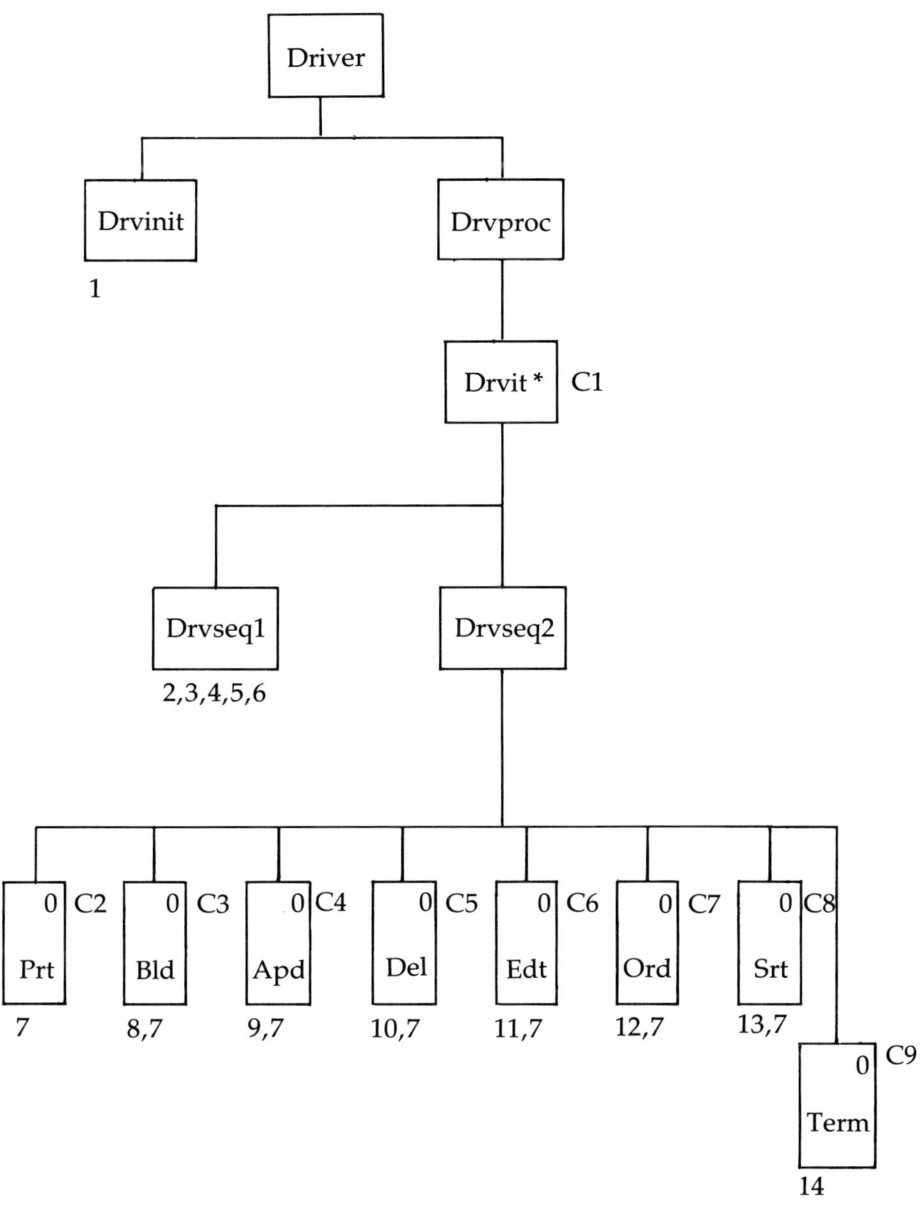

9. Append
10. Delete
11. Edit
12. Order
13. Sort
14. Mainchoice := 'N'

C6 Option = 5
C7 Option = 6
C8 Option = 7
C9 Option = 8

```
PROCEDURE Drvseq1;
BEGIN
        WRITELN('Choose one option :');
        WRITELN('1 : Display all records');
        WRITELN('2 : New file of records');
        WRITELN('3 : Append new records');
        WRITELN('4 : Delete a record');
        WRITELN('5 : Edit a record');
        WRITELN('6 : Sort');
        WRITELN('7 : Insert a record');
        READLN(Option);
END:
```

```
PROCEDURE Drvseq2;
BEGIN
        CASE Option OF
                1 : Printfile;
                2 : BEGIN
                        Buildfile;
                        Printfile
                   END;
                3: BEGIN
                        Append;
                        Printfile
                   END;
                4 : BEGIN
                        Delete;
                        Printfile
                   END;
                5 : BEGIN
                        Edit;
                        Printfile
                   END;
```

```
                6 : BEGIN
                        Order;
                        Sort;
                        Printfile
                    END;
                7 : BEGIN
                        Append;
                        Order;
                        Sort;
                        Printfile
                    END;
                8 : Mainchoice := 'N'
        END;
END;
```

```
PROCEDURE Driver;
VAR Mainchoice : CHAR;
 Option : INTEGER;
```

```
PROCEDURE Drvinit;
BEGIN
        Mainchoice := 'Y'
END;
```

```
PROCEDURE Drvproc;
        PROCEDURE Drvit;
        BEGIN
                Drvseq1;
                Drvseq2
        END;
BEGIN
        WHILE Mainchoice = 'Y' DO
        Drvit
END;
```

```
BEGIN
        Drivinit;
        Drvproc
END;

BEGIN
        Driver
END.
```

12.7 SUMMARY

- 1. To manipulate sequential files we need a separate file that we can transfer our records to during the file processes of append, update, delete and edit.
- 2. We need a special procedure to restore the original file name. Note that this can be done at the operating system level.
- 3. In the delete procedure the record to be deleted is not copied across to the temporary file.
- 4. The file is sorted 'internally', ie a complete copy of the file is transferred into main memory, sorted, and then transferred out again. To do this we must form an array of records – we can do this using a separate procedure.
- 5. The edit procedure only allows one field to be altered; alter this so that the other fields can be changed. This will be more appropriate if your record design has many fields.

12.8 PROBLEMS

- 1. Modify your program to perform the file processes append, update, delete, edit and sort.
- 2. Rewrite the bubble sort using non-procedural structuring.
- 3. Investigate other sorting algorithms such as shell sort and quick sort. Comment on their relative advantages.
- 4. Code another sort method and include this as an option in your program menu.
- 5. The edit procedure only allows one field to be altered, change this so that the other fields can be changed. This will be more appropriate if your record design has many fields.

– 6. For the more adventurous, write a user option that will allow one or more records to be selected by their primary keys. Then modify this to allow selection by other fields.

13 BASIC

13.1 INTRODUCTION

For many people BASIC is synonymous with computer programming. Why BASIC?

'BASIC has become the most widely known computer language. Why? Simply because there are more people in the world than there are programmers. If ordinary people are to use a computer, there must be simple computer languages for them to use' Thomas Kurtz, *'BASIC'*, 1981.

However, in the words of Edsger Dijkstra:

'It is practically impossible to teach good programming to students that have had a prior exposure to BASIC: as potential programmers they are mentally mutilated beyond hope of regeneration'

'How Do We Tell Truths That Might Hurt?' *Selected Writings on Computing*, 1975.

Much has been written on BASIC, and this text does assume at least some familiarity with this language. The role of computing that Kemeny and Kurtz proposed when developing BASIC was in many ways as important as the language itself. They determined to:

- 1. Devise a computer system that would be friendly, easy to learn and use, and not require students to go out of their way.
- 2. Develop a new language that is easy to learn and use.
- 3. Introduce students to computing as an adjunct to another course.
- 4. Operate the computer with open access.

Without doubt BASIC has been a successful language as measured against these goals. As a language it has evolved. It has changed from being an unstructured language to a structured language. Also, as more languages have made their appearance with complex data and control structures, later versions of BASIC have incorporated these new features.

Debate about the choice of a language for educational purposes usually centres around BASIC and Pascal. As we have seen, the elegance of

Pascal is that with a single call to a procedure, such as Buildfile, the main program can invoke code that is in another part of the program. Line numbers are not used. The main part of the program is therefore succinct. The detail is appropriate to the level on which we are working. However in BASIC all parts of the program operate together. It is not as visually powerful as Pascal. In recognition of this, versions of BASIC now include SBASIC. This is a structured version of BASIC that incorporates many of the ideas of structured programming. SBASIC does not use line numbers, GOTO statements, subroutines etc. The last words on this should be left to one of the founding fathers of BASIC.

'The GOTO statement has an attractive simplicity for novices, but . . . should be discarded at an early stage in favour of structured constructs' Thomas Kurtz, 1978.

13.2 BASIC BASIC

Some knowledge of BASIC is assumed in this text. For convenience here is a summary of aspects of BASIC that are required in order to fully understand the following BASIC coding. Do note versions of BASIC will differ.

Program structure

The BASIC program structure is a single block of statements with ascending statement numbers. Functions and subroutines form part of the program block.

Statement layout

There is only one line per statement; however, multiple statements can appear in a single line. Statements are executed sequentially with the exception of GOTO and GOSUB statements.

```
10 INPUT F

20 LET C = (F - 32)/1.8

30 PRINT "TEMPERATURE IS "; C
```

Data types – elementary

Standard BASIC has numeric and string data types.

Type	*Example*
Numeric	123
String	"ABC"

Identifiers and assignment

Identifiers are the names of variables and constants. Numeric variable identifiers may be a letter or a letter followed by a digit. String variable identifiers consist of a letter or letter and digit, followed by a dollar sign.

Numeric	A, A1
String	A$, A1$

Unlike Pascal declarations are not needed. The variable data type is implied in the variable name.

A = 1.23 signifies A is a numeric variable

A$ = "1.23" signifies A is a string variable

MAINCHOICE$ = "Y"

Data types – structured

Arrays may be one or two dimensional. The subscripts can range from zero to ten without the need for declaration. The use of subscripts is flexible as they can be constants, variables, function references or expressions as long as the values are integers.

10 DIM A(100)

DIM SORTNO$(100), SORTNAME$(100), SORTCODE$(100)

SORTNO$(INDEX) = WORKNUMBER$

Operators

BASIC has the standard arithmetic operators for arithmetic manipulation – exponentiation, multiplication, division, addition and subtraction. Logical and relational operators are also used. The use of parentheses raise the order of precedence of operators.

Expressions

Expressions can be numeric or logical. The assignment is performed by use of the LET, READ or DATA statements.

LET A = 1.23

LET A$ = "ABC"

READ A

DATA 100

Selection – conditional and unconditional branching

Unconditional branching is achieved by the GOTO and GOSUB statements. Explicit RETURN statements are needed.

Conditional branching is by means of the IF condition THEN and the ON condition GOTO statements.

```
ON VAL(OPT$) + 1 GOSUB 500, 1000, 2000

IF WORKSNUMBER$ <> CANCEL$ THEN GOSUB 4400 ELSE GOSUB
4500
```

Iteration

Iteration is by use of the FOR... and NEXT... statements.

```
10 FOR I = 1 TO 10

20 READ A

30 LET B = B + A

40 PRINT B

50 NEXT I

WHILE WORKSNUMBER$ <> SENTINEL$

WHILE MAINCHOICE$ = "Y"

        GOSUB 300 : REM Main Menu

WEND

FOR INDEX2 = INDEX1 – 1 TO STEP – 1

        GOSUB 6650

NEXT INDEX2
```

Subroutines

These are blocks of code that perform a specific function or functions. Subroutines are called by a GOSUB statement and ended by a RETURN.

```
GOSUB 100 : REM Main Initialise

RETURN
```

File handling

Files must be opened for input or output and closed after use. Files can then be written to or read from.

```
OPEN "I", 1, MASTER$

OPEN "O", 2, COPY$

INPUT #1, WORKSNUMBER$, WORKER$, TAXCODE$

PRINT #1, WORKSNUMBER$; ","; WORKER$; ","; TAXCODE$

PRINT #2, WORKSNUMBER$; ","; WORKER$; ","; TAXCODE$

CLOSE #1
```

Input and output

Data input and output is achieved by the INPUT and PRINT statements. Data can be entered in free format using commas as separators.

```
PRINT "1 : Display all records"

PRINT WORKSNUMBER$

INPUT " Choose an option ", OPT$

INPUT "More records, type Y or N ", CHOICE$
```

Termination

The STOP halts the program execution but maintains the status of the variables. The END statement clears the variables.

Documentation

Documentation is by REM statements.

```
10 REM THIS ROUTINE GENERATES A FILE
```

For each structured diagram there will be two versions of the associated BASIC code. The first version will be perhaps more typical, full use being made of the GOTO control statement. The second version is relatively free of the GOTO statement. But in either case we are using the same language independent structured diagrams that were used to code in Pascal. The main differences are due to the fact that it is not necessary to close files in Pascal; in BASIC and other languages this is essential. From our designs we will produce two versions of BASIC code to allow files to be manipulated.

The following programs were written with all the correct line numbers. For convenience they have been broken up into modules and are given after the associated structured diagrams.

13.3 THE MENU

Functions	*Conditions*
1. Initialise Mainchoice to 'Y'	C1 While Mainchoice = 'Y'
2.. 5 User prompts	C2 Option = 1
6. Read user Option	C3 Option = 2
7. Printfile	C4 Option = 3
8. Buildfile	C5 Option = 4
9. Append	C6 Option = 5
10. Delete	C7 Option = 6

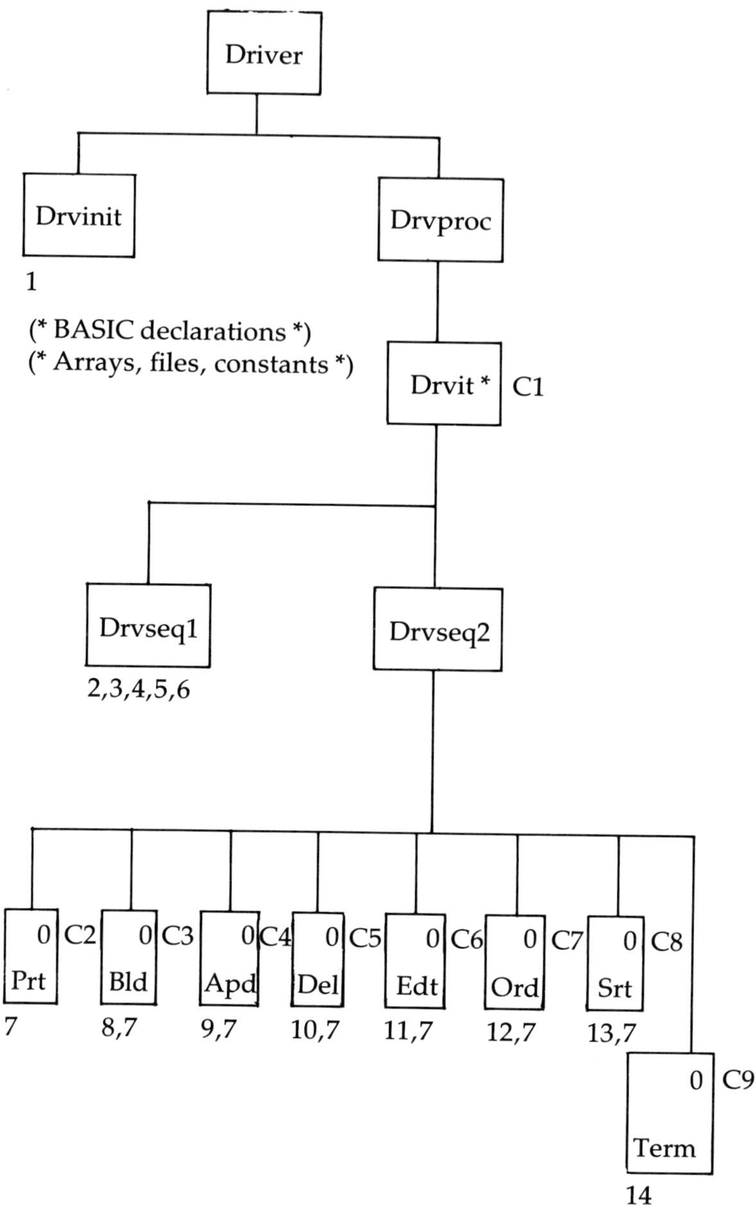

11. Edit
12. Order
13. Sort
14. Mainchoice := 'N'

C8 Option = 7

C9 Option = 8

This is the same in both versions of BASIC.

```
10 REM Microsoft BASIC program version 1.0
```

```
40 REM Driver
50    GOSUB 100: REM Drvinit
60    GOSUB 200: REM Drvproc
70 END
100 REM ---------------------------------------------------------------------------
110 REM Drvinit
120 REM ---------------------------------------------------------------------------
130 DIM SORTNO$(100), SORTNAME$(100), SORTCODE$(100)
SORTCODE$(100)
140        MAINCHOICE$ = "Y"
150        MASTER$ = "MASTER"
160        COPY$ = "TEMPFILE"
170        SENTINEL$ = "9999"
180        DUMMY$="X"
190 RETURN
200 REM ---------------------------------------------------------------------------
210 REM Drvproc
220 REM ---------------------------------------------------------------------------
230 REM Main Program
240        WHILE MAINCHOICE$ = "Y"
260           GOSUB 300: REM Drvit
270        WEND
280 RETURN
300 REM ---------------------------------------------------------------------------
310 REM Drvit
320 REM ---------------------------------------------------------------------------
330        GOSUB 400 : REM Drvseq1
340        GOSUB 500 : REM Drvseq2
400 REM ---------------------------------------------------------------------------
410 REM Drvseq1
420 REM ---------------------------------------------------------------------------
430        REM CLS for users with graphics commands
```

```
440      PRINT "1 : Display all records"
450      PRINT "2 : New file of records"
460      PRINT "3 : Append new records"
470      PRINT "4 : Delete a record"
480      PRINT "5 : Edit"
490      PRINT "6 : Sort"
500      PRINT "7 : Insert"
510      PRINT "8 : End program"
520      INPUT "Choose an option ", OPT$
530 RETURN
550 REM --------------------------------------------------------------------------
560 REM Drvseq2
570 REM --------------------------------------------------------------------------
580      ON VAL(OPT$) GOSUB 1000, 2000, 3000, 4000, 5000, 6000,
         7000, 600
590 RETURN
600 REM --------------------------------------------------------------------------
610 REM Term
620 REM --------------------------------------------------------------------------
630      MAINCHOICE$ = "N"
640 RETURN
700 REM --------------------------------------------------------------------------
710 REM
720 REM The following code is the main code for each option
730 REM Option 1 Lines 1000–1999 Option 2 Lines 2000–2999 etc
740 REM
750 REM --------------------------------------------------------------------------
```

13.4 DISPLAY A FILE

Functions	*Conditions*
1. Open file Master for reading	C1 While not Sentinel
2. Read record (first) from Master	

3. Write all record fields to screen
4. Read record (next) from Master

(5. Close file, no need in Pascal)

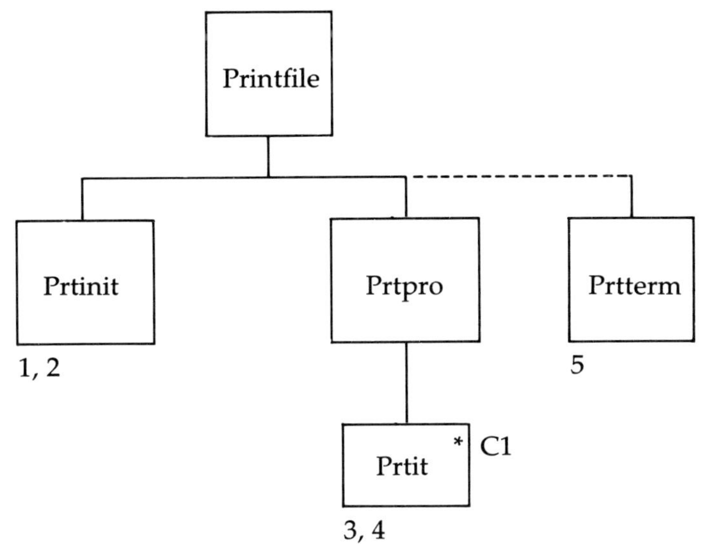


```
1000 REM ***********************************************************
1010 REM Printfile Version 1
1020 REM -----------------------------------------------------------
1030      GOSUB 1100: REM Prtinit
1040      GOSUB 1200: REM Prtpro
1070      GOSUB 1400: REM Prtterm
1080 RETURN
1100 REM -----------------------------------------------------------
1110 REM Prtinit
1120 REM -----------------------------------------------------------
1130      OPEN "I", 1, MASTER$
1140      INPUT #1, WORKSNUMBER$, WORKER$, TAXCODE$
1150 RETURN
1200 REM -----------------------------------------------------------
1210 REM Prtpro
1220 REM -----------------------------------------------------------
1230      WHILE WORKSNUMBER$ <> SENTINEL$
```

```
1240         GOSUB 1300: REM Prtit
1250       WEND
1260 RETURN
1300 REM -----------------------------------------------------------------------
1310 REM Prtit
1320 REM -----------------------------------------------------------------------
1330       PRINT WORKSNUMBER$
1340       PRINT WORKER$
1350       PRINT TAXCODE$
1360       INPUT #1, WORKSNUMBER$, WORKER$, TAXCODE$
1370 RETURN
1400 REM -----------------------------------------------------------------------
1410 REM Prtterm
1420 REM -----------------------------------------------------------------------
1430       CLOSE #1
1440 RETURN

1000 REM ************************ Printfile Version 2 **************
1010       REM ---------------------------- Prtinit ------------------------------
1020         OPEN "I", 1, MASTER$
1030         INPUT #1, WORKSNUMBER$, WORKER$, TAXCODE$
1100       REM ---------------------------- Prtpro ------------------------------
1110         WHILE WORKSNUMBER$ <> SENTINEL$
1120         REM ---------------------------- Prtit ------------------------------
1130           PRINT WORKSNUMBER$
1140           PRINT WORKER$
1150           PRINT TAXCODE$
1160           INPUT #1, WORKSNUMBER$, WORKER$, TAXCODE$
1170         WEND
1200       REM ---------------------------- Prtterm ----------------------------
1210         CLOSE #1
1220 RETURN
```

13.5 BUILD A FILE

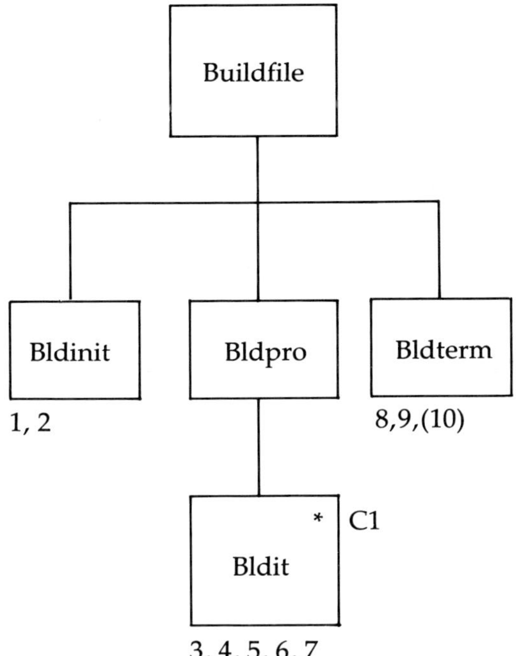

Functions

1. Open file Master for Writing
2. Initialise Choice to 'Y'
3. User prompt
4. Read record fields
5. Write record to file Master
6. User prompt
7. Read user choice
8. Lastrecord
9. Write Lastrecord to file Master

(10. Close file – done for you in Pascal)

Conditions

C1 While choice = 'Y'

```
2000 REM ************************************************************
2010  REM Buildfile Version 1
2020 REM ------------------------------------------------------------
2030       GOSUB 2100: REM Bldinit
```

```
2040      GOSUB 2200: REM Bldpro
2050      GOSUB 2400: REM Bldterm
2060 RETURN
2100 REM ------------------------------------------------------------------
2110 REM Bldinit
2120 REM ------------------------------------------------------------------
2130      OPEN "O", 1, MASTER$
2140      CHOICE$ = "Y"
2150 RETURN
2200 REM ------------------------------------------------------------------
2210 REM Bldpro
2220 REM ------------------------------------------------------------------
2230      WHILE CHOICE$ = "Y"
2240        GOSUB 2300: REM Bldit
2250      WEND
2260 RETURN
2300 REM ------------------------------------------------------------------
2310 REM Bldit
2320 REM ------------------------------------------------------------------
2330      INPUT "Worksnumber ", WORKSNUMBER$
2340      INPUT "Name  ",        WORKER$
2350      INPUT "Taxcode  ",     TAXCODE$
2360        PRINT #1, WORKSNUMBER$; ","; WORKER$; ",";
            TAXCODE$
2370      INPUT "More records, type Y or N <ENTER>", CHOICE$
2380 RETURN
2400 REM ------------------------------------------------------------------
2410 REM Bldterm
2420 REM ------------------------------------------------------------------
2430      GOSUB 10500 : REM Lastrecord
2440      PRINT #1, WORKSNUMBER$;",";WORKER$;",";TAXCODE$
2450      CLOSE #1
```

```
2460 RETURN

2000 REM ************************ Buildfile Version 2***************
2010      REM ----------------------------- Bldinit -----------------------------
2020        OPEN "O", 1, MASTER$
2030        CHOICE$ = "Y"
2100      REM ----------------------------- Bldpro ------------------------------
2110        WHILE CHOICE$ = "Y"
2120        REM ---------------------------- Bldpit -----------------------------
2130          INPUT "Worksnumber ", WORKSNUMBER$
2140          INPUT "Name     ", WORKER$
2150          INPUT "Taxcode", TAXCODE$
2160           PRINT #1, WORKSNUMBER$; ","; WORKER$; ",";
               TAXCODE$
2170          INPUT "More records, type Y or N <ENTER>",CHOICE$
2180        WEND
2200      REM ----------------------------- Bldterm ----------------------------
2210        GOSUB 10500 : REM Lastrecord
2220             PRINT     #1,
WORKSNUMBER$;",";WORKER$;","; TAXCODE$
2230        CLOSE #1
2240 RETURN
```

13.6 APPEND A RECORD

Functions	*Conditions*
1. Open file Master for reading	C1 While not Sentinel
2. Open file Copy for writing	C2 While Appendchoice is 'Y'
3. Initialise Appendchoice to 'Y'	
4. Read record (first) from Master	
5. Write record (current) to file Copy	
6. Read record (next) from Master	
7. User prompt	
8. Read fields	

9. Write record to file Copy
10. User prompt
11. Read user option Appendchoice
12. Lastrecord
13. Write record (last) to file Copy
14. Updatefile

(15. Close files)

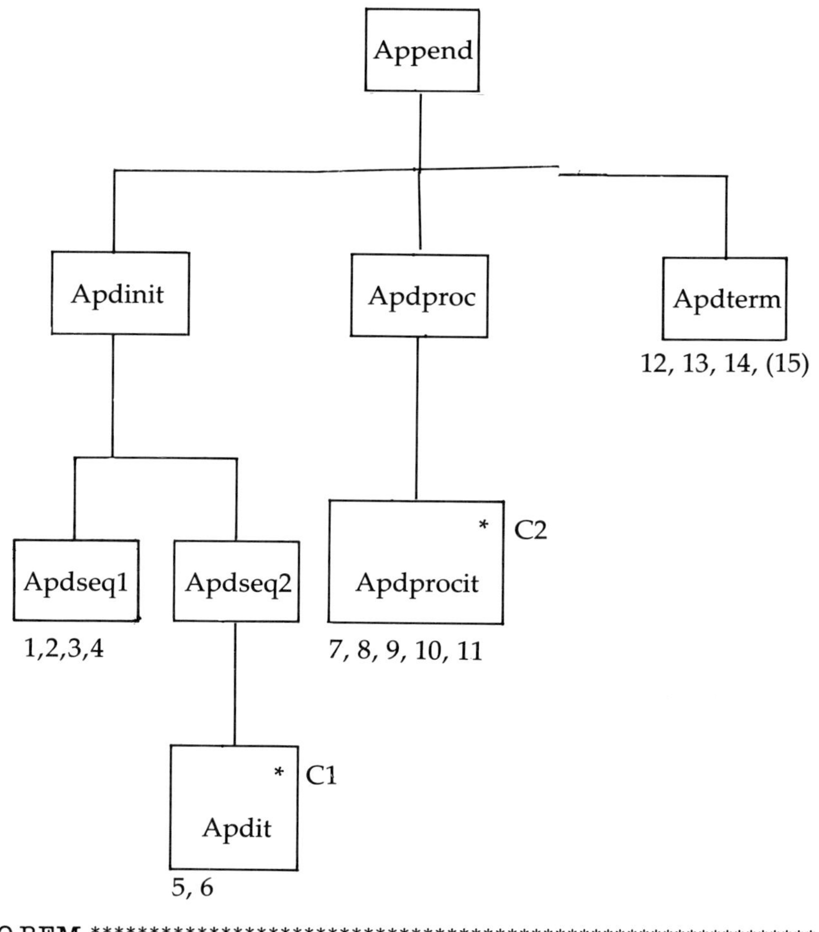


```
3000 REM ***********************************************************
3010 REM Append Version 1
3020 REM ------------------------------------------------------------
3030      GOSUB 3100: REM Apdinit
3040      GOSUB 3500: REM Apdproc
```

```
3050      GOSUB 3700: REM Apdterm
3060 RETURN
3100 REM ---------------------------------------------------------------------------
3110 REM Apdinit
3120 REM ---------------------------------------------------------------------------
3130      GOSUB 3200: REM Apdseq1
3140      GOSUB 3300: REM Apdseq2
3150 RETURN
3200 REM ---------------------------------------------------------------------------
3210 REM Apdseq1
3220 REM ---------------------------------------------------------------------------
3230      OPEN "I", 1, MASTER$
3240      INPUT #1, WORKSNUMBER$, WORKER$, TAXCODE$
3250      OPEN "O", 2, COPY$
3260      APPENDCHOICE$ = "Y"
3270 RETURN
3300 REM ---------------------------------------------------------------------------
3310 REM Apdseq2
3320 REM ---------------------------------------------------------------------------
3340      WHILE WORKSNUMBER$ <> SENTINEL$
3350        GOSUB 3400: REM Apdit
3360      WEND
3380 RETURN
3400 REM ---------------------------------------------------------------------------
3410 REM Apdit
3420 REM ---------------------------------------------------------------------------
3430       PRINT #2, WORKSNUMBERS$; ","; WORKERS$; ",";
           TAXCODES$
3440      INPUT #1, WORKSNUMBER$, WORKER$, TAXCODE$
3450 RETURN
3500 REM ---------------------------------------------------------------------------
3510 REM Apdproc
```

```
3520 REM -------------------------------------------------------------------------
3530      WHILE APPENDCHOICE$ = "Y"
3540        GOSUB 3600: REM Apdprocit
3550      WEND
3560 RETURN
3600 REM -------------------------------------------------------------------------
3610 REM Apdprocit
3620 REM -------------------------------------------------------------------------
3630      INPUT "Worksnumber ", WORKSNUMBER$
3640      INPUT "Name        ", WORKER$
3650      INPUT "Taxcode     ", TAXCODE$
3660       PRINT #2, WORKSNUMBER$; ","; WORKER$; ",";
           TAXCODE$
3670       INPUT "More records, type Y or N <ENTER>",
           APPENDCHOICE$
3680 RETURN
3700 REM -------------------------------------------------------------------------
3710 REM Apdterm
3720 REM -------------------------------------------------------------------------
3730      GOSUB 10500 : REM Lastrecord
3740      PRINT #2, WORKSNUMBER$;",";WORKER$;",";TAXCODE$
3750      CLOSE #2
3760      CLOSE #1
3770      GOSUB 10000 : REM Updatefile
3780 RETURN

3000 REM ************************* Append Version 2 ***************
3010      REM ----------------------------- Apdinit ------------------------------
3020        REM -------------------------- Apdseq1 ----------------------------
3030          OPEN "I", 1, MASTER$
3040          INPUT #1, WORKSNUMBER$, WORKER$, TAXCODE$
3050          OPEN "O", 2, COPY$
3060          APPENDCHOICE$ = "Y"
```

```
3100      REM -------------------------- Apdseq2 ---------------------------
3110        WHILE WORSKNUMBER$ <> SENTINEL$
3120          PRINT #2, WORKSNUMBER$; “,”; WORKER$;“,”;
              TAXCODE$
3130          INPUT #1, WORKSNUMBER$, WORKER$,
              TAXCODE$
3140        WEND
3200    REM ---------------------------- Apdproc -----------------------------
3210      WHILE APPENDCHOICE$ = “Y”
3220      REM ------------------------- Apdprocit --------------------------
3230        INPUT “Worksnumber ”, WORKSNUMBER$
3240        INPUT “Name     ”, WORKER$
3250        INPUT “Taxcode”, TAXCODE$
3260         PRINT #2, WORKSNUMBER$; “,”; WORKER$; “,”;
             TAXCODE$
3270         INPUT “More records, type Y or N <ENTER>”,
             APPENDCHOICE$
3280      WEND
3300    REM ---------------------------- Apdterm ----------------------------
3310      GOSUB 10500 : REM Lastrecord
3320         PRINT #2, WORKSNUMBER$;“,”;WORKER$;“,”;
             TAXCODE$
3330      CLOSE #2
3340      CLOSE #1
3350      GOSUB 10000 : REM Updatefile
3360 RETURN
```

13.7 DELETE A RECORD

Functions	*Conditions*
1. Open file Master for reading	C1 While not Sentinel
2. Open file Copy for writing	C2 If Worksnumber <> Cancel
3. Read record (first) from Master	
4. User prompt	C3 If Worksnumber = Cancel
5. Read Cancel	

6. Write record (current) to file Copy
7. Read record (next) from file Master
8. Read record (next) from file Master
9. Lastrecord
10. Write record (last) to file Copy
11. Updatefile
(12. Close files)

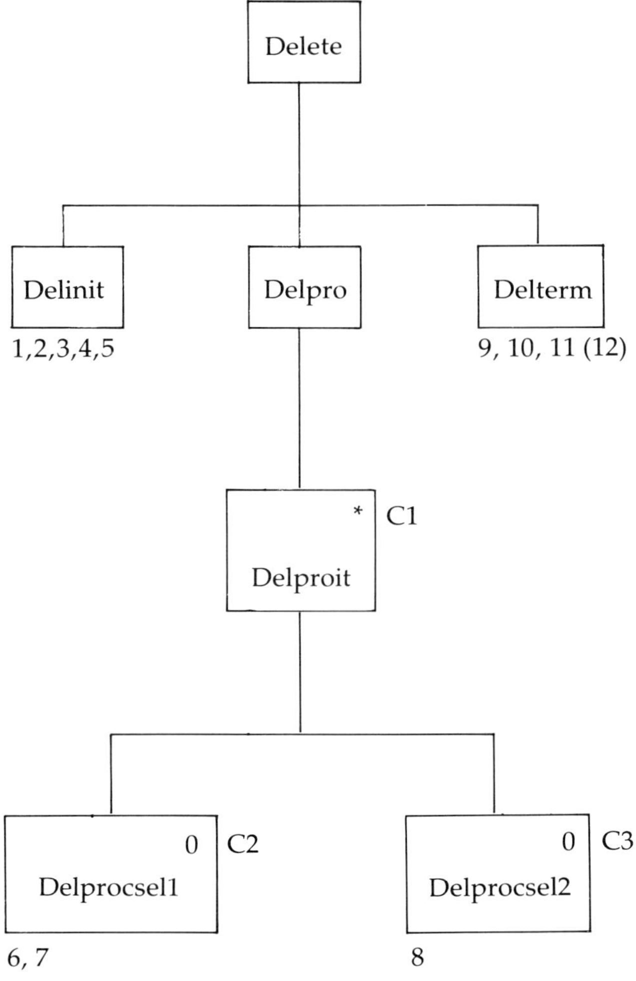


```
4000 REM ************************************************************
4010  REM Delete a record Version 1
4020 REM -------------------------------------------------------------------------
```

```
4030        GOSUB 4100: REM Delinit
4040        GOSUB 4200: REM Delpro
4050        GOSUB 4600: REM Delterm
4060 RETURN
4100 REM ------------------------------------------------------------------------
4110 REM Delinit
4120 REM ------------------------------------------------------------------------
4130        OPEN "I", 1, MASTER$
4140        INPUT #1, WORKSNUMBER$, WORKER$, TAXCODE$
4150        OPEN "O", 2, COPY$
4160        INPUT "Enter number of record to delete ", CANCEL$
4170 RETURN
4200 REM ------------------------------------------------------------------------
4210 REM Delpro
4220 REM ------------------------------------------------------------------------
4230        WHILE WORKSNUMBER$ <> SENTINEL$
4240          GOSUB 4300: REM Delproit
4250        WEND
4260 RETURN
4300 REM ------------------------------------------------------------------------
4310 REM Delproit
4320 REM ------------------------------------------------------------------------
4330        IF WORKSNUMBER$ <> CANCEL$ THEN GOSUB 4400
            ELSE GOSUB 4500
4340 RETURN
4400 REM ------------------------------------------------------------------------
4410 REM Delprocsell
4420 REM ------------------------------------------------------------------------
4430          PRINT #2, WORKSNUMBER$; ","; WORKER$; ",";
              TAXCODE$
4440        INPUT #1, WORKSNUMBER$, WORKER$, TAXCODE$
4450 RETURN
```

```
4500 REM ----------------------------------------------------------------------------
4510 REM Delprocsel2
4520 REM ----------------------------------------------------------------------------
4530      INPUT #1, WORKSNUMBER$, WORKER$, TAXCODE$
4540 RETURN
4600 REM ----------------------------------------------------------------------------
4610 REM Delterm
4620 REM ----------------------------------------------------------------------------
4630      GOSUB 10500 : REM Lastrecord
4640      PRINT #2, WORKSNUMBER$;",";WORKER$;",";TAXCODE$
4650      CLOSE #2
4660      CLOSE #1
4670      GOSUB 10000: REM Update file
4680 RETURN

4000 REM ************************* Delete Version 2 ****************
4010      REM ----------------------------- Delinit ------------------------------
4020        OPEN "I", 1, MASTER$
4030        INPUT #1, WORKSNUMBER$, WORKER$, TAXCODE$
4040        OPEN "O", 2, COPY$
4050        INPUT "Enter number of record to delete ", CANCEL$
4200      REM ----------------------------- Delpro ------------------------------
4210        WHILE WORKSNUMBER$ <> SENTINEL$
4220        REM --------------------------- Delproit ----------------------------
4230           IF WORKSNUMBER$ <> CANCEL$ THEN GOSUB
               4400 ELSE GOSUB 4500
4240        WEND
4300      REM ---------------------------- Delterm -----------------------------
4310        GOSUB 10500 : REM Lastrecord
4320           PRINT #2, WORKSNUMBER$;",";WORKER$;",";
               TAXCODE$
4330        CLOSE #2
4340        CLOSE #1
```

```
4350        GOSUB 10000 : REM Update file
4360 RETURN
4400 REM ------------------------------------------------------------------------
4410 REM Delprocsel1
4420 REM ------------------------------------------------------------------------
4430        PRINT #2, WORKSNUMBER$; ","; WORKER$; ",";
            TAXCODE$
4440      INPUT #1, WORKSNUMBER$, WORKER$, TAXCODE$
4450 RETURN
4500 REM ------------------------------------------------------------------------
4510 REM Delprocsel2
4520 REM ------------------------------------------------------------------------
4530      PRINT #1, WORKSNUMBER$;",";WORKER$;",";TAXCODE$
4540 RETURN
```

13.8 EDIT A RECORD

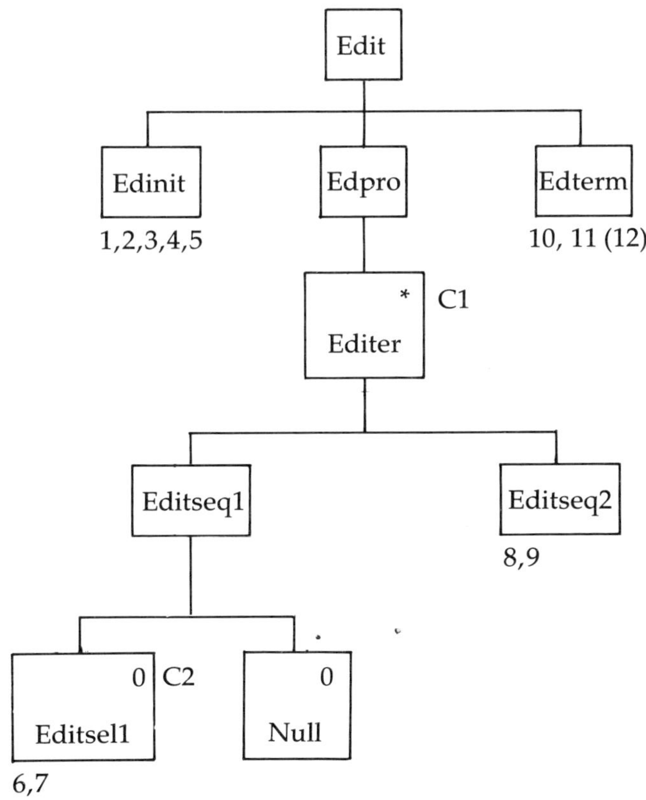

Functions	*Conditions*
1. Open file Master for reading	C1 While not Sentinel
2. Open file Copy for writing	C2 If Worksnumber = Change
3. Read record (first) from Master	
4. User prompt	
5. Read Change	
6. User prompt	
7. Read new Worksnumber	
8. Write record to file Copy	
9. Read record from Master	
10. Write record (last) to file Copy	
11. Updatefile	
(12. Close files)	

```
5000 REM ************************************************************
5010 REM Edit record Version 1
5020 REM ------------------------------------------------------------
5030       GOSUB 5100 : REM Edinit
5040       GOSUB 5200 : REM Edpro
5050       GOSUB 5700 : REM Edterm
5060 RETURN
5100 REM ------------------------------------------------------------
5110 REM Edinit
5120 REM ------------------------------------------------------------
5130       OPEN "I" , 1 , MASTER$
5140       OPEN "O" , 2 , COPY$
5150       INPUT #1, WORKSNUMBER$, WORKER$, TAXCODE$
5160       INPUT "Record to be changed :",CHANGE$
5170 RETURN
5200 REM ------------------------------------------------------------
5210 REM Edpro
5220 REM ------------------------------------------------------------
```

```
5230      WHILE WORKSNUMBER$<>SENTINEL$
5240         GOSUB 5300 : REM Editer
5250      WEND
5260 RETURN
5300 REM --------------------------------------------------------------------------------
5310 REM Editer
5320 REM --------------------------------------------------------------------------------
5330      GOSUB 5400 : REM Editseq1
5340      GOSUB 5600 : REM Editseq2
5350 RETURN
5400 REM --------------------------------------------------------------------------------
5410 REM Editseq1
5420 REM --------------------------------------------------------------------------------
5430      IF WORKSNUMBER$=CHANGE$ THEN GOSUB 5500
5440 RETURN
5500 REM --------------------------------------------------------------------------------
5510 REM Editsel1
5520 REM --------------------------------------------------------------------------------
5530      INPUT "New number of the record ?",WORKSNUMBER$
5540 RETURN
5600 REM --------------------------------------------------------------------------------
5610 REM Editseq2
5620 REM --------------------------------------------------------------------------------
5630      PRINT #2,WORKSNUMBER$;",";WORKER$;",";TAXCODE$
5640      INPUT #1,WORKSNUMBER$,WORKER$,TAXCODE$
5650 RETURN
5700 REM --------------------------------------------------------------------------------
5710 REM Edterm
5720 REM --------------------------------------------------------------------------------
5730      PRINT #2,WORKSNUMBER$;",";WORKER$;",";TAXCODE$
5740      CLOSE #1
```

```
5750        CLOSE #2
5760        GOSUB 10000 : REM Updatefile
5770 RETURN

5000  REM ******************* Edit Version 2 *************************
5010 REM Edit record
5020        REM Edinit
5030          OPEN "I" , 1 , MASTER$
5040          OPEN "O" , 2 , COPY$
5050          INPUT #1, WORKSNUMBER$,WORKER$,TAXCODE$
5060          INPUT "Record to be changed :",CHANGE$
5100        REM Edpro
5110          WHILE WORKSNUMBER$<>SENTINEL$
5120          REM Editer
5130            REM Editseq1
5140                IF  WORKSNUMBER$=CHANGE$  THEN  GOSUB
                    5500
5150            GOSUB 5600 : REM Editseq2
5160          WEND
5200        REM Edterm
5210                PRINT        #2,WORKSNUMBER$;",";WORKER$;",";
                    TAXCODE$
5220          CLOSE #1
5230          CLOSE #2
5240          GOSUB 10000 : REM Updatefile
5250 RETURN
5500 REM ------------------------------------------------------------------------
5510 REM Editsel1
5520 REM ------------------------------------------------------------------------
5530        INPUT "New number of the record ?",WORKSNUMBER$
5540 RETURN
5600 REM ------------------------------------------------------------------------
5610 REM Editseq2
```

```
5620 REM -----------------------------------------------------------------------
5630        PRINT #2,WORKSNUMBER$;",";WORKER$;",";TAXCODE$
5640        INPUT #1,WORKSNUMBER$,WORKER$,TAXCODE$
5650 RETURN
```

13.9 SORT A FILE

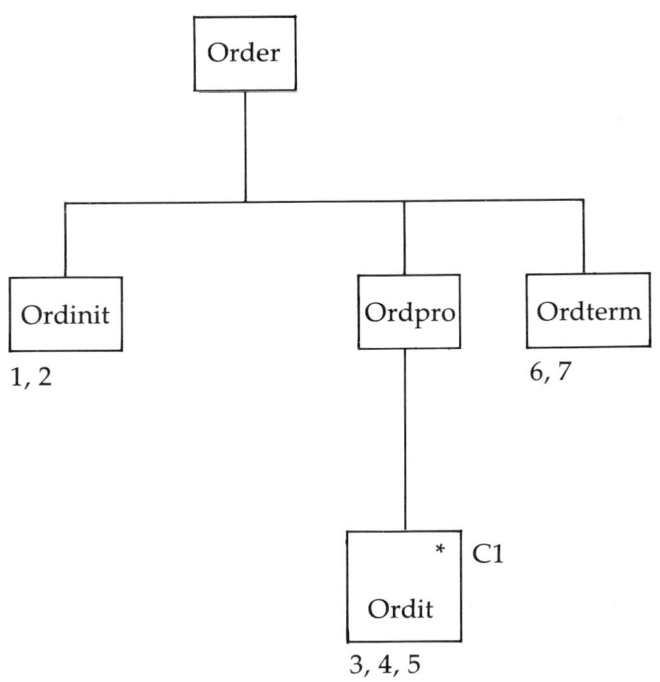

Functions	*Conditions*
1. Open file Master for writing	C1 While not Sentinel
2. Initialise Index to 0	
3. Increment Index	
4. Read record from file Master	
5. Place record in array	
6. Recordcount := Index	
(7. Close files)	

Functions	*Conditions*
1. Sorted := TRUE	C1 Repeat until Sorted TRUE
2. Sorted := FALSE	

3. Temp := Sortarray[Index2]
4. Sortarray[Index2] :=
   Sortarray[Index2 + 1]
5. Sortarray[Index2 +1] := Temp
6. Open file Master for writing
7. Write Sortarray[Index1] to file Master

(8. Close files)

C2 For Index2 := 1
to Recordcount –1

C3 If Sortarray[Index2].Worksnumber
>Sortarray[Index2 +1].Worksnumber

C4 For Index1 := 1 to Recordcount +1

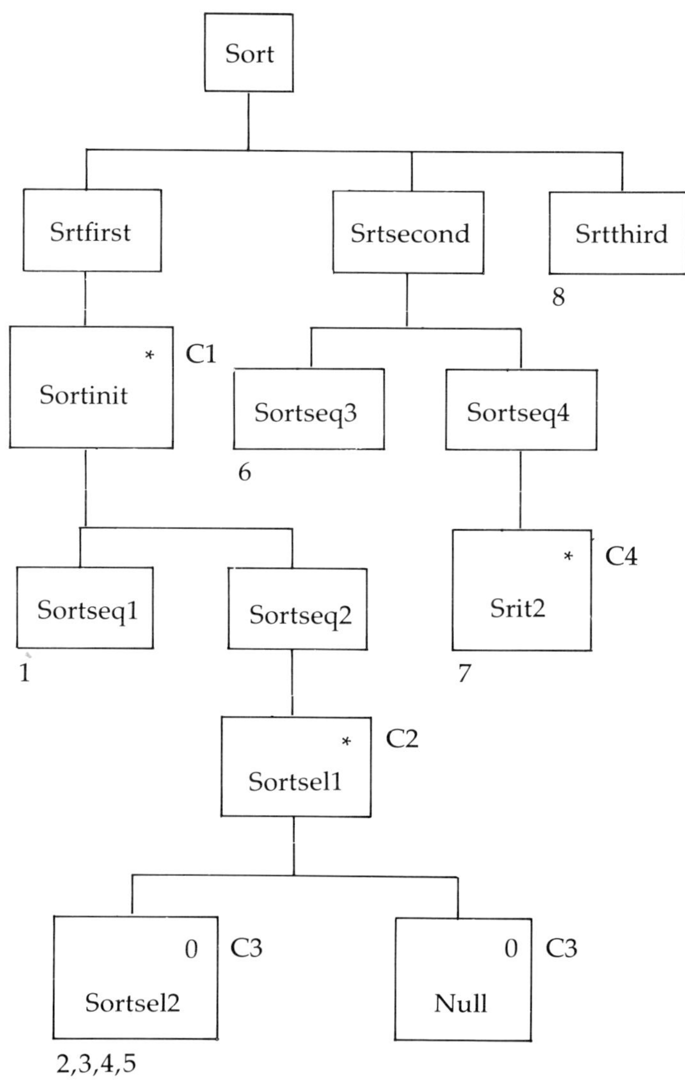

```
6000 REM ************************************************************
6010 REM Sort records Version 1
6020 REM -------------------------------------------------------------------
6030      GOSUB 6100: REM Order
6040      GOSUB 6500: REM Sort
6050 RETURN
6100 REM -------------------------------------------------------------------
6110 REM Order
6120 REM -------------------------------------------------------------------
6130      GOSUB 6200: REM Ordinit
6140      GOSUB 6250: REM Ordpro
6150      GOSUB 6400: REM Ordterm
6160 RETURN
6200 REM ------------------------------ Ordinit ------------------------------
6210      INDEX = 0
6220      OPEN "I", 1, MASTER$
6230      WORKSNUMBER$ = "DUMMY"
6240 RETURN
6250 REM ------------------------------ Ordpro ------------------------------
6260      WHILE WORKSNUMBER$ <> SENTINEL$
6270         GOSUB 6300: REM Ordit
6280      WEND
6290 RETURN
6300 REM ------------------------------ Ordit ------------------------------
6310      INPUT #1, WORKSNUMBER$, WORKER$, TAXCODE$
6320      INDEX = INDEX + 1
6330      SORTNO$(INDEX) = WORKSNUMBER$
6340      SORTNAME$(INDEX) = WORKER$
6350      SORTCODE$(INDEX) = TAXCODE$
6360 RETURN
6400 REM ------------------------------ Ordterm ------------------------------
6410      CLOSE #1
```

```
6420      RECORDCOUNT=INDEX
6430 RETURN
6500 REM --------------------------------------------------------------------
6510 REM Sort
6520 REM --------------------------------------------------------------------
6530      GOSUB 6600: REM Srtfirst
6540      GOSUB 6800: REM Srtsecond
6550 RETURN
6600 REM ------------------------------- Srtfirst -------------------------------
6605      SORTED=0
6610      WHILE SORTED=0
6615        GOSUB 6650 : REM Srtinit
6620      WEND
6625 RETURN
6650 REM ------------------------------- Srtinit -------------------------------
6655      GOSUB 6670 : REM Srtseq1
6660      GOSUB 6690 : REM Srtseq2
6665 RETURN
6670 REM ------------------------------- Srtseq1 -------------------------------
6675      SORTED=1
6680 RETURN
6690 REM ------------------------------- Srtseq2 -------------------------------
6695      FOR INDEX3 = 1 TO RECORDCOUNT-1
6797        GOSUB 6700
6798      NEXT INDEX3
6799 RETURN
6700 REM ------------------------------- Sortsel1 -------------------------------
6710      IF VAL( SORTNO$(INDEX3) ) > VAL( SORTNO$(INDEX3
          + 1 ) ) THEN GOSUB 6750
6720 RETURN
6750 REM ------------------------------- Sortsel2 -------------------------------
6755      SORTED=0
```

```
6760      REM Move index3 record to temporary record
6771      TEMPNO$ = SORTNO$(INDEX3)
6772      TEMPNAME$ = SORTNAME$(INDEX3)
6773      TEMPCODE$ = SORTCODE$(INDEX3)
6780      REM Move index3+1 record to index3 record
6781      SORTNO$(INDEX3) = SORTNO$(INDEX3 + 1)
6782      SORTNAME$(INDEX3) = SORTNAME$(INDEX3 + 1)
6783      SORTCODE$(INDEX3) = SORTCODE$(INDEX3 + 1)
6790      REM Move temporary record to index3+1 record
6791      SORTNAME$(INDEX3 + 1) = TEMPNAME$
6792      SORTNO$(INDEX3 + 1) = TEMPNO$
6793      SORTCODE$(INDEX3 + 1) = TEMPCODE$
6795 RETURN
6800 REM ------------------------------ Srtsecond ------------------------------
6810      GOSUB 6850: REM Srtseq3
6820      GOSUB 6900: REM Srtseq4
6830      GOSUB 6980: REM Srtseq5
6840 RETURN
6850 REM ------------------------------- Srtseq3 -------------------------------
6860      OPEN "O", 1, MASTER$
6870 RETURN
6900 REM ------------------------------- Srtseq4 -------------------------------
6910      FOR INDEX2 = 1 TO INDEX
6920         GOSUB 6950: REM Srtit2
6930      NEXT INDEX2
6940 RETURN
6950 REM -------------------------------- Srtit2 --------------------------------
6960         PRINT #1, SORTNO$(INDEX2); ",";
             SORTNAME$(INDEX2); ","; SORTCODE$(INDEX2)
6970 RETURN
6980 REM ------------------------------- Srtseq5 -------------------------------
6990      CLOSE #1
```

```
6995 RETURN
6000 REM ****************** Sortrecords Version 2 ****************
6010 REM Sort records
6020 REM --------------------------------------------------------------------------
6030      GOSUB 6100 : REM Order
6040      GOSUB 6400 : REM Sort
6050 RETURN
6100 REM --------------------------------------------------------------------------
6110 REM Order
6120 REM --------------------------------------------------------------------------
6130      REM ----------------------------- Ordinit -----------------------------
6140        INDEX = 0
6150        OPEN "I", 1, MASTER$
6160        WORKSNUMBER$ = "DUMMY"
6200      REM ----------------------------- Ordpro ------------------------------
6210        WHILE WORKSNUMBER$ <> SENTINEL$
6220        REM ----------------------------- Ordit -----------------------------
6230          INPUT #1, WORKSNUMBER$, WORKER$, TAXCODE$
6240          INDEX = INDEX + 1
6250          SORTNO$(INDEX) = WORKSNUMBER$
6260          SORTNAME$(INDEX) = WORKER$
6270          SORTCODE$(INDEX) = TAXCODE$
6280        WEND
6300      REM ---------------------------- Ordterm -----------------------------
6310        CLOSE #1
6320        RECORDCOUNT=INDEX
6330 RETURN
6400 REM **********************************************************
6410 REM Sort
6420 REM --------------------------------------------------------------------------
6430      GOSUB 6500 : REM Srtfirst
6440      GOSUB 6900 : REM Srtsecond
```

```
6450 RETURN
6500 REM ------------------------------- Srtfirst -------------------------------
6510      SORTED=0
6520      WHILE SORTED=0
6530      REM ---------------------------- Srtinit ----------------------------
6540        REM -------------------------- Srtseq1 --------------------------
6550          SORTED=1
6560        REM -------------------------- Srtseq2 --------------------------
6570          FOR INDEX3 = 1 TO RECORDCOUNT-1
6580          REM ------------------------ Sortsel1 ------------------------
6590          IF VAL( SORTNO$(INDEX3) ) > VAL
              ( SORTNO$(INDEX3 + 1 ) ) THEN GOSUB 6700
6600          NEXT INDEX3
6610      WEND
6620 RETURN
6700 REM ------------------------------- Sortsel2 -------------------------------
6710      SORTED=0 : REM Flag list not sorted
6720      REM Move index3 record to temporary record
6730        TEMPNO$      = SORTNO$(INDEX3)
6740        TEMPNAME$ = SORTNAME$(INDEX3)
6750        TEMPCODE$  = SORTCODE$(INDEX3)
6760      REM Move index3+1 record to index3 record
6770        SORTNO$(INDEX3)      = SORTNO$(INDEX3 + 1)
6780        SORTNAME$(INDEX3) = SORTNAME$(INDEX3 + 1)
6790        SORTCODE$(INDEX3)  = SORTCODE$(INDEX3 + 1)
6800      REM Move temporary record to index3+1 record
6810        SORTNAME$(INDEX3 + 1)   = TEMPNAME$
6820        SORTNO$(INDEX3 + 1)        = TEMPNO$
6830        SORTCODE$(INDEX3 + 1)    = TEMPCODE$
6840 RETURN
6900 REM ------------------------------ Srtsecond ------------------------------
6910      REM ---------------------------- Srtseq3 ----------------------------
```

```
6920       OPEN "O", 1, MASTER$
6930     REM ----------------------------- Srtseq4 -----------------------------
6940       FOR INDEX2 = 1 TO INDEX
6950       REM ---------------------------- Srtit2 -----------------------------
6960         PRINT #1, SORTNO$(INDEX2); ",";
             SORTNAME$(INDEX2); ","; SORTCODE$(INDEX2)
6970       NEXT INDEX2
6980     REM ----------------------------- Srtseq5 -----------------------------
6990       CLOSE #1
6995 RETURN
```

13.10 INSERT A RECORD

This is the same in both versions of BASIC.

```
7000 REM ***********************************************************
7010 REM insert a record
7020 REM -----------------------------------------------------------
7030     GOSUB 3000: REM Append a record
7040     GOSUB 6000: REM Sort list
7050 RETURN
```

13.11 UPDATE THE FILE

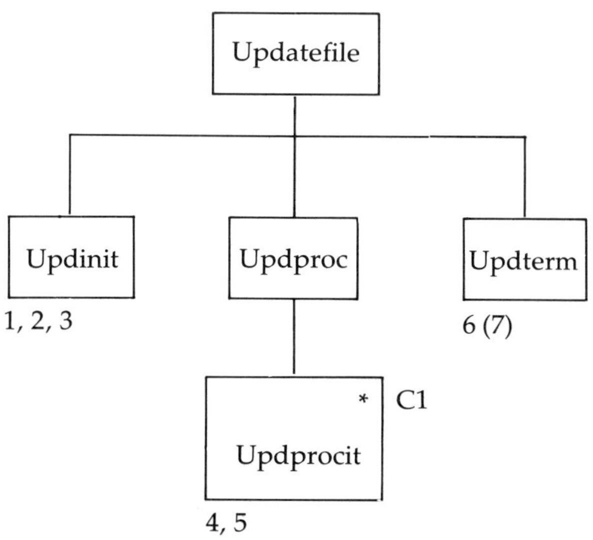

Functions	*Conditions*
1. Open file Copy for reading	C1 While not Sentinel
2. Open file Master for writing	
3. Read record (first) from Copy	
4. Write record to file Master	
5. Read record from Copy	
6. Write record (last) to file Master	
(7. Close files)	

```
10000 REM  *******************************************************
10010  REM Update file Version 1
10020 REM  -----------------------------------------------------------------
10030      GOSUB 10100: REM Updinit
10040      GOSUB 10200: REM Updproc
10050      GOSUB 10400: REM Updterm
10060 RETURN
10100 REM  -----------------------------------------------------------------
10110 REM Updinit
10120 REM  -----------------------------------------------------------------
10130      OPEN "O", 2, MASTER$
10140      OPEN "I", 1, COPY$
10150      INPUT #1, WORKSNUMBER$, WORKER$, TAXCODE$
10160 RETURN
10200 REM  -----------------------------------------------------------------
10210 REM Updproc
10220 REM  -----------------------------------------------------------------
10230      WHILE WORKSNUMBER$ <> SENTINEL$
10240        GOSUB 10300: REM Updprocit
10250      WEND
10260 RETURN
10300 REM  -----------------------------------------------------------------
10310 REM Updprocit
```

```
10320 REM ---------------------------------------------------------------
10330     PRINT #2, WORKSNUMBER$; ","; WORKER$; ",";
          TAXCODE$
10340     INPUT #1, WORKSNUMBER$, WORKER$, TAXCODE$
10350 RETURN
10400 REM ---------------------------------------------------------------
10410 REM Updprocit
10420 REM ---------------------------------------------------------------
10430     PRINT #2, WORKSNUMBER$; ","; WORKER$; ",";
          TAXCODE$
10440     CLOSE #1
10450     CLOSE #2
10460 RETURN
10000 REM ********************** Update file Version 2 *************
10010     REM ---------------------------- Updinit ----------------------------
10020       OPEN "O", 2, MASTER$
10030       OPEN "I", 1, COPY$
10040       INPUT #1, WORKSNUMBER$, WORKER$, TAXCODE$
10100     REM ---------------------------- Updproc ----------------------------
10110       WHILE WORKSNUMBER$ <> SENTINEL$
10120       REM ------------------------ Updprocit --------------------------
10130         PRINT #2, WORKSNUMBER$; ","; WORKER$; ",";
              TAXCODE$
10140         INPUT #1, WORKSNUMBER$, WORKER$,
              TAXCODE$
10150       WEND
10200     REM ---------------------------- Updterm ----------------------------
10210       PRINT #2, WORKSNUMBER$; ","; WORKER$; ",";
            TAXCODE$
10220       CLOSE #1
10230       CLOSE #2
10240 RETURN
```

13.12 LAST RECORD

This is the same for both versions of BASIC.

```
10500 REM ------------------------------------------------------------------------
10510 REM Lastrecord
10520 REM ------------------------------------------------------------------------
10530     WORKSNUMBER$     = SENTINEL$
10540     WORKER$          = DUMMY$
10550     TAXCODE$         = SENTINEL$
10560 RETURN
```

13.13 SUMMARY

– 1. Original versions of BASIC do not support structured programming. Contemporary versions are much more structured.

– 2. The uncontrolled use of the GOTO statement should be avoided at all costs.

– 3. With very little modification the structured diagrams can be converted to another target language.

13.14 PROBLEMS

– 1. Modify the above structured diagrams and associated code to handle your record design.

– 2. For the more adventurous, code the diagrams in another target language. This will obviously require extensive reading on another language. However you should be in the position now of quickly being able to define the key features of another language.

14 Modular Programming

14.1 INTRODUCTION

The concept of modules in programming has been touched upon in the preceding chapters. As a rule of thumb we have determined that a good module will be no larger than a page and have no more than three or four levels of indentation. It is now time to be more rigorous. In doing so it is necessary to identify the characteristics of our good module. For further reading a book called *Structured Design* by Yourdon and Constantine is to be recommended.

14.2 LEVELS OF ABSTRACTION

When a modular solution is used different levels of abstraction are considered:

– 1. Highest level: the solution in broad terms, ie the problem environment.

– 2. Lower level: procedural orientation, ie the major software tasks.

– 3. Lowest level: direct implementation.

Each level is a refinement of the preceding one.

Wasserman succinctly provides a definition of abstraction:

". . . the psychological notion of 'abstraction' permits one to concentrate on a problem at some level of generalisation without regard to irrelevant low levels of detail; use of abstraction also permits one to work with concepts and terms that are familiar in the problem environment without having to transform them into an unfamiliar structure. . .".

We can therefore talk about stepwise refinement of a given problem. Stepwise refinement can be defined as 'a transformation applied to a single step of a process description in a sequence of one or more commands expressed in a form more closely related to the problem and the set of available executable primitives'. In this context it is important to achieve a singlemindedness in that each module should address a specific group of needs and have a simple interface when viewed from other parts of the program. It is then possible to have plug-in modules. A suitably designed module can be replaced by an equivalent module with little or no change to other parts of the program. This has obvious advantages for maintenance, portability, etc. This independence is measured in the cohesion and coupling potential of the program.

14.3 COHESION

Cohesion is the measure of relative functional strength of a module. There are different degrees of cohesion. The highest level of cohesion is referred to by Yourdon and Constantine as 'functional cohesion' in which every element or statement is 'an integral part of and essential to the performance of a single function'. In this case module replacement is simple and there are minimal side effects. Similarly error detection and correction are easier in that the module can quickly be identified or eliminated as a source of the error.

This can be contrasted with the other extreme of 'coincidental cohesion' in which the association between statements is minimal or zero. This would occur if a monolithic program were arbitrarily subdivided into modules.

There are other levels and classifications of cohesion. Others you may meet are:

- 1. Coincidental: In monolithic (single structure) programs functional groupings tend to be coincidental.
- 2. Logical: structure is based on logical functions.
- 3. Temporal/Chronological: structure is based on tasks that are executed in the same time periods.
- 4. Procedural: structure is based on tasks that occur in a specific order.
- 5. Functional: single function.

14.4 INFORMATION HIDING

Information hiding suggests that modules can be characterised by design decisions that each hide from all others. A module is only aware of another if it has to be, ie on a need-to-know basis. Hiding implies that modularity can be achieved by defining a set of independent modules that communicate with one another only that information necessary to achieve the software function. Each module should be allowed access only to variables that are needed to implement the functions appropriate to that module. Access to other objects, if not needed, should be denied. The reader should remember 'hidden information cannot be corrupted'. The resulting program is more secure with greater data independence. Information is therefore a design criterion with implications in testing, maintenance etc. There is also better readability as the variables are declared only where they are needed. Pascal, unlike Ada, has no specific constructs to restrict access on a need-to-know basis; hence the need for disciplined programming.

For those new to programming it is important to realise that programs are often developed as part of a team. Certainly when you are developing a program by yourself you know that one part of your program will not corrupt the data used by another part! Consider therefore the situation when there are a team of programmers working on a very large project over a considerable period of time. Team members leave, others join. It's 'open season' for global data.

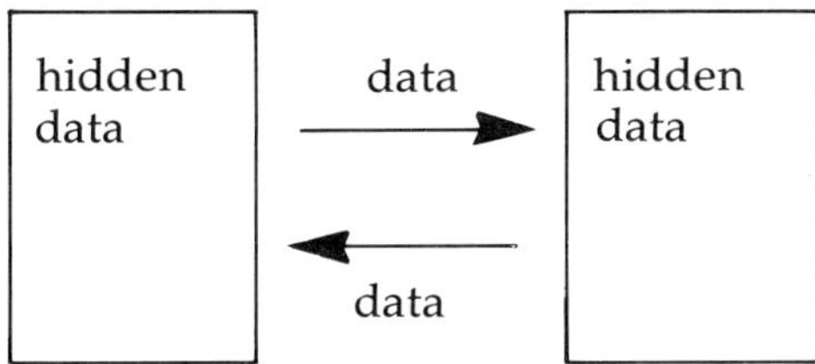

access on a 'need-to-know basis'

14.5 COUPLING

Coupling is a measure of the strength of the interconnection between or interdependence of modules. Modules are uncoupled if they can function independently of each other. This is perhaps rarely the case. Modules have to interact and therefore have to be coupled. Again Yourdon and Constantine suggest different types of coupling whose strength can be estimated.

The term minimal connection is used to describe a fully parameterised transfer of control to a single entry point within a called module with an implicit return to a single point in the calling module. By fully parameterised we mean that all information transfer between different modules is explicit or visible by module parameters. There are no hidden or implicit information flows via global variables. Global variables are available to all modules in the program. Are you sure no one is going to modify the global variable you are using? Shared data makes error detection and correction much harder as potentially any part of the code can change any data value. Program modification is also more difficult.

Coupling and cohesion are essentially linked. If there are multiple entry points this implies that the module has multiple functions and therefore has low cohesion. Using variable entry points implies a much stronger coupling between modules as the calling module needs-to-know more about the called one.

Another measure of the strength of coupling is the complexity of the interface between communicating modules. A module that has to import or export ten parameters has a more complex coupling than one that has only to pass one parameter.

What is passed between modules has a bearing on the coupling strength. If data is passed between modules there is a looser coupling than if control information passes between them.

Again there are other levels and classifications of cohesion. Others you may meet are:

- 1. Global coupling: all data is available to all modules and can therefore be modified by all modules.
- 2. Data coupling: simple argument passed to another module, ie local variables.
- 3. Control: a flag is passed on which the receiving module can then make decisions.
- 4. Common: modules can access common data areas.

In the case of COBOL all parts of the program share a common data area, the DATA DIVISION. This is called common environment coupling by Yourdon and Constantine.

14.6 MODULE SPAN

The consequences of stepwise refinement is a hierarchical structure that we have met before. The span-of-control of a module is the number of subordinate modules which it immediately calls. Yourdon and Constantine suggest that very high or very low spans-of-control indicate poor structure.

The suggested critical figure is ten modules. A figure in excess of this, ie a wide span-of-control is caused by the failure to define intermediate levels correctly. This can be corrected by defining cohesive groups in order to form the intermediate level.

A wide span-of-control can be reduced by breaking up the subordinate modules into smaller cohesive groups.

14.7 MODULE SIZE

How big should a module be?

Let C(x) be a function that defines the complexity of a problem x.

Let E(x) be a function that defines the effort to solve the problem x.

Given that we have two problems P1 and P2.

If C(P1) > C(P2)

then E(P1) > E(P2)

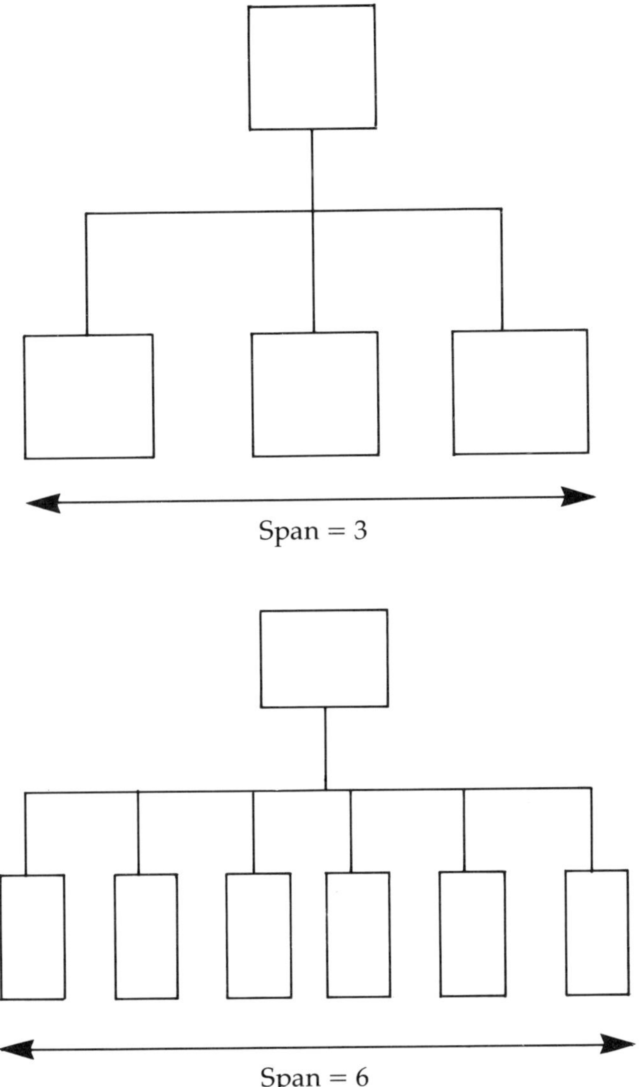

It is possible to show that

$$C(P1 + P2) > C(P1) + C(P2)$$

therefore $E(P1 + P2) > E(P1) + E(P2)$

What we have is larger problems with greater complexity and therefore greater effort is needed to solve them. The converse of this is divide-and-conquer – smaller problems are easier to solve. But how small? The problem comes with coupling – the more modules there are the greater the amount of coupling. A lot of small modules will have a higher interface overhead than a reduced number of larger modules.

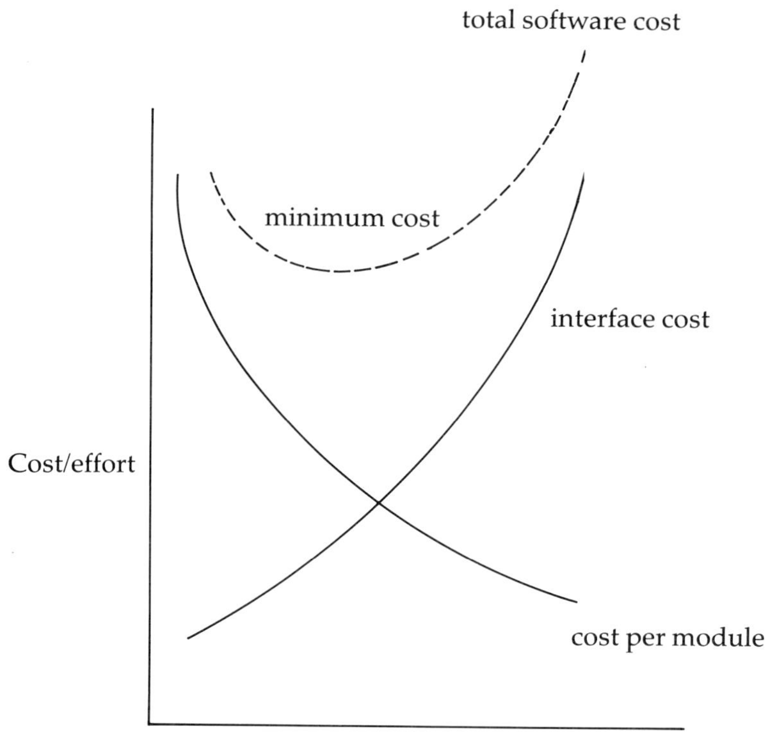

14.8 MODULE CHARACTERISTICS

The aims for module design are *high cohesion* and *low coupling* with a medium *span-of-control* and *optimum size*.

14.9 MENU DRIVEN PROGRAMS

With our file handling program we require a significant amount of user interaction. We can therefore design our program around a menu-driven interface. A menu can be defined as a list of options which is presented to the user who can then select an option. The selection of an option may result in action or in another menu presentation.

Menus are common forms of user interface as they present to the user a controlled environment. Similarly they are useful for programmers in that they suggest a breakdown of the modules.

14.10 SUMMARY

– 1. A 'good' module should be no larger than a page and have no more than three or four levels of indentation.

- 2. A module should address a specific group of needs and have a simple interface to other parts of the program.
- 3. With suitably designed modules it should be possible to easily replace a module with an equivalent module with little or no side effects.
- 4. The measures of module independence are cohesion and coupling.
- 5. Cohesion is the measure of relative functional strength, ie are the internal functions suitably related?
- 6. Information hiding is data availability on a 'need to know basis'. Hidden information cannot be corrupted.
- 7. Coupling is a measure of the strength of the interconnection or interdependence of modules.
- 8. The span of control is the number of subordinate modules.
- 9. Menus are often a convenient guide to program structure.
- 10. It bears repeating that our aims are high cohesion, low coupling, medium span of control and optimum size.

14.11 PROBLEMS

- 1. Global data is sometimes said to be concerned with implicit or hidden data manipulation. This can be contrasted with parameter passing that is said to be explicit with regard to data manipulation. What is meant by these terms?
- 2. A real-time system must respond to external events within a guaranteed response time suitable to the application. Applications include robots, navigation systems, chemical plants, etc, but they are typically safety critical. Ada was specifically designed for the development of real-time systems. The key construct in Ada is the package which supports information hiding. How is this done? This will require a little reading but knowing Pascal you should be able to read an Ada book with relative ease.

15 Procedures and Parameter Passing

15.1 INTRODUCTION

Much of the preceding chapter was of a theoretical nature. Let us now consider some practical examples.

Procedures and functions in Pascal should be relatively independent subprograms which may be invoked to perform a certain task or tasks. Standard procedures and functions are supplied with the compiler, eg WRITE. WRITE (A, B, C) is a procedure statement which invokes WRITE and A, B, and C are parameters which are passed to this procedure. The structure of a subprogram is similar to that of the main program; the main program which is identified in the program heading is known as the main procedure. All programs consist of one main procedure and zero or more secondary procedures and functions.

Both procedures and functions appear as the last declarations in the main program.

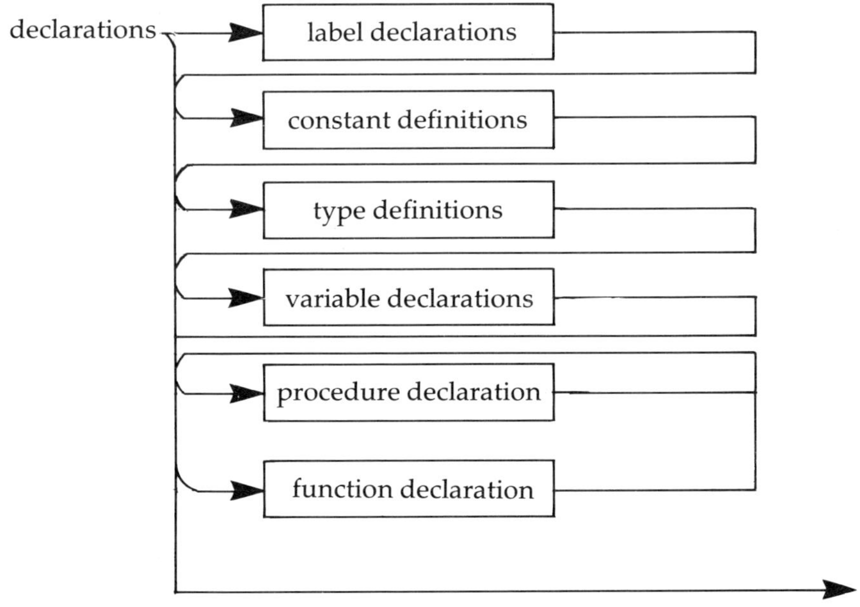

All procedures and functions that are invoked within the program must be declared. For subprograms defined elsewhere and compiled separately a dummy declaration is made.

The subprogram facility in BASIC is crude as it does not allow parameter passing or the declaration of local variables. Only Pascal will be considered in this chapter.

15.2 PROCEDURES RECONSIDERED

As with a program, a procedure (or function) block consists of label declarations, constant and type definitions, variable declarations and a statement part.

procedure declaration

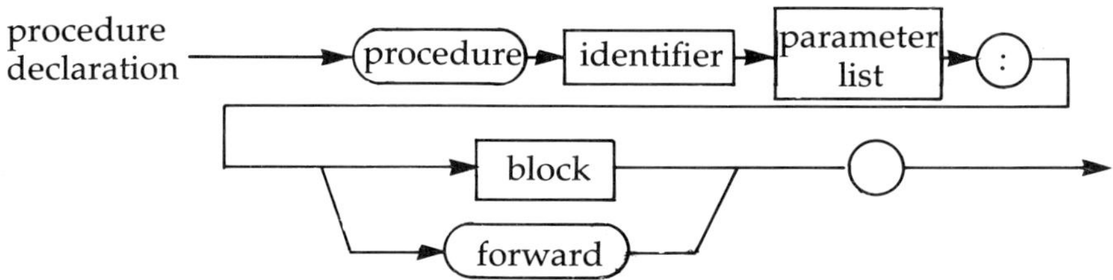

Consider the following simple program, Ch15P1, to calculate Basearea, Perimeter and Volume. The variables, Length, Width and Height are global. All parts of the program have access to them. The difficulty is that real life problems are usually very large and the associated complex programs are designed and developed by teams of analysts and programmers. Global variables can be modified by any programmer working on any part of the program. Communication is hidden or implicit in that it can occur without being specified.

```
PROGRAM Ch15P1 (INPUT, OUTPUT);

VAR Length, Width, Height : INTEGER;
```

```
PROCEDURE Inputdata;
BEGIN
    WRITELN('Length, Width and Height?');
    READLN(Length, Width, Height)
END;
```

```
PROCEDURE Basearea;
BEGIN
    WRITELN('Area of base', Length * Width)
END;
```

```
PROCEDURE Perimeter;
BEGIN
        WRITELN('Perimeter is', 2 * (Length + Width)
END;
```

```
PROCEDURE Volume;
BEGIN
        WRITELN('Volume is', Length * Width * Height)
END;
```

```
BEGIN
        Inputdata;
        Basearea;
        Perimeter;
        Volume
END.
```

Each module should only have access to variables that are needed to implement its own specific functions. The required data should be explicitly defined. Access to other data, if not needed, should be denied. Recall the maxim that hidden information cannot be corrupted, therefore the program is more secure. For large programs, as the variables are declared as needed, there is better readability. Unlike Ada, Pascal has no specific construction to restrict access on a need-to-know basis hence the need for disciplined and structured programming. As a step in this direction the variables can of course be made local to each procedure, as in program Ch15P2.

```
PROGRAM Ch15P2 (INPUT, OUTPUT);
```

```
PROCEDURE Inputdata;
VAR Length1, Width1 : INTEGER;
BEGIN
        WRITELN('Length, Width ?');
        READLN(Length1, Width1);
        WRITELN('Area of base', Length1 * Width1)
END;
```

```
PROCEDURE Basearea;
VAR Length2, Width2 : INTEGER;
BEGIN
        WRITELN('Length, Width ?');
        READLN(Length2, Width2);
        WRITELN('Area of base', Length2 * Width2)
END;
```

```
PROCEDURE Perimeter;
VAR Length3, Width3 : INTEGER;
BEGIN
        WRITELN('Length, Width ?');
        READLN(Length3, Width3);
        WRITELN('Perimeter is', 2 * (Length3 + Width3)
END;
```

```
PROCEDURE Volume;
VAR Length4, Width4, Height4 : INTEGER;
BEGIN
        WRITELN('Length, Width, Height ?');
        READLN(Length4, Width4, Height4);
        WRITELN('Volume is', Length4 * Width4 * Height4)
END;
```

```
BEGIN
        Inputdata;
        Basearea;
        Perimeter;
        Volume
END.
```

Procedures can have their own local declarations. Local variables are created dynamically when procedure is called and are then disposed of when the procedure is exited. Local declarations are known only to the procedure that declares them and to any other procedures embedded within the declaring procedure. To other procedures these local variables are undefined. It is sometimes said that variables are local to the declaring procedure and non-local to the embedded procedure. Local variables in one procedure could have the same names as those in another procedure; this could however cause confusion and is best avoided. Program Ch15P2, whilst offering a degree of information hiding, contains a lot of duplication of effort.

15.3 FORMAL AND ACTUAL PARAMETERS

This can be solved by parameter passing. The format of our code must now include formal and actual parameters.

```
PROGRAM ChXPX (INPUT, OUTPUT);
global declarations
        PROCEDURE Nameofprocedure (Formal parameter list);
        local declarations
        BEGIN
                statements;
                .
                .
        END;
BEGIN
        statements;
        Nameofprocedure (Actual parameter list)
        .
        .
END.
```

The procedure to be executed is called by name. Communication with the called procedure is by specified data items being passed via the actual to the formal parameter list. Parameter passing must conform to the following rules:

– 1. The number of parameters in the formal and actual lists must be the same.

– 2. Corresponding pairs of parameters between the lists must correspond in data type, ie parameters must match in number and type.

It is worth noting that the control variable for the FOR iteration statement must be declared as a local variable.

In order to achieve minimum coupling there must be a fully parameterised transfer of control. Data communication must therefore be explicit or visible. As a step in this direction in program Ch15P3 the global variables are Length, Width and Height. However, when the procedure Basearea is called, data is passed from the actual parameter list, in this case Length and Width, to the formal parameter list, A and B. The formal parameters A and B are replaced by the actual parameters Length and Width. The procedure Basearea is then able to use this data. Data that is not passed to it is not used. In the case of Volume, three parameters are passed. Do note that parameters must match in both number and type.

Parameters are the medium through which procedures share information. Procedures declare and use formal parameters with their identifiers. These formal parameters are substitutes for actual parameters, which are passed to the procedure when it is called by a procedure statement.

```
PROGRAM Ch15P3 (INPUT, OUTPUT);

VAR Length, Width, Height : INTEGER;
```

```
PROCEDURE Inputdata;
BEGIN
        WRITELN('Length, Width, Height ?');
        READLN(Length, Width, Height);
END;
```

```
PROCEDURE Basearea (A, B : INTEGER);
VAR Basearea : INTEGER;
BEGIN
        Basearea := A * B;
        WRITELN('Area of base', Basearea)
END;
```

```
PROCEDURE Perimeter (C, D : INTEGER);
VAR Perimeter : INTEGER;
BEGIN
        Perimeter := 2 * (C + D);
        WRITELN('Perimeter is', Perimeter)
END;
```

```
PROCEDURE Volume (E, F, G : INTEGER);
VAR Volume : INTEGER;
BEGIN
    Volume := E * F * G;
    WRITELN('Volume is',Volume)
END;
```

```
BEGIN
    Inputdata;
    Basearea(Length, Width);
    Perimeter(Length, Width);
    Volume(Length, Width, Height)
END.
```

Formal parameters are only place holders. This can be demonstrated by Ch15P4 where the procedures are called a second time but different actual parameters are used – L, W and H. The third time the procedures are called constant values of 1, 2, and 3 are passed. The same procedure can thus be called from different parts of the program, or indeed by different programs, with a variety of actual parameters; the formal parameters are constant. The procedures accept any data passed as parameters as long as the items are consistent in both number and data type.

```
PROGRAM Ch15P4 (INPUT, OUTPUT);
(* Repeated procedure calls using formal parameters *)
VAR Length, Width, Height, L, W, H : INTEGER;
```

```
PROCEDURE Indata1;
BEGIN
    WRITELN('Length, Width, Height ?');
    READLN(Length, Width, Height);
END;
```

```
PROCEDURE Indata2;
BEGIN
    WRITELN('Length, Width, Height ?');
    READLN(L, W, H)
END;
```

```
PROCEDURE Basearea (A, B : INTEGER);
VAR Basearea : INTEGER;
BEGIN
        Basearea := A * B;
        WRITELN('Area of base', Basearea)
END;
```

```
PROCEDURE Perimeter (C, D : INTEGER);
VAR Perimeter : INTEGER;
BEGIN
        Perimeter := 2 * (C + D);
        WRITELN('Perimeter is', Perimeter)
END;
```

```
PROCEDURE Volume (E, F, G : INTEGER);
VAR Volume : INTEGER;
BEGIN
        Volume := E * F * G;
        WRITELN('Volume is', Volume)
END;
```

```
BEGIN
        Indata1;
        Basearea(Length, Width);
        Perimeter(Length, Width);
        Volume(Length, Width, Height)
        Indata2;
        Basearea(L, W);
        Perimeter(L, W);
        Volume(L, W, H);
        Basearea(1, 2);
        Perimeter(1, 2);
        Volume(1, 2, 3)
END.
```

15.4 SCOPE

The scope, or range, of an identifier within which it is visible is the entire block in which it is defined. Each block may be viewed as a level that can correspond to the structured diagram.

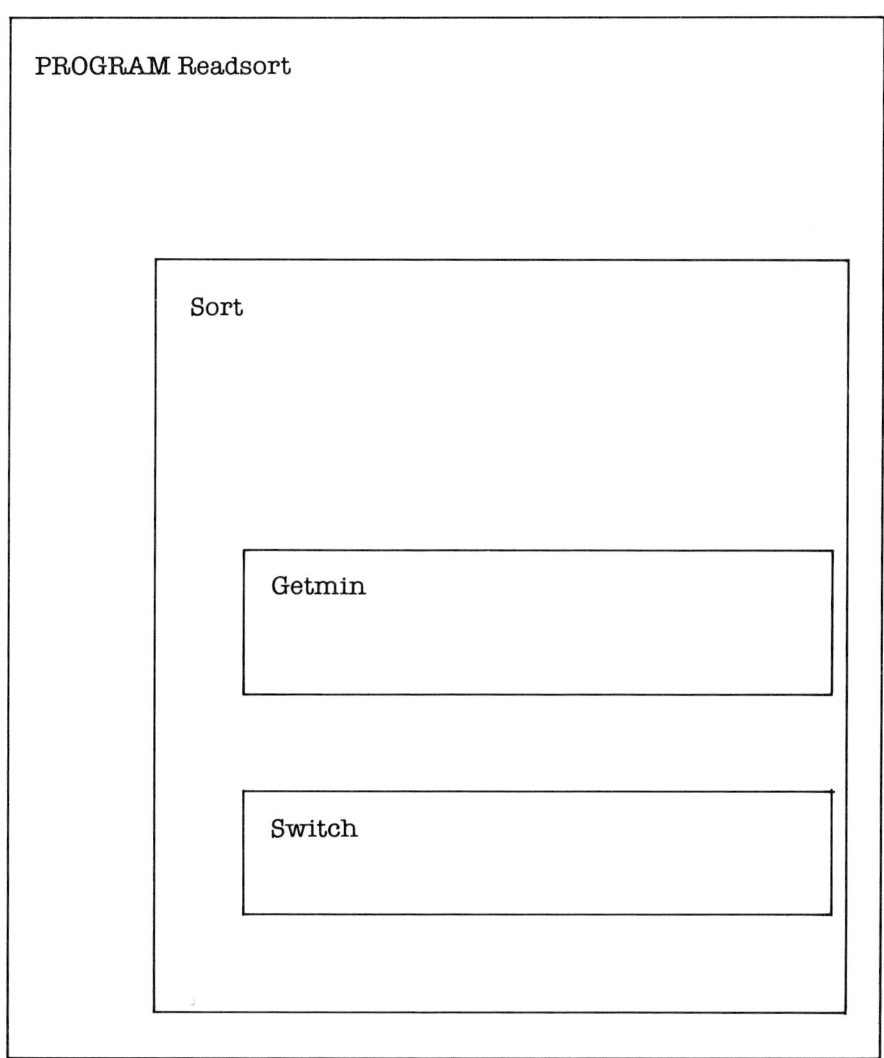

Figure 15.1 Block structuring

Readsort exists at the highest and outermost level. Definitions at this level are global. Sort is one level below Readsort, with Getmin and Switch existing at the lowest level within Sort. (See Figure 15.1.) The labels and the constant, type, variable and procedure identifiers accessible from each level are as follows:

Objects defined in	*Accessible only from procedures*
1. Readsort	Readsort, Sort, Getmin, Switch ie all procedures
2. Sort	Sort, Getmin, Switch
3. Getmin	Getmin
4. Switch	Switch

Objects defined in procedure Readsort are said to have a high visibility. Objects defined in procedures Switch and Getmin have a low visibility.

The scope will depend upon the block structuring. Figure 15.2 can be implemented in two main ways, as in Figures 15.3 and 15.4.

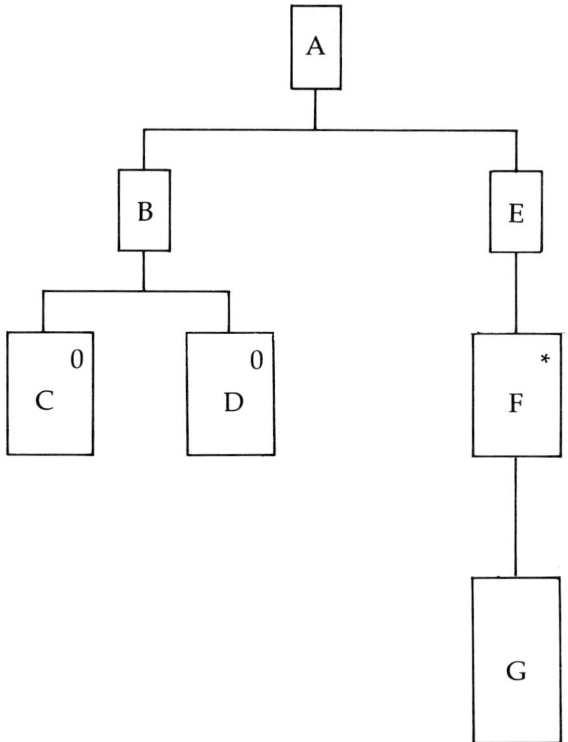

Figure 15.2 Typical structured diagram

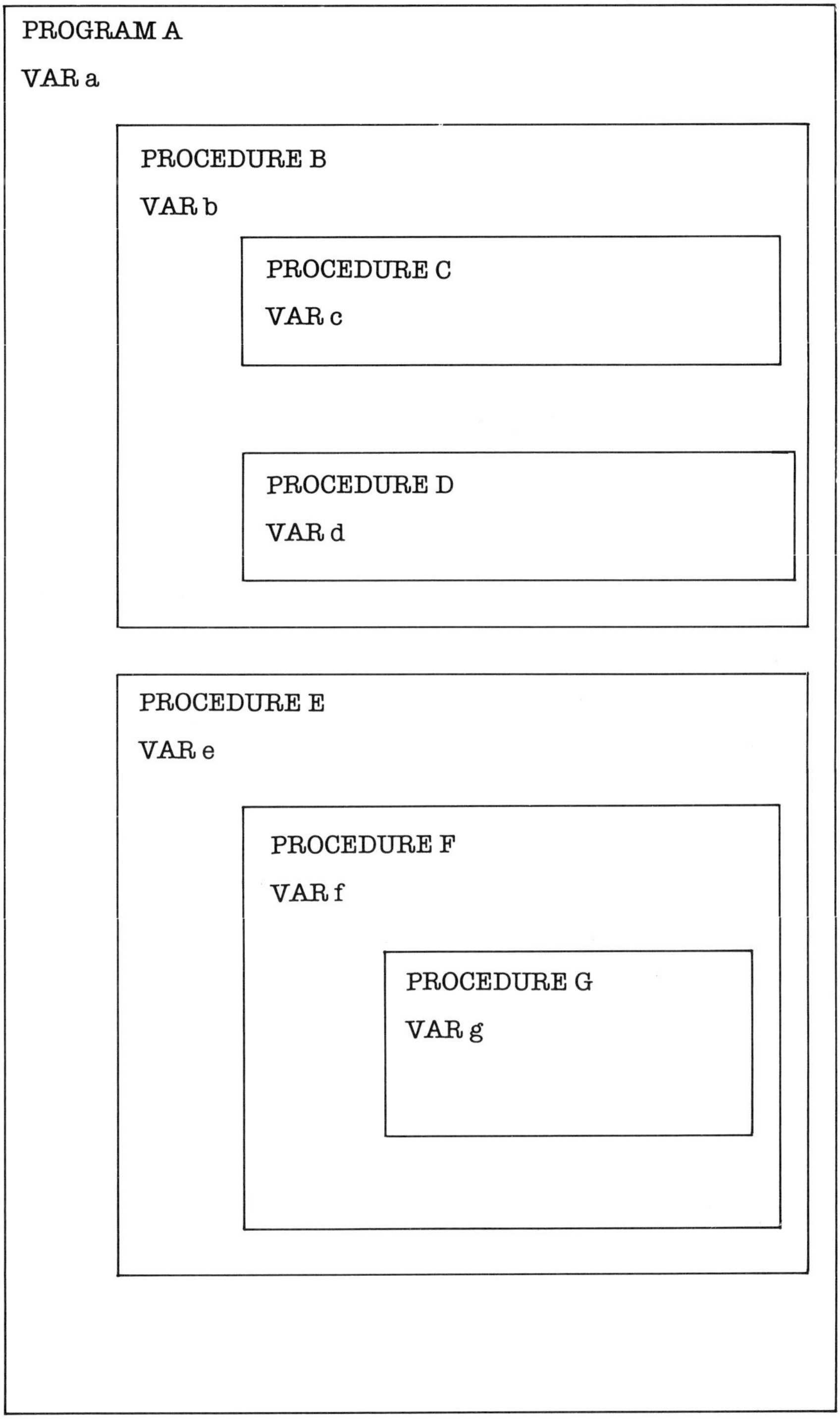

PROGRAM A
VAR a

PROCEDURE B
VAR b

PROCEDURE C
VAR c

PROCEDURE D
VAR d

PROCEDURE E
VAR e

PROCEDURE F
VAR f

PROCEDURE G
VAR g

Figure 15.3 First implementation

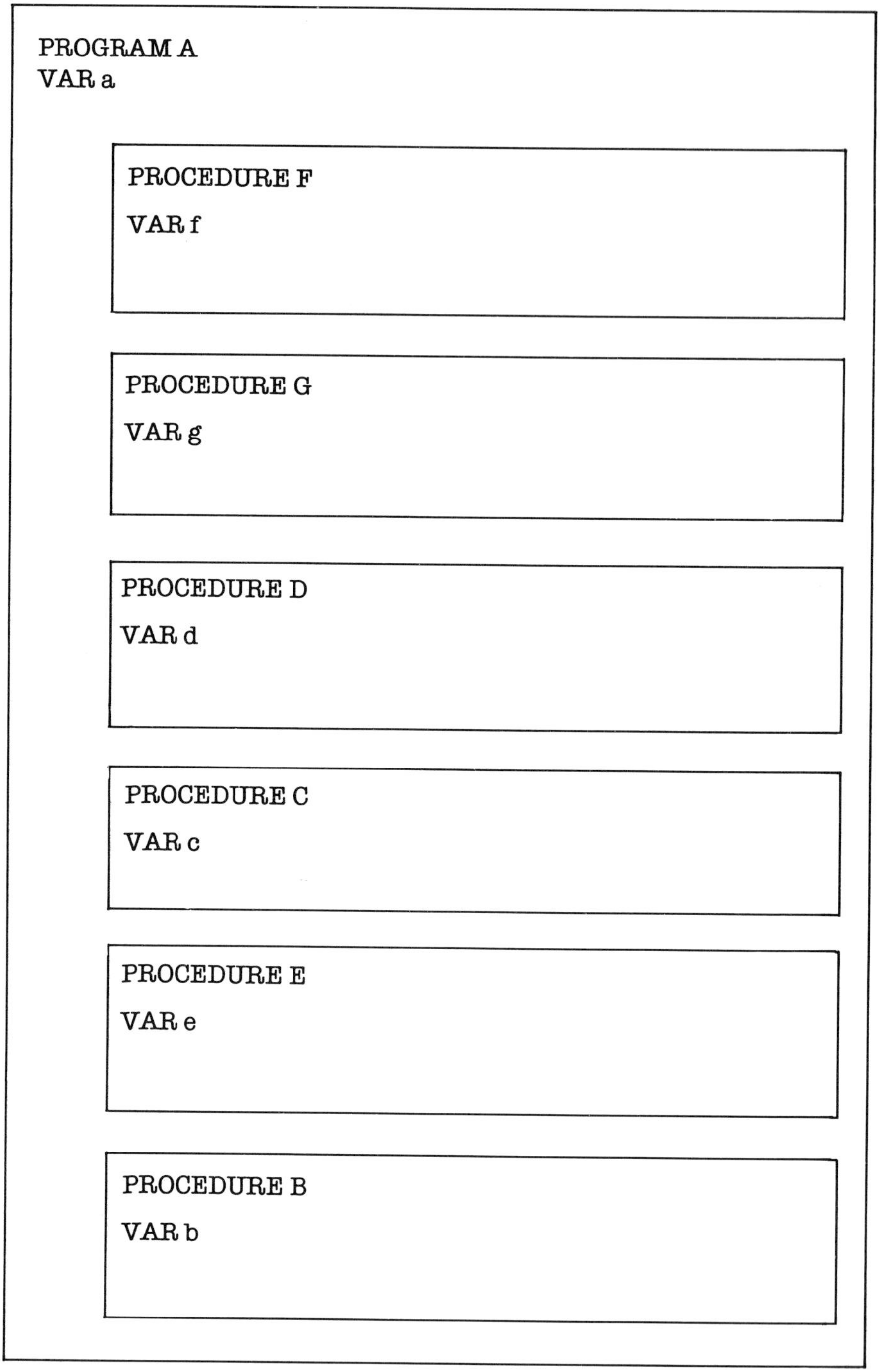

```
PROGRAM A
VAR a

    PROCEDURE F
    VAR f

    PROCEDURE G
    VAR g

    PROCEDURE D
    VAR d

    PROCEDURE C
    VAR c

    PROCEDURE E
    VAR e

    PROCEDURE B
    VAR b
```

Figure 15.4 Second implementation

The consequences with respect to variables and their scope is as follows:

Variables declared in Figure 15.3	*Scope – can be referenced by*
A a	A, B, C, D, E, F, G
B b	B, C, D
C c	C
D d	D
E e	E, F, G
F f	F, G
G g	G
Figure 15.4	
A a	A, B, C, D, E, F, G
B b	B
C c	C
D d	D
E e	E
F f	F
G g	G

Table 15.1 Variables and their scope

15.5 PROCEDURES AT EQUIVALENT LEVELS – THE FORWARD DIRECTIVE

In addition to variables, constants, etc, a procedure has access to procedure and function identifiers previously declared at a higher level or at the same level as its own declaration.

In the following program the procedures Alpha and Beta exist at the same level and have full access to all labels, constants, types, etc, defined in Main. Procedure Beta also has access to the identifier Alpha, whose declaration precedes Beta's. Beta can thus invoke Alpha. However Alpha cannot invoke Beta as Beta will be undefined to Alpha as it is declared after Alpha.

The forward directive makes it possible for each of the two procedures declared at the same level to call each other.

This requires a dummy declaration of one procedure using the format:

Procedure-heading FORWARD;

Definition of the specified procedure block is then deferred until the actual declaration, which appears later.

```
PROGRAM Main
VAR Number1, Number2 : INTEGER;

        PROCEDURE Alpha (a : INTEGER);

        PROCEDURE Beta (b : INTEGER);

BEGIN
        Alpha(Number1);
        Beta(Number2)
END.
```

The form of the deferred actual declaration is:

PROCEDURE Procedure-identifier; block

```
PROGRAM Main
VAR Number1, Number2 : INTEGER;
PROCEDURE Beta(b : INTEGER); FORWARD;
(* Dummy declaration of Beta *)

        PROCEDURE Alpha (a : INTEGER);

        PROCEDURE Beta;
        (* Actual declaration of Beta *)

BEGIN
        Alpha(Number1);
        Beta(Number2)
END.
```

Note that in the actual declaration of procedure Beta, the parameter list is not repeated. The procedure alone serves as the heading.

15.6 VALUE AND REFERENCE PARAMETERS

Both data and references to memory locations that hold data can be passed to procedures when they are called. The procedure headings allow the parameters to be defined as value or reference parameters. The expressions commonly used are parameters 'passed or called by value' or 'passed or called by reference'. (See Figure 15.5.)

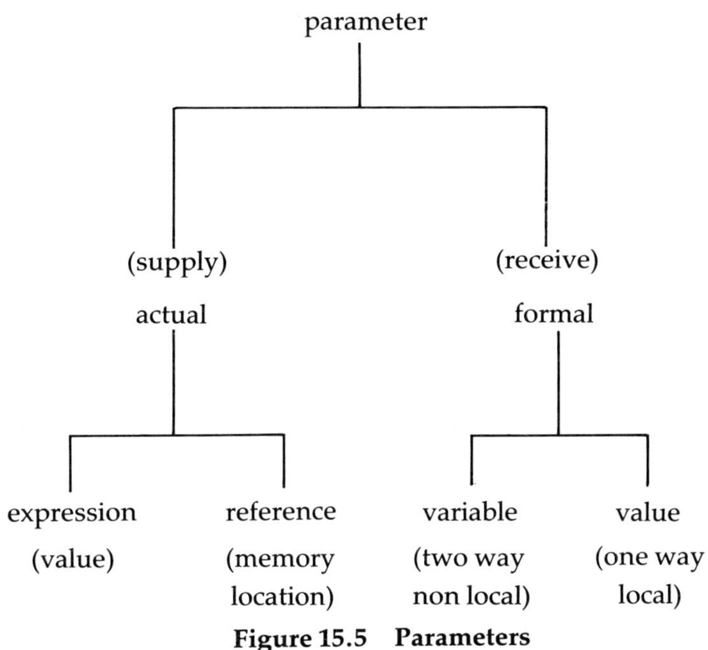

Figure 15.5 Parameters

15.7 VALUE PARAMETERS

Value parameters receive values from actual parameters when a procedure with value parameters is activated.

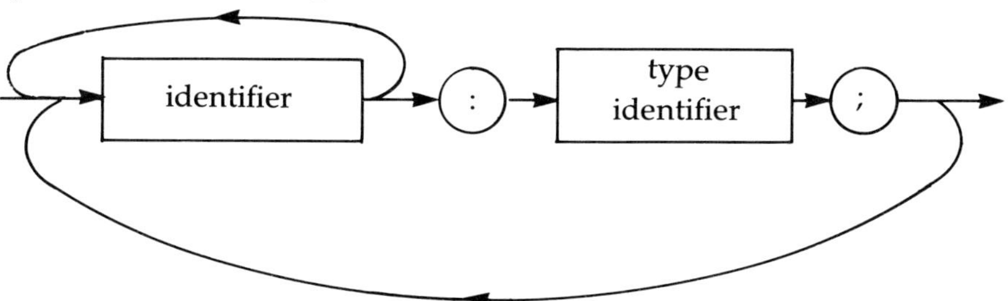

In program Ch15P5 Numb is a local variable. The processes that happen to this variable inside the procedure Incdata do not change the value of the actual parameter, Number. What happens to Numb is local.

```
PROGRAM Ch15P5 (INPUT, OUTPUT);
VAR Number : INTEGER:
(* Pass by value – one way local *)

PROCEDURE Inputdata;
BEGIN
        WRITELN('Input number');
        READLN(Number)
END;

PROCEDURE Incdata (Numb : INTEGER);
BEGIN
        Numb := Numb + 1;
        WRITELN('Incremented value of Numb is', Numb)
END;

PROCEDURE Outputdata;
BEGIN
        WRITELN('The input number is the same', Number)
END;

BEGIN
        Inputdata;
        Incdata(Number);
        Outputdata
END.
```

15.8 REFERENCE PARAMETERS

When a procedure with a variable, formal parameter is activated, the data it receives is the address of the associated actual parameter. A variable parameter is used to hold a reference to a memory location. The result of a procedure with a variable parameter can be used outside the procedure because both the actual and formal parameters use the data held in the same address. The identifier names may differ but they still use the same memory location.

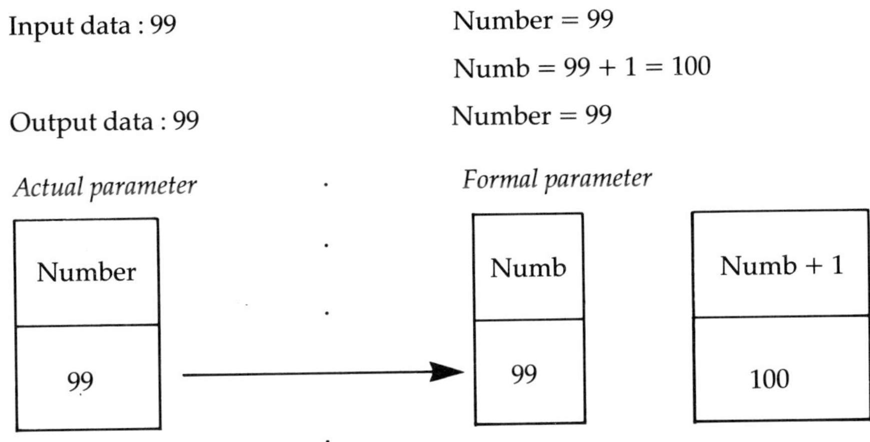

Figure 15.6 Effect of program Ch15p5

Number is not affected by changes to Numb Pass by value is one way and local. (See Figure 15.6.)

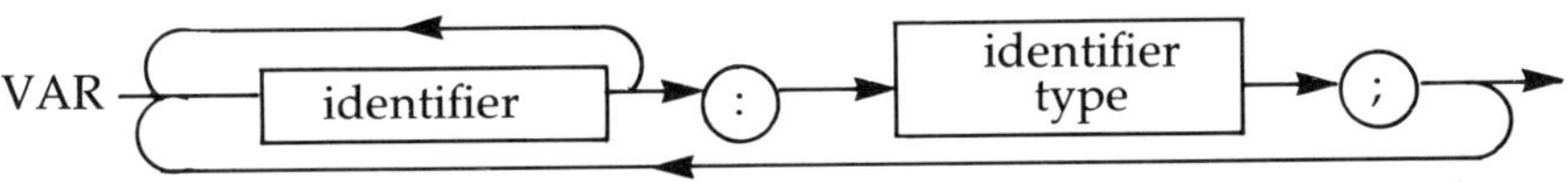

In program Ch15P6, the original value of Number has been incremented. What happens inside the procedure Incdata is recorded in the referenced storage area. (See Figure 15.7.)

```
PROGRAM Ch15P6 (INPUT, OUTPUT);

VAR Number : INTEGER:

(* Pass by reference – two way non-local *)
```

```
PROCEDURE Inputdata;

BEGIN
        WRITELN('Input number');
        READLN(Number)
END;
```

```
PROCEDURE Incdata (VAR Numb : INTEGER);
BEGIN
        Numb := Numb + 1;
        WRITELN('Incremented value of Numb is', Numb)
END;
```

```
PROCEDURE Outputdata;
BEGIN
        WRITELN(The input number has been changed', Number)
END;
```

```
BEGIN
        Inputdata;
        Incdata(Number);
        Outputdata
END.
```

Input data : 99 — Number = 99

Numb = 99 + 1 = 100

Output data : 100 — Number = 100

Actual parameter — *Formal parameter*

Number
99

→

Numb
99

Numb + 1
100

Number
100

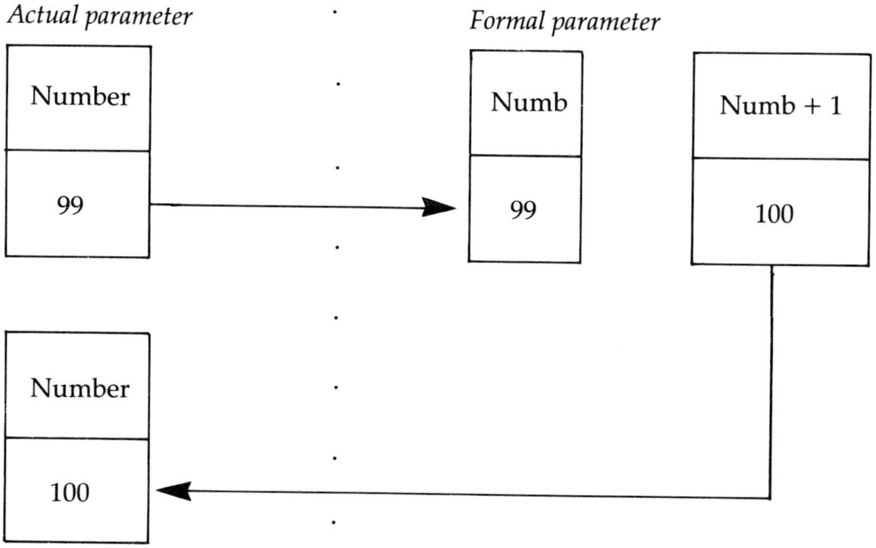

Pass by reference is two way and non-local.

Figure 15.7 Effect of Program Ch15p6

Consider a program, Ch4P1, that we have previously seen. Let us look at how to set parameters for the procedures.

```
PROGRAM Ch4P1 (INPUT, OUTPUT);
(* Sequential procedure calls *)
CONST Density = 5.0;
VAR Length, Width, Height, Mass, Basearea,
        Perimeter, Volume : REAL;
```

```
PROCEDURE Inputdata;
BEGIN
        WRITELN('Please enter Length, Width and Height');
        READ(Length);
        READ(Width);
        READ(Height)
END;
```

```
PROCEDURE Processdata;
BEGIN
        Basearea := Length * Width;
        Perimeter := 2 * (Length + Width);
        Volume := Perimeter * Height;
        Mass := Density * Volume
END;
```

```
PROCEDURE Outputdata;
BEGIN
        WRITELN('Basearea', Basearea : 6 :2);
        WRITELN('Perimeter', Perimeter : 6 : 2);
        WRITELN('Volume', Volume :6 :2);
        WRITELN('Mass', Mass :6 :2)
END;
```

```
BEGIN
        Inputdata;
        Processdata;
        Outputdata
END.
```

The data read in by procedure Inputdata must be made available to other procedures in the program. This is obviously done by parameters being passed by reference. Procedure Inputdata is therefore assigned the variable parameters L, W and H. When the procedure is called the variable L uses the same address as the variable Length, the variable W uses the same address as Width, and H, the same address as Height. Operations on the formal parameters L, W and H within that procedure therefore affect the actual parameters. However procedure Inputdata has no direct access to the variables Length, Width and Height. Furthermore it is necessary for data to be passed to the procedure before it can be accessed.

Procedure Processdata needs access to the three variables Length, Width and Height. This is done via value parameters L, W and H. There are no data manipulations that require the results to be made available to other procedures. We therefore declare L, W and H as value parameters. However, the calculations performed within this procedure that need to be made available to other parts of the program are the variable parameters B, P, V and M.

Finally we can assign the value parameters B, P, V and M to procedure Outputdata.

```
PROGRAM Ch15P7 (Input, Output);
(* Parameter passing – by value and by reference *)
CONST Density = 5.0;
VAR Length, Width, Height, Mass, Basearea,
      Perimeter, Volume : REAL;
```

```
PROCEDURE Inputdata(VAR L, W, H, : REAL);
BEGIN
        WRITELN('Please enter Length, Width and Height');
        READ(Length);
        READ(Width);
        READ(Height);
END;
```

```
PROCEDURE Processdata(L, W, H : REAL;
                      VAR B, P, V, M : REAL);
BEGIN
  B := L * W;
  P := 2 * (L + W);
  V := P * H;
  M := Density * V
END;
```

```
PROCEDURE Outputdata(B, P, V, M : REAL);
BEGIN
    WRITELN('Basearea', B : 6 :2);
    WRITELN('Perimeter', P : 6 : 2);
    WRITELN('Volume', V :6 :2);
    WRITELN('Mass', M :6 :2)
END;
```

```
BEGIN
    Inputdata(LENGTH, WIDTH, HEIGHT);
    Processdata(LENGTH, WIDTH, HEIGHT, BASEAREA,
                PERIMETER, VOLUME, MASS);
                 VOLUME, MASS);
    Outputdata(BASEAREA, PERIMETER, VOLUME, MASS)
END.
```

What are appropriate names for parameters? In program Ch15P7 the names of the actual and formal parameters are different but we have used the same formal names in different procedures. If we wished, they could be different, as in program Ch15P8.

```
PROGRAM Ch15P8 (Input, Output);
(* Parameter passing – by value and by reference *)
(* Parameter names all kept the same *)
CONST Density = 5.0;
VAR Length, Width, Height, Mass, Basearea,
    Perimeter, Volume : REAL;
```

```
PROCEDURE Inputdata(VAR Len, Wid, Hei :REAL);
BEGIN
        WRITELN('Please enter Length, Width and Height');
        READ(Len);
        READ(Wid);
        READ(Hei)
END;
```

```
PROCEDURE Processdata(L, W, H : REAL;
                        VAR B, P, V, M : REAL);
BEGIN
        B := L * W;
        P := 2 * (L + W);
        V := P * H;
        M := Density * V
END;
```

```
PROCEDURE Outputdata(B, P, V, M : REAL);
BEGIN
        WRITELN('Basearea', B : 6 :2);
        WRITELN('Perimeter', P : 6 : 2);
        WRITELN('Volume', V :6 :2);
        WRITELN('Mass', M :6 :2)
END;
```

```
BEGIN
        Inputdata(LENGTH, WIDTH, HEIGHT);
        Processdata(LENGTH, WIDTH, HEIGHT, BASEAREA,
                        PERIMETER, VOLUME, MASS);
                        VOLUME, MASS);
        Outputdata(BASEAREA, PERIMETER, VOLUME, MASS)
END.
```

Indeed we could use the same names for our formal and actual parameters. This is demonstrated in program Ch15P9. Do note that the actual parameter Length shares the same address as the formal value parameter Length in procedure Inputdata. The actual parameter being eclipsed by the formal parameter of the same name. In process Inputdata the actual parameter Length is passed to the formal value parameter Length, etc; perhaps a little confusing.

```
PROGRAM Ch15P9 (Input, Output);

(* Parameter passing – by value and by reference *)

(* Parameter names all the same *)

CONST Density = 5.0;

VAR Length, Width, Height, Mass, Basearea,
        Perimeter, Volume : REAL;
```

```
PROCEDURE Inputdata(VAR Length, Width, Height :REAL);

BEGIN

        WRITELN('Please enter Length, Width and Height');
        READ(Length);
        READ(Width);
        READ(Height)
 END;
```

```
PROCEDURE Processdata(Length, Width, Height : REAL;
                                    VAR Basearea, Perimeter, Volume,
                                          Mass : REAL);

BEGIN
        Basearea := Length * Width;
        Perimeter := 2 * (Length + Width);
        Volume := Perimeter * Height;
        Mass := Density * Volume
END;
```

```
PROCEDURE Outputdata(Basearea, Perimeter, Volume,
                         Mass : REAL);
BEGIN
       WRITELN('Basearea', B : 6 :2);
       WRITELN('Perimeter', P : 6 : 2);
       WRITELN('Volume', V :6 :2);
       WRITELN(Mass', M :6 :2)
END;
```

```
BEGIN
       Inputdata(LENGTH, WIDTH, HEIGHT);
       Processdata(LENGTH, WIDTH, HEIGHT, BASEAREA,
                   PERIMETER, VOLUME, MASS);
       Outputdata(BASEAREA, PERIMETER, VOLUME, MASS)
END.
```

Recall that our procedures will probably be written once and used many times. The procedures will be called many times by other different procedures. We should therefore aim for formal names of a general nature to account for this.

To summarise, what we should aim for is a procedure that is about one page long with no more than three or four levels of indentation. Further our procedure will not access any global variables. All data manipulation must be via parameter passing ie on a need-to-know basis.

15.9 FILES REVISITED

So far we have only looked at parameters of type INTEGER. The same principles can however be applied to more complex data types. The program Ch15P10, used to handle strings, can be modified to incorporate parameter passing.

```
PROGRAM Ch15P10 (INPUT, OUTPUT, MASTER);
CONST Namelength = 10;
        Keylength = 4;
        Sentinel = '9999';
        Dummy = '    ';
TYPE Namestring = PACKED ARRAY[ 1..Namelength ] OF CHAR;
```

```
      Keystring = PACKED ARRAY[ 1..Keylength ] OF CHAR;
      Employee = RECORD
                       Worksnumber : Keystring;
                       Name        : Namestring;
                       Taxcode     : INTEGER;
                     END;
      Personnel = FILE of Employee;
VAR Employeerecord : Employee;
     Master: Personnel;
```

```
PROCEDURE Getnamestring (VAR Str : Namestring);
VAR
     i : INTEGER;
BEGIN
     FOR i := 1 to Namelength do
        IF EOLN THEN
          Str[i] := ' '
        ELSE
          READ(Str[i]);
     READLN
END;
```

```
PROCEDURE Getkeystring (VAR Str : Keystring);
VAR
     i : INTEGER;
BEGIN
        FOR i := 1 to Keylength DO
          IF EOLN THEN
            Str[i] := ' '
        ELSE
          READ(Str[i]);
        READLN
END;
```

```
PROCEDURE Buildfile;
VAR Choice : CHAR;

    PROCEDURE Bldinit;
    BEGIN
        REWRITE(Master);
        Choice := 'Y'
    END;

    PROCEDURE Bldpro;

        PROCEDURE Bldit;
        BEGIN
            WITH Employeerecord DO
                BEGIN
                    WRITELN('Worksnumber ?');
                    Getkeystring(Worksnumber);
                    WRITELN('Name ?');
                    Getnamestring(Name);
                    WRITELN('Taxcode ?');
                    READLN(Taxcode)
                END;
            WRITE(Master, Employeerecord);
            WRITELN('More records, type Y or N');
            READLN(Choice)
        END;

    BEGIN
        WHILE Choice = 'Y' DO
        Bldit
    END;
```

```
PROCEDURE Bldterm;
BEGIN
      Lastrecord;
      WRITE(Master, Employeerecord)
END;
```

```
BEGIN
      Bldinit;
      Bldpro;
      Bldterm
END;
```

The variables Gname and Gkey of type Namestring and Keystring respectively have been deleted. The procedure Getnamestring has been modified to:

```
PROCEDURE Getnamestring (VAR Str : Namestring);
```

and procedure Getkeystring is now:

```
PROCEDURE Getkeystring (VAR Str : Keystring);
```

and the conditions modified accordingly. These procedures can then be called by reference from other procedures.

The statements

```
Getkeystring;
Worksnumber := Gkey;
```

and

```
Getnamestring;
Name := Gname;
```

have been replaced by

Getkeystring(Worksnumber) and Getnamestring(Name) respectively.

15.10 FUNCTIONS RECONSIDERED

The function designator consists of a function identifier and a parameter list. The function designator then activates the function in order to return a single result. Recall that it is the function name that is assigned the result produced by the function. The function designator rules are:

- 1. A function designator activates a function to produce (return) a single value.
- 2. A function designator consists of a function identifier and a parameter list (if any).
- 3. A function designator can never appear by itself. It must always be part of a larger instruction.
- 4. A function identifier is limited to a scalar or pointer type (simple, enumerated, subrange or pointer).
- 5. The function name always gets assigned the result produced by the function.

Program Ch3P2 uses what is called an implicit function.

```
PROGRAM Ch3P2 (INPUT, OUTPUT);

VAR Number : INTEGER;

PROCEDURE Inputdata;
BEGIN
        WRITELN('Input a number');
        READLN(Number)
END;

PROCEDURE Outputdata;
BEGIN
        WRITELN('Number squared is', Number := SQR(Number)
END;

BEGIN
        Inputdata;
        Outputdata
END.
```

As well as the functions ROUND, MOD, DIV, PRED, SUCC, CHR, ORD and TRUNC other implicit functions in Pascal are:

Function	*Action*	*Parameters*	*Result*
ABS	absolute value of argument	REAL/INTEGER	same as argument
ARCTAN	arc tan of argument	REAL/INTEGER	REAL
COS	cosine of argument	REAL/INTEGER	REAL

EXP	value of e raised to power of argument	REAL/INTEGER	REAL
LN	logarithm to the base e of argument	REAL/INTEGER	REAL
ODD	TRUE if argument is odd	INTEGER	BOOLEAN
SIN	sine of argument	REAL/INTEGER	REAL
SQR	square of argument	REAL/INTEGER	Same as argument
SQRT	positive square root of argument	REAL/INTEGER	REAL

In each case the argument or parameter is passed to the function and the associated result returned, eg ABS(–1.23) will return the value of 1.23.

It is possible to have user defined or explicit functions, thus giving the programmer the power to enhance the language accordingly.

Consider the fragment of code to return the largest of two values supplied to an explicit function. It is necessary to:

- 1. Name the function, Largest in this case.
- 2. Define the type and number of data items to be supplied to our function.
- 3. Define the type of value that will be generated

```
FUNCTION Largest(x, y :INTEGER) : INTEGER;
BEGIN
    IF x >= y THEN
      Larger := x
    Else
      Larger := y
END;
```

Our function can then be manipulated as part of a larger instruction. The statement WRITELN(Larger(a, b)) passes the values associated with the variables a and b to our function Larger. The resulting value is then assigned to Largest which has to be part of a larger instruction.

```
READLN(a, b);
WRITELN(Larger(a, b), 'is the largest');
```

Once written, the function can be used many times with different variables.

```
READLN(c, d);

WRITELN(Larger(c, d), 'is the largest');
```

As Larger represents a single value it can be manipulated in arithmetic expressions.

```
Difference := larger(a, b) – larger(c, d);
```

15.11 SUMMARY

- 1. Global data can be corrupted. The data requirements of each module should be specifically defined on a 'need to know basis'.
- 2. In program Ch5P1 we made use of a procedure that would swap the order of two numbers. Modify the program using parameter passing (pass by reference).
- 3. Communication with procedures can be by parameter passing. Data is passed from the actual parameter list to the formal parameter list of the receiving procedure.
- 4. Parameters must match in both number and type.
- 5. Procedures with parameters can be used as often as required.
- 6. The scope of an identifier depends upon where it is defined – they can have 'high' or 'low' visibility.
- 7. The forward directive makes it possible for procedures declared at the same level to call each other.
- 8. Value parameter passing is 'one way and local'.
- 9. Reference parameter passing is 'two way and non-local'.
- 10. Pascal provides a range of implicit functions. This range can be enhanced by user defined or explicit functions.

15.12 PROBLEMS

- 1. Rewrite program Ch2P9 in a procedure based structured form using parameter passing.
- 2. In program Ch5P1 we made use of a procedure that would swap the order of two numbers. Modify the program using parameter passing (pass by reference).
- 3. Write a program that will display on the screen the following:

A
BB
CCC
DDDD
EEEEE

To do this sequentially call a procedure each time passing the parameters associated with each line. For example the parameters for the third line are procedurecall('C', 3).

16 Program Development and Testing

16.1 INTRODUCTION

A major objective and outcome of structured design is to produce programs that are more likely to be correct. Much work is being done on formal specification techniques that allow the generation of proof of correctness. Formal techniques are however complex; hence for the time being programs must be tested. Design methods help us to produce correct designs. The emphasis should be on the design process. The act of coding should then be a simple, mechanical process. Any errors at this stage will be trivial, eg transcription errors.

It is important at this point to realise that 'bits do not rot', 'bytes do not decay' and the 'system is not stressed'. Software does not wear out, errors are introduced and errors propagate. Therefore the next time you purchase a software package there is every chance that it will be defective. Errors can be introduced at all stages of development. Further, if errors are inherent in the design we could well be in the position of cementing-in bugs. The aim of testing is to find errors. The algorithm for testing can be simplified to 'find errors early and find all errors'. It is essential therefore to incorporate testing as an integral part of the design, thus reducing the likelihood of designing errors into the system.

The validation of a software system is a continuous process through each stage of the software life cycle. Program testing is the most widely used system validation technique. Program testing is that part of the validation process which is normally carried out prior to and during implementation. Testing involves exercising the program using data similar to the real data the program is designed to execute, observing the program outputs and deducing the existence of program errors or inadequacies from anomalies in that output.

Do note, testing is the process of establishing the existence of errors. Debugging is the process of locating and correcting these errors. It has been said many times, and bears repeating again, 'testing cannot show that a program is error free'; testing can only show the presence, not the absence, of errors.

If you are still not convinced about structured design methods consider the system development cycle. There are various figures quoted for the relative percentage times involved in good program design, development and testing, but I feel the following figures are an accurate reflection:

- 1. Design 35%
- 2. Coding 15%
- 3. Testing 50%

As much time can be spent testing a program as designing and coding. Similarly the cost ratio of software development to maintenance is between one to five and one to fifty. This means the maintenance costs far exceed the design costs.

16.2 DATA VETTING

Data vetting is the process of checking the quality of input data. The program must be able to respond in a meaningful manner to any data that can be presented to it. Data vetting procedures can therefore be quite extensive. Accordingly data can be classified:

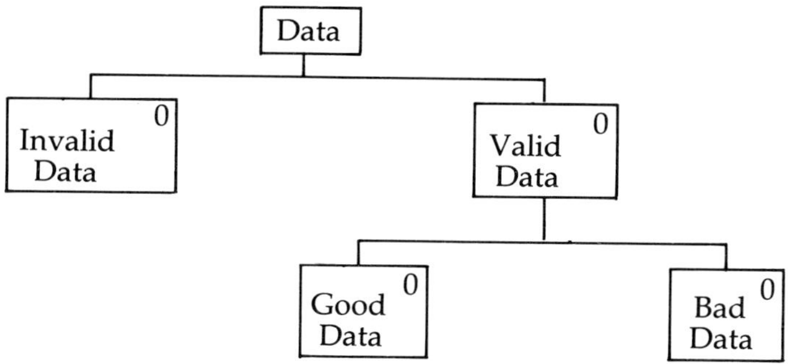

Invalid data: will cause systems corruption and therefore have unacceptable consequences.

Valid data: can be dealt with by the program in an acceptable manner. Valid data can be either good or bad data.

Good data: data that will be processed according to the program specification.

Bad data: data that will not be processed but will be detected and the appropriate action taken.

16.3 SYSTEMATIC TESTING

The modular approach we have been using can be employed in the testing process. In this case it is possible to identify five distinct stages:

- 1. Function testing. This is to ensure that a module performs to specification. It should be possible to test each module as a stand alone entity.
- 2. Module testing. A module is made up of a number of functions which may co-operate with each other. After each individual function has been tested, it is necessary to test the co-operation process.
- 3. Subsystem testing. For very large systems there may be many hierarchical levels.
- 4. System testing. Does the system provide the functions specified in the acceptance document?
- 5. Acceptance testing. Prior to this all testing has been artificial. Acceptance testing is the process of testing using real or live data.

There are two main methods for testing programs, Black Box testing and White Box testing (also known as Glass Box). They are complementary rather than mutually exclusive testing methods.

16.4 BLACK BOX TESTING

In this approach the program is seen as a black box. It is a piece of software the contents of which are unknown to the tester. However we do know the specification and we can therefore test the external interfaces. Input data is generated systematically and the associated output results inspected accordingly.

System test cases can include:

- 1. Valid input
- 2. Invalid input
- 3. System corruption
- 4. Performance

The basic ideas that support Black Box Testing are 'equivalence partitioning' and 'boundary value analysis'. Programs expect data input; this data may be valid, invalid or cause system corrpution and perhaps failure. Equivalence partitioning is a technique for determining which classes of input data have common properties. It is then possible to test only one member of that set, our aim being to establish a reasonable level of confidence with a minimum set of test cases.

For a given data item there will be a defined range of values. An equivalence class is a collection of values that will have the same effect on the program.

Consider one of our earlier programs Ch5P7 which displays 'One' when

1 is typed in, 'Two' when 2 is typed in etc. The program expects data in the range zero to four inclusive. There are four equivalence classes:

– 1.	input data < 0	invalid
– 2.	input data >= 0 and <= 4	valid
– 3.	input data > 4	invalid
– 4.	input data is a non-integer value	invalid

Using equivalence partitioning we can identify that –1, –2, –3, etc are all in the set of data corresponding to our first class. Similarly 0, 1, 2, 3 and 4 all belong to the same class. In order to test our program at least one member from each set should be included. This may seem trivial but what if the range of input data is zero to one thousand?

It is often the case that errors are due to equivalent class boundary values, typically a misunderstanding regarding the use of 'greater than' rather than 'greater than or equal to'. In boundary value testing, the test data consists of the boundary values. In our example valid data is zero to four inclusive. Boundary values are therefore :

– 1.	–1	invalid
– 2.	0	valid
– 3.	4	valid
– 4.	5	invalid

16.5 WHITE BOX TESTING

In this approach we know the internal workings of the program. Test data is designed in conjunction with this knowledge. Knowing the specification we can conclude that testing to see if the program will meet the specification is all that we need to do. All the sequence, selection and iteration routes can be tested.

Consider for a moment an automatic washing machine program:

10 'programs'	10 x
Biological or non-biological	2 x
Full or economy load	2 x
Extra spin option	2 x
No rinse option	2 x

This gives rise to 160 combinations. Consider now a multi-user operating system with some users multitasking. The total number of combinations is pretty much incalculable.

16.6 CONCLUSION

The key here is quality rather than the quantity of test data. Test strategies should be defined along with the test data, and the test documents fully documented.

16.7 SUMMARY

- 1. Errors are introduced into software.
- 2. Testing can only establish the existence, not the absence of errors.
- 3. Test strategies should be defined along with the test data and the test documentation.
- 4. The two main methods for testing are black box and white box testing. They should be seen as complementary rather than exclusive testing methods.
- 5. Black box testing employs equivalence testing in order to ensure the minimum effective test data set.
- 6. White box testing involves exercising logical routes through the program.

16.8 PROBLEMS

In this short text it is not possible to cover all the topics one would like to. In this context the reader may like to further develop some aspects of programming only touched upon; perhaps to further enhance the program on files. What is needed is to validate the worksnumber and the taxcode to ensure that they are within predefined limits. They should have both the correct number and type of values. Remember it is essential to protect your program from invalid data.

17 Where to Next? Jackson Structured Programming (JSP)

17.1 INTRODUCTION

Where to next? The problems so far considered have been relatively small with a commensurate development time. Further, the programs developed have been written by yourself for yourself. This can be contrasted with a commercial environment where the problems to be solved are large and complex and the associated code must work for its living! Hence the development times are longer and involve teams of analysts and programmers, ie 'man years'. Further, the trend today is very much concerned with the development of 'Information Systems'. An Information System can be defined as 'a system that collects, processes, stores and delivers the information that is relevant to all parts of an organisation in a manner that is both timely and appropriate'. As such, there has to be integrated corporate data processing. We can therefore identify an information hierarchy, Figure 17.1.

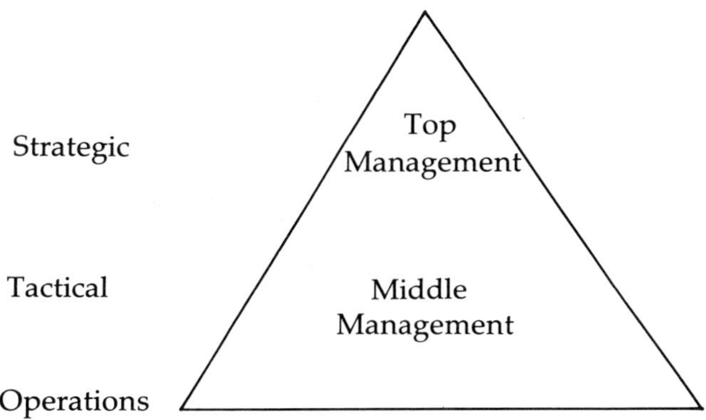

Figure 17.1 Data hierarchy

The method employed to help co-ordinate all of these 'man-years' of development is an important factor in determining the final success of the project. Certainly the method must represent an integrated set of standards that is generally applicable for widely differing project circumstances. It must have:

- Structure, ie it must be possible to describe the project in clearly defined stages.
- Techniques, ie the techniques employed should be proven, preferably in common use and have detailed guide-lines for their use.
- Documentation, ie the record of the project activity must be consistent, complete and correct.

17.2 HARD AND SOFT METHODS

There are many analysis and design methods based on different principles. The 'Soft' methods aim to optimise people as a resource and as such are more 'open' methods , often dealing with complex and non-deterministic situations. The 'Hard' methods typically aim to optimise equipment as the primary resource and are of a 'closed' nature with deterministic properties. The relationship between the two is shown in Figure 17.2.

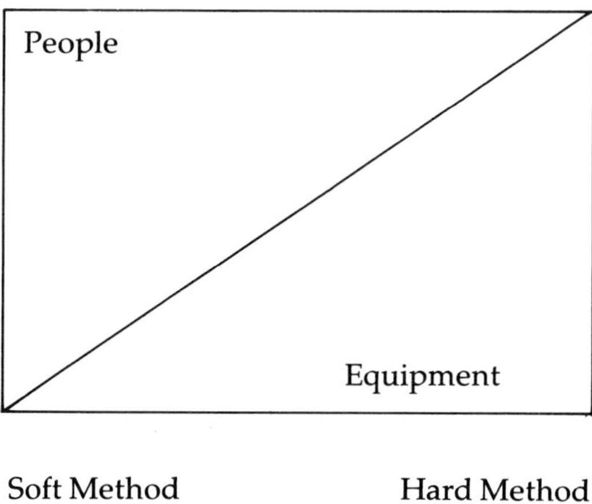

Soft Method Hard Method

Figure 17.2 Soft and Hard Methods

Methods also vary in their project scope, as shown in Figure 17.3. The phases of a large project are:

- Strategic (S)
- Feasibility (F)
- Analysis (A)
- Design (D)
- Implementation (I)
- Maintenance (M)

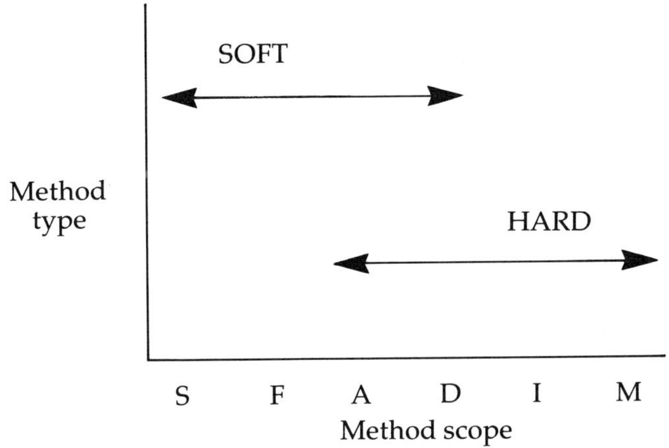

Figure 17.3 Method scope

The Soft methods address the ill defined problems associated with people working in an organisation, the organisation itself interacting with its environment. The Hard methods are concerned primarily with the development of system software.

17.3 JACKSON STRUCTURED PROGRAMMING (JSP) FUNDAMENTALS

JSP, by many considered to be primarily a Hard method, was developed by Michael Jackson and readers may like to read his book *Principles of Program Design*. In common with other design methods JSP is based on top-down decomposition using step-wise refinement and as such employs the three constructs of sequence, selection and iteration (SSI). However, Michael Jackson also applies these principles to data. All systems have an underlying data structure that changes little with time and forms an ideal basis for analysis and design. JSP is often referred to as a data driven method. The underlying principle is that in a correct program design the data structure and the program structure must correspond; the program structure in fact reflects the data structures. Jackson Structured Programming (JSP) is a program design method characterised by:

- Program structure modelled on the data of the system under investigation.
- Clearly defined stages and techniques that tend to produce standard results. Given the same problem different JSP programmers will produce very similar solutions. This has important maintenance considerations.
- Intrinsic documentation. Hence documentation is produced as part of the method, and has a better chance of being accurate and

complete. Again, this is an important factor in maintenance.

Starting with the program specification JSP has the following stages:

- 1. Draw the data structure diagrams.
- 2. Combine the data structures into a program structured diagram.
- 3. List the program operations and conditions, then allocate them to the program structured diagram.
- 4. Convert the program structured diagram to the target language.

Packages are available to automate the generation of code and to support the use of graphics.

Here only an outline of JSP is given. A more detailed consideration must address the problems of structure clashes, program inversion, optimisation, etc. What we will be doing here is :

- 1. Defining the data structures for the input and output files.
- 2. Identifying correspondences between input and output data structures.
- 3. Forming a composite data structure.
- 4. Defining the initial program structure.

17.3.1 Data structures

The first stage is JSP is to analyse the input and output data in order to define its structure using structured diagrams. This data is analysed in the topdown, stepwise manner we have seen. Consider the example of a sequential file. This consists of a series of records terminated by a Lastrecord holding our sentinel. We can therefore define a sequence of 'File body' followed by our 'Last record'. Further, that 'Record' is an iteration of 'File body', as seen in Figure 17.4

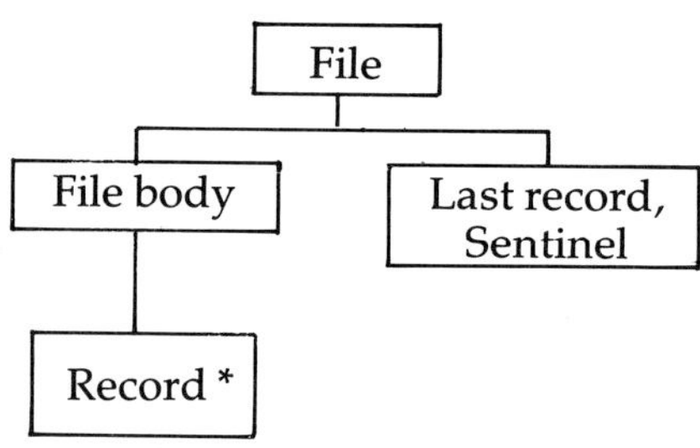

Figure 17.4 A file of records

In the case of a simple stock file, we have a record for each stock item. Each Part and therefore each record has a part number that is used as the primary key. Part is an iteration of File body, shown in Figure 17.5.

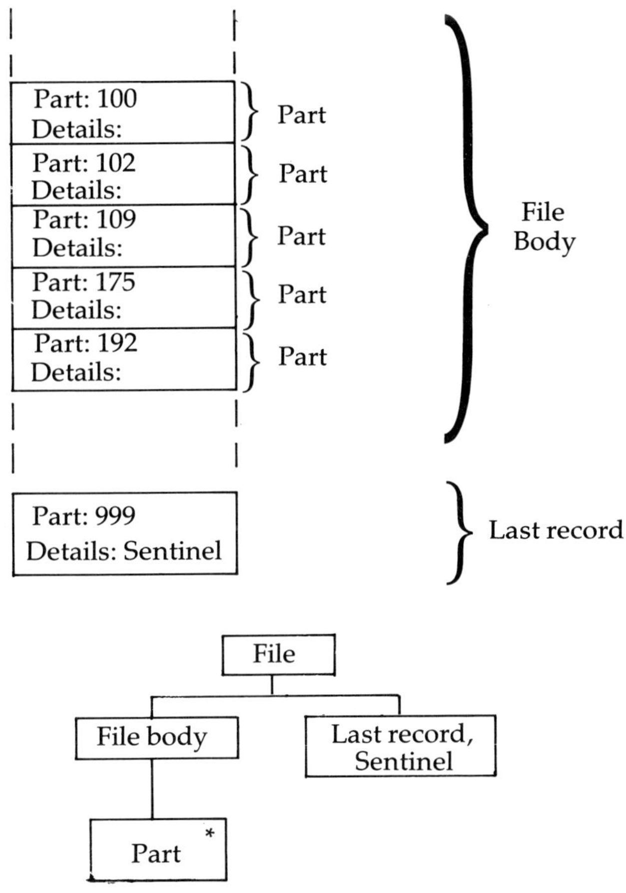

Figure 17.5 Simple stock file

A more practical data processing application is stock control. A stock movement file consists of a sequence of records ordered by part number. Each data record may be one of two types, either stock out or stock in. As a record of the movement of stock in and out of the stores there may be more than one record with the same part number. This can be seen in Figure 17.6.

Our structured diagram is modified accordingly. Movement is an iteration of Part with Stock in and Stock out being selections of Movement, Figure 17.7.

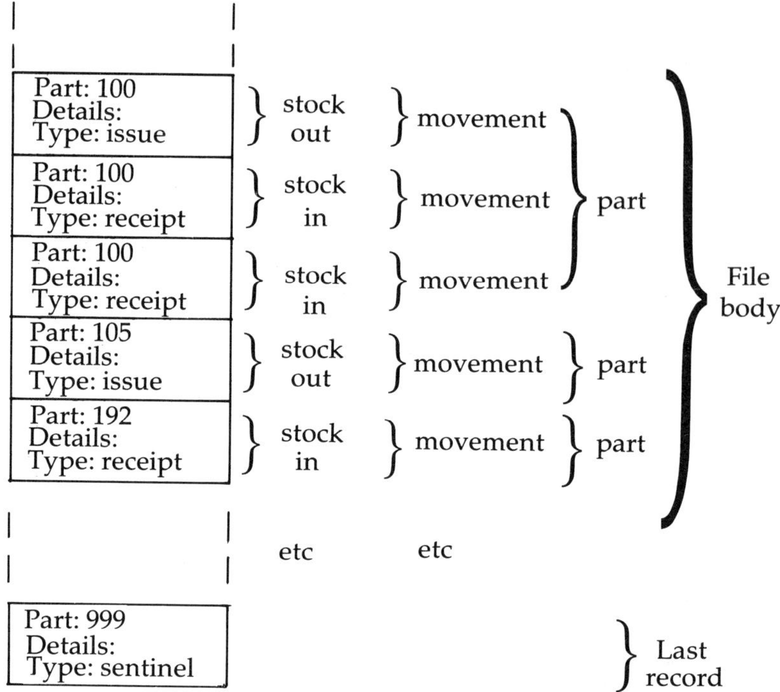

Figure 17.6 Stock movement file

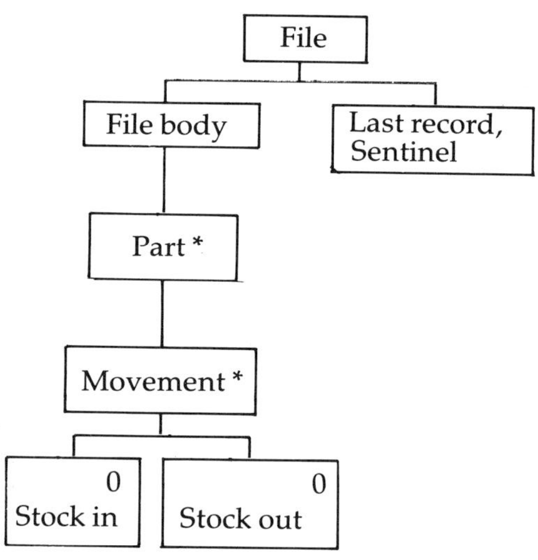

Figure 17.7 Stock movement file – structured diagram

As previously mentioned, a menu based system can be used as the interface to the user. Thus we have an 'interactive' program in which there is a dialogue between the program and the user.

A simple dialogue may be something like this:

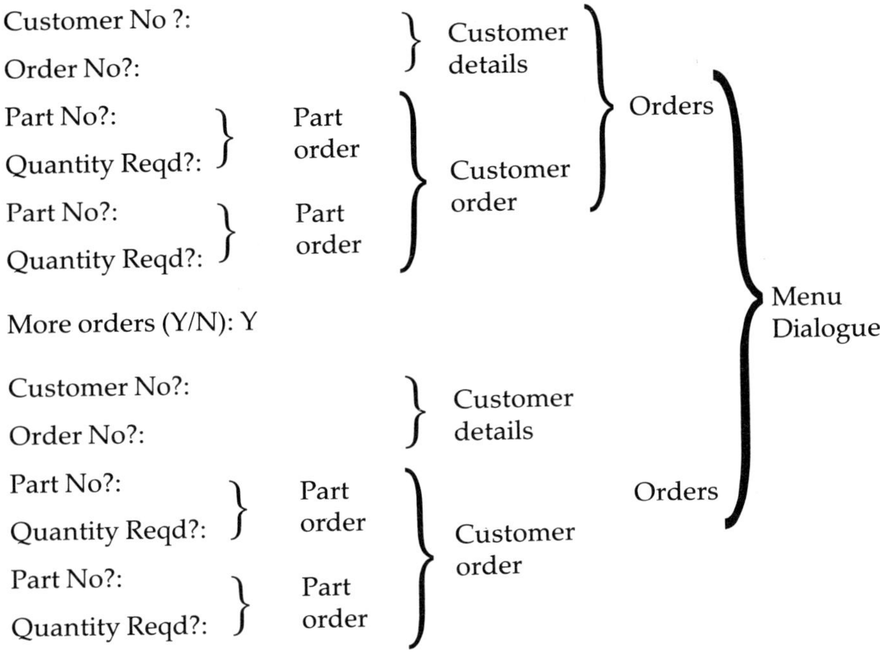

More orders (Y/N): N

In this dialogue the program prompts the user to supply the Customer number and then the Order number. Then for each Customer order number the required parts can be ordered.

The diagram for the Menu dialogue has an iteration of Orders, as in figure 17.8. Each Order has Customer details followed by the Customer order which has an iteration of Part order.

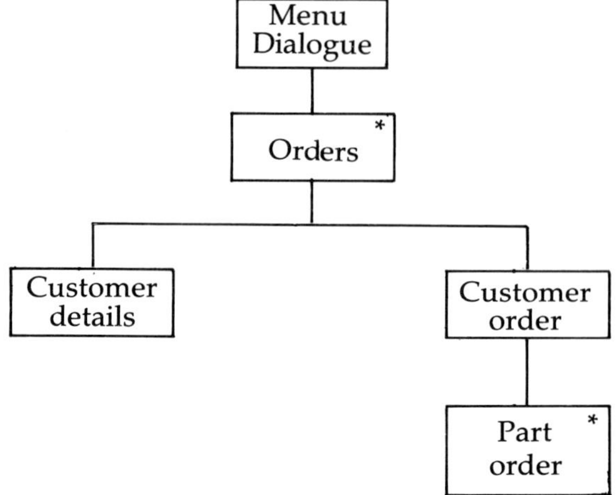

Figure 17.8 Menu dialogue structured diagram

The above diagram is obviously part of the complete menu system, as we can see in Figure 17.9, which includes menu initialisation and termination.

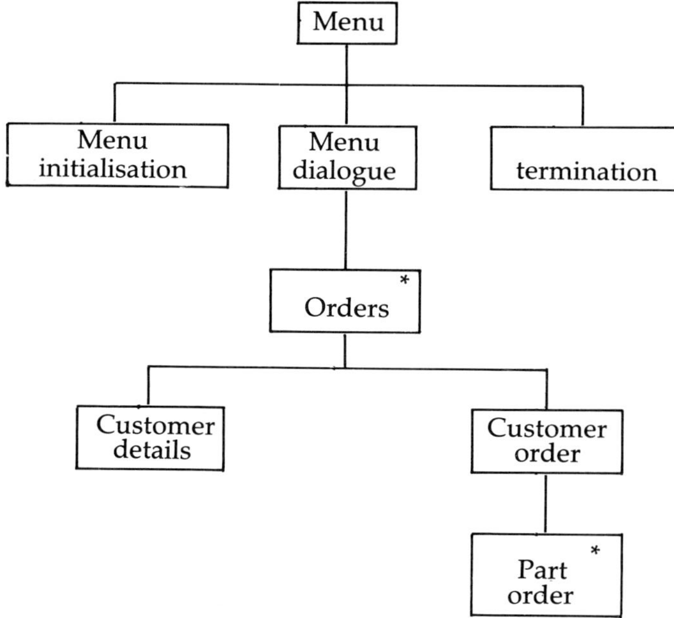

Figure 17.9 Complete menu system

Further refinements include data validation to take into account invalid order numbers, etc.

17.3.2 Program structure

After the data structures for input and output have been defined the next stage is to produce an initial program structure based on these data structures. This relationship ensures that there is an identifiable program module that is responsible for the processing of each data module. The series of stages is:

- 1. Identify and list correspondences between the two data structures for input and output. Do note, it is unlikely, but there may not be two data structures.
- 2. Form a composite data structure by merging the two data structures. This process is helped by a set of rules – correspondence rules.
- 3. Define the initial program structure. Then produce the detailed design with conditions and terminal functions.

For our example we will take a very simple library system. Our input data structure for the Members loan file is shown in Figure 17.10.

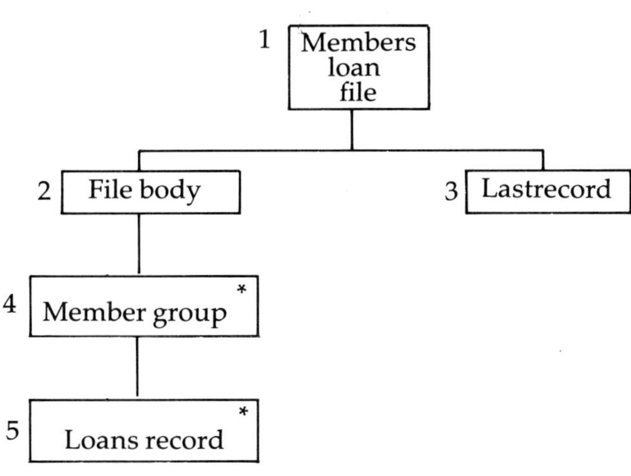

Figure 17.10 Input data structure

Further, our system has an output data structure based on a report generator, which is shown in Figure 17.11.

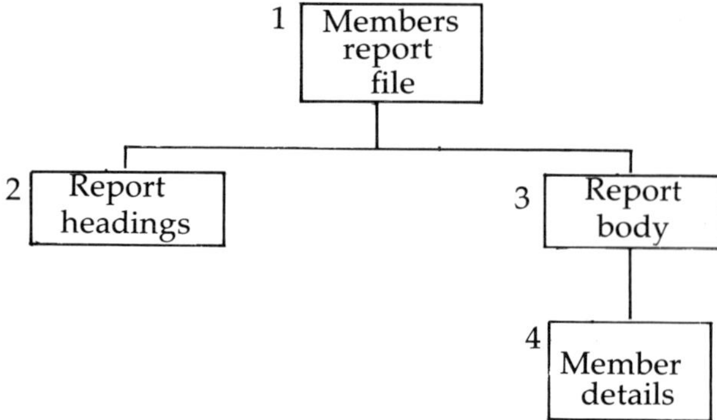

Figure 17.11 Output data structure

1 Identify and list correspondences

Number the modules in each data structure. Starting with the root module (the top of the hierarchy), work top to bottom and left to right. This results in the numbering shown above. For each module define the number of instances, ie quantify the number of each type of module. There is, for example, only one instance of 'File Body'. There are however many instances of 'Member group'; the number of instances in this case is the number of members. It sometimes helps to tabulate, eg Table 17.1, Table 17.2.

Module number	Module name	Instances
1	Members file	1
2	File body	1
3	Lastrecord	1
4	Member group	number of members
5	Loans record	number of books

Table 17.1 Input data structure tabulation

Module number	Module name	Instances
1	Member report	1
2	Report headings	1
3	Report body	1
4	Member details	number of members

Table 17.2 Output data structure tabulation

2 Form a composite data structure

The modules must, where possible, be linked in a sequential manner. The constraints are:

- A module in one data structure may have at most only one corresponding module in the other data structure. There may be instances where there are no correspondences.
- For corresponding data modules there have to be corresponding 'instances'. For example, it is possible to link Input number 1 with Output numbers 1 or 2 or 3. Similarly Input number 2 could be linked to Output1 or 2 or 3. Finally Input number 3 could be linked to Output1 or 2 or 3. Input4 can be linked with Output4. We can see that Input5 cannot be linked to any Output module.
- Links must not cross. If a link is formed between Input1 and Output2, no link may be formed between Input2 and Output1, Figure 17.12.

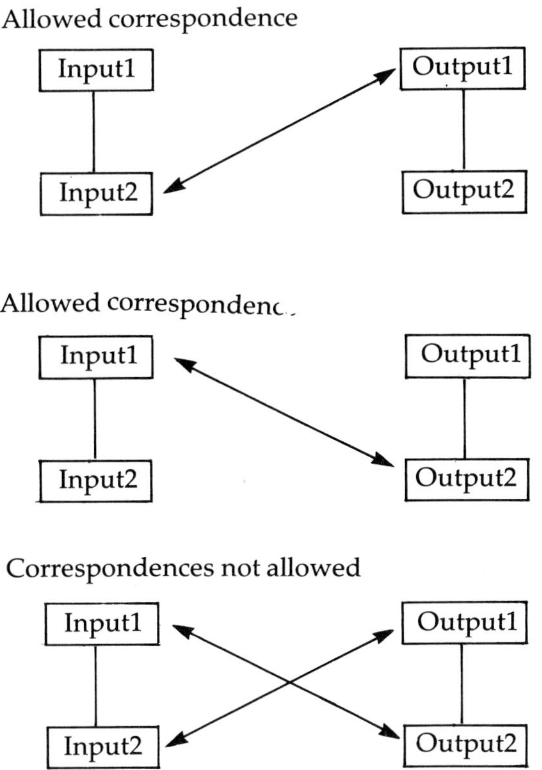

Figure 17.12 Allowed and disallowed correspondences

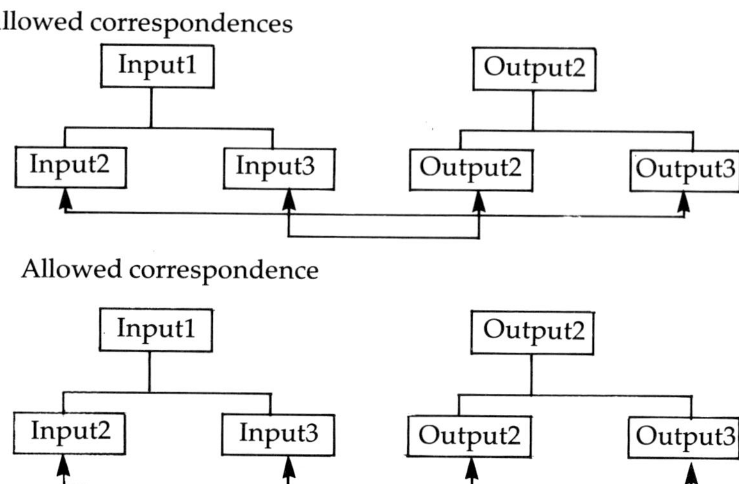

Figure 17.13 Disallowed and allowed correspondence

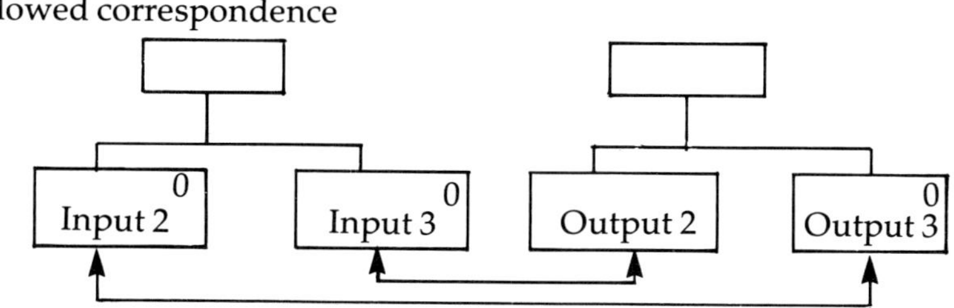

Figure 17.14 Allowed correspondence

– Maintain the sequential chronology by linking only in sequence. Input2 will occur before Input3, similarly for Output2 and Output3. Linking Input2 with Output3 is possible, ie they then occupy the

Input number	**Module name**	**Processing relationship**	**Output number**	**Module name**
1	Members loan file	⟷	1	Members report file
2	File body	⟷	3	Report body
4	Member group	⟷	4	Member details

Table 17.3

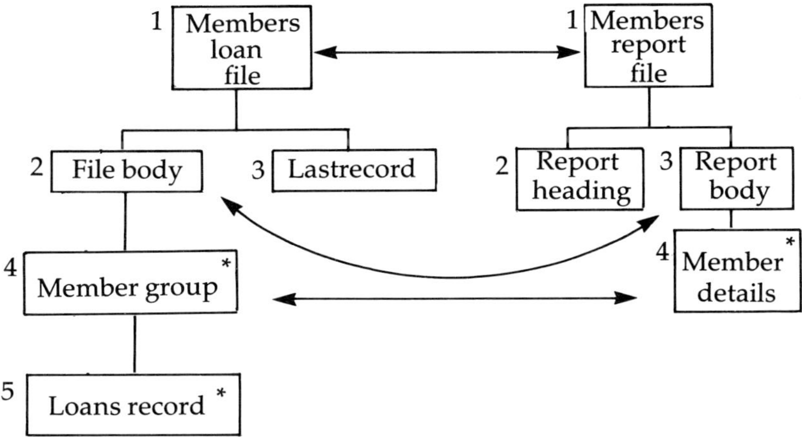

Figure 17.15

same 'time frame'. However it is not then possible to link Input3 and Output2 as in Figure 17.13. This does not however apply when the modules refer to data items of records. When the record has been accessed the data fields may be processed in any order and as often as required.

– selected components may be linked in any order, as in Figure 17.14.

Applying the rules to our input and output data structures we obtain the results in Table 17.3 and Figure 17.15.

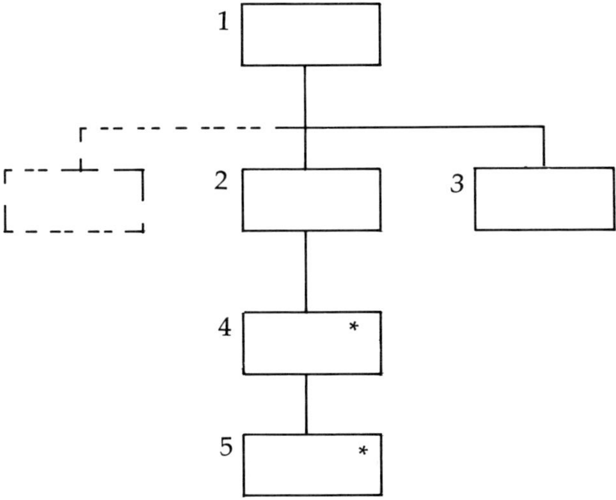

Figure 17.16 'Complete' input data structure

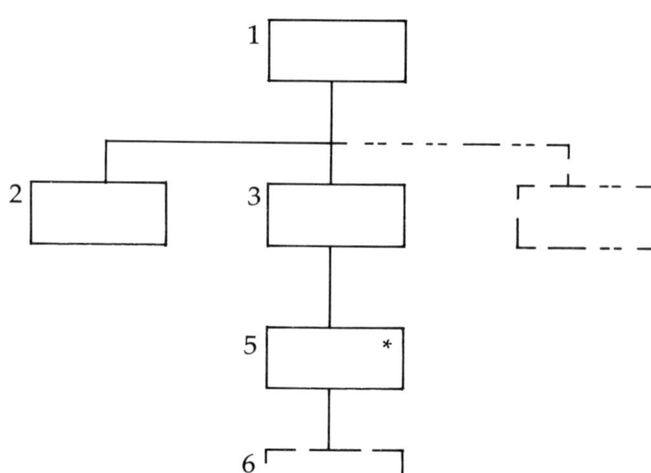

Figure 17.17 'Complete' output data structure

The correct links between the two data structures have been identified. The final result gives 'dummy' modules in the input and output data structures, Figures 17.16 and 17.17.

3 Define the initial program structure

The program structure is derived from the composite data structure. This can be seen in Figure 17.18 and Table 17.4.

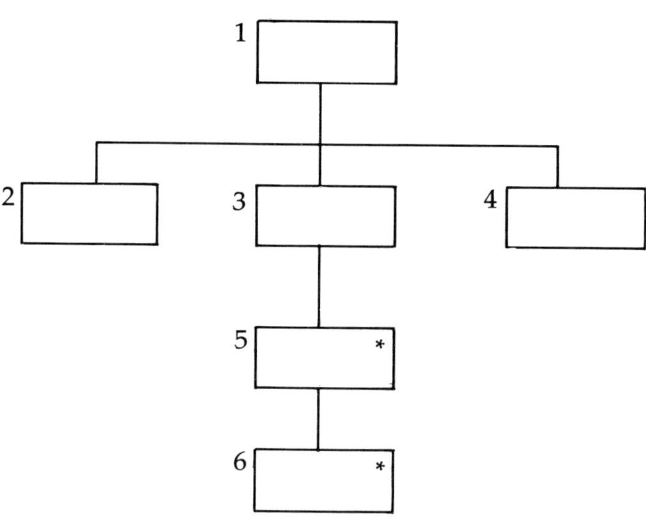

Figure 17.18 Initial program structure

Program module number	Process
1	Process members files for report generation
2	Generate report headings
3	Process members file
4	Process Lastrecord ie file processing termination
5	Process each member
6	Process loans

Table 17.4 Processing modules

Certainly the hardest part has now been done. What remains is to flesh out the program structure by identifying conditions and terminal functions.

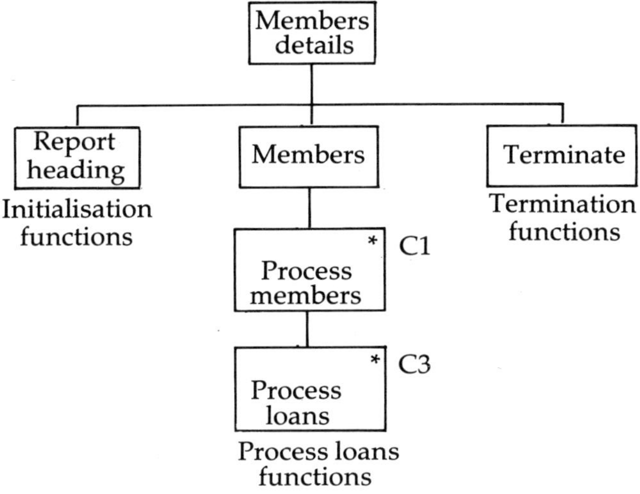

17.19 Program structure

17.4 SUMMARY

- 1. Large computer based systems take man years to develop; therefore methods are needed to provide guidance over the project life cycle.
- 2. Methods differ in their approach, ranging from people based 'soft' to equipment based 'hard' methods.

– 3. Jackson Structured Programming (JSP) is a data driven method.

– 4. The data of a given system tends to be stable over extended periods of time. This data can be analysed to produce data structures that are used to define the structured diagrams for the associated code.

17.5 PROBLEMS

What is to be recommended here is to further investigate JSP. Certainly there are many excellent texts available. Note – do not confuse JSP with Jackson Structured Development (JSD). JSD is an expansion of JSP and therefore includes aspects of JSP.

In Conclusion

I hope you have enjoyed this book. The emphasis throughout has been on demonstrating some of the basic principles that are mappable to different languages, and to this end the problems have been kept simple in order to focus on the concepts that are being taught. That the approach is perhaps different from others you may have come across needs no apology. If you have learnt something then this book has served its purpose. I would welcome any comments from readers.

Appendix 1

PASCAL SYNTAX DIAGRAMS

Simple type

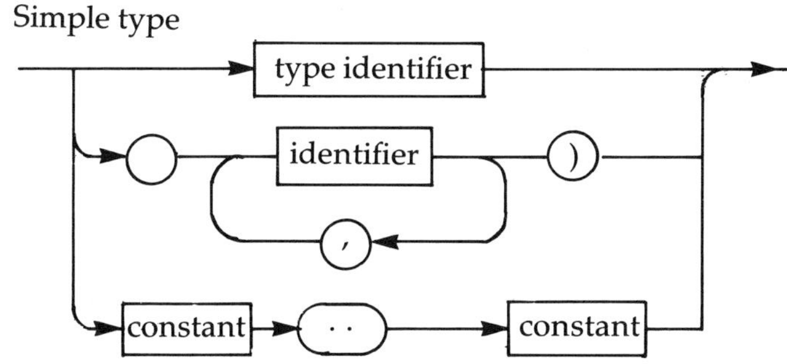

Type

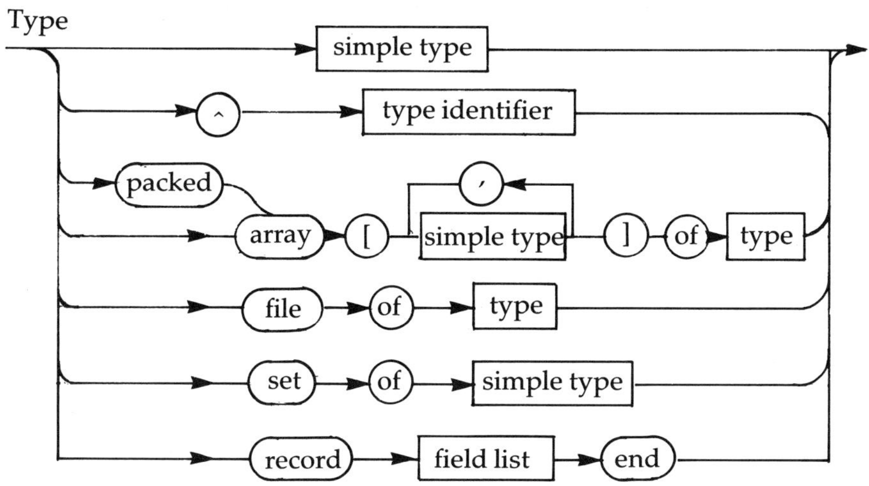

Parameter list

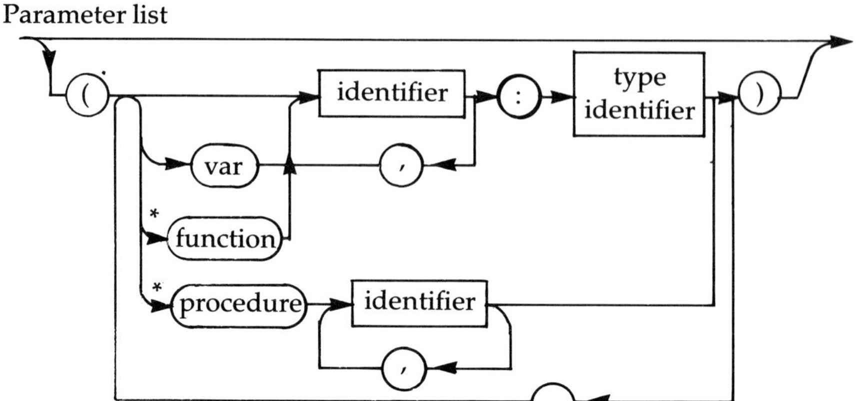

Conditional statement

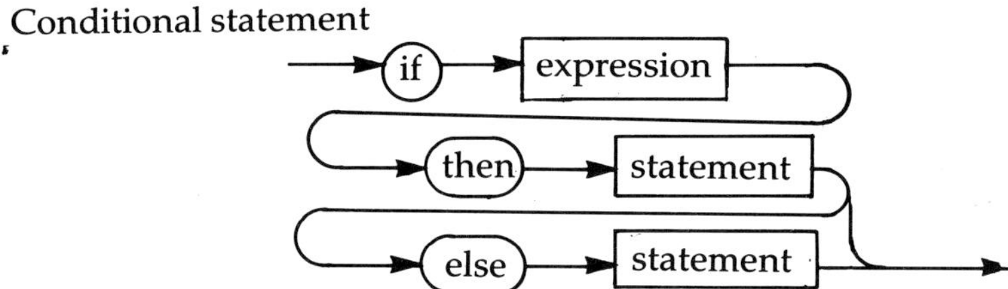

Case statement

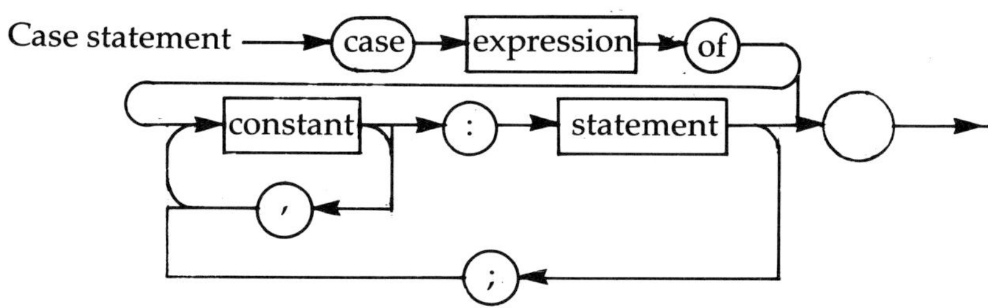

While statement

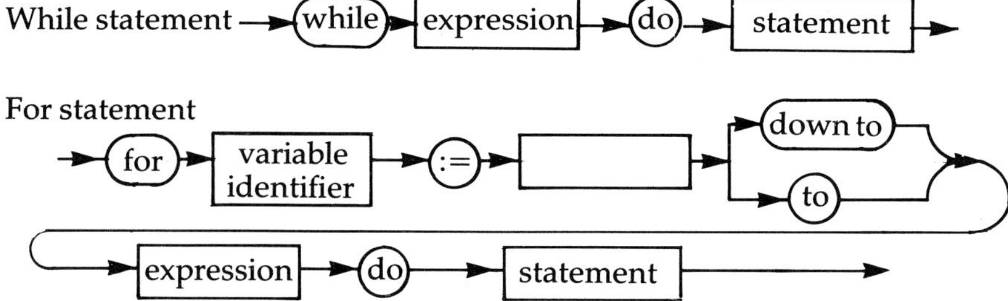

Repeat statement

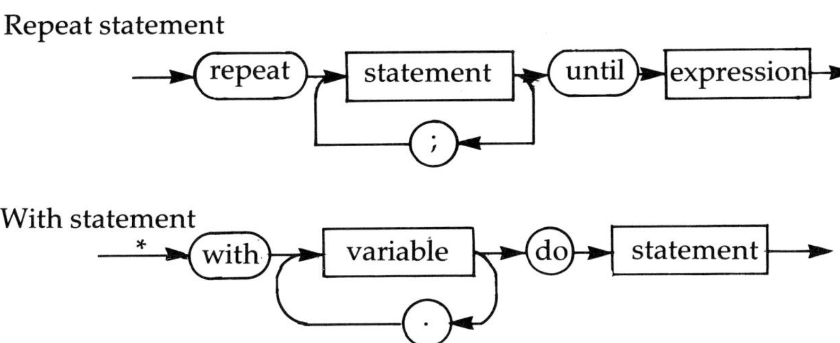

Goto statement

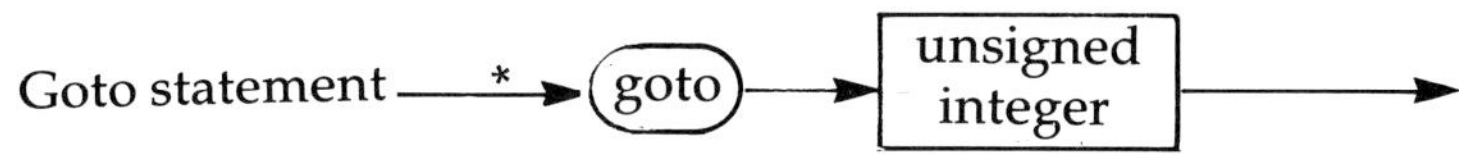

Procedure declaration

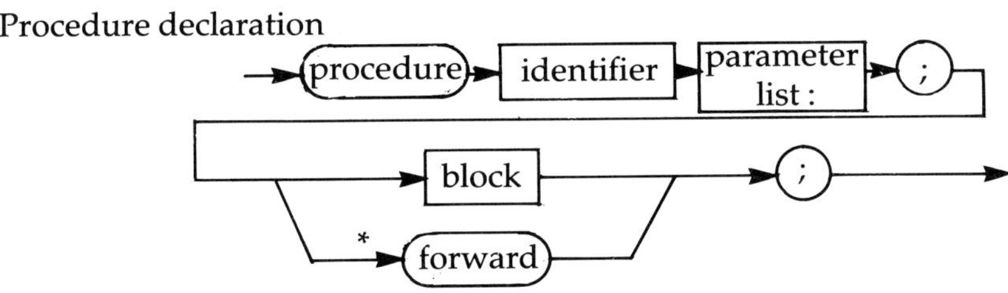

Function declaration

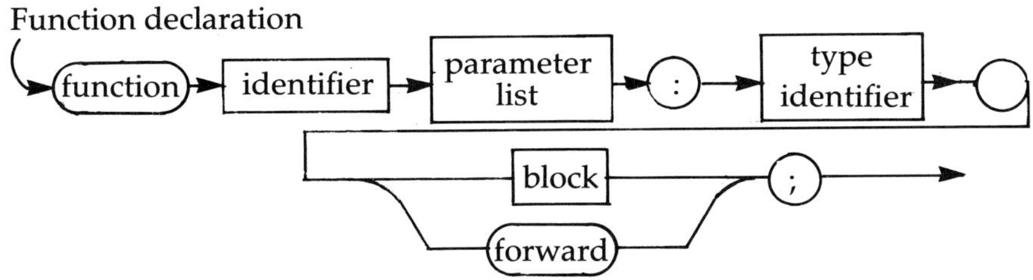

Statement

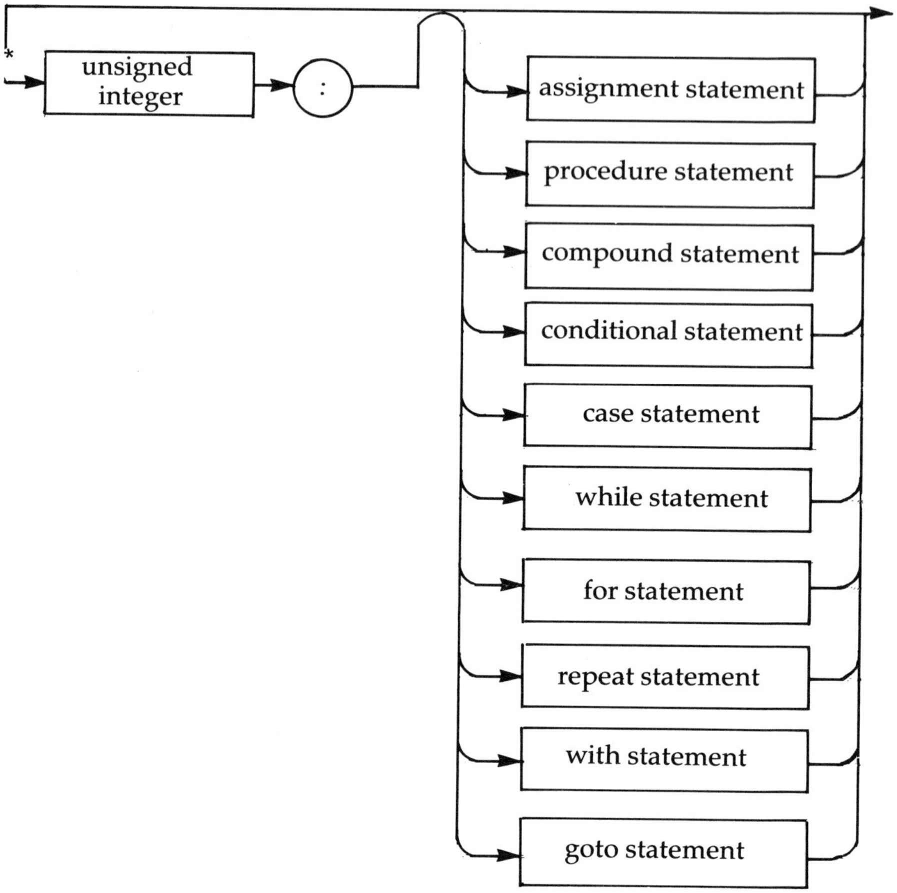

*

unsigned integer

:

assignment statement

procedure statement

compound statement

conditional statement

case statement

while statement

for statement

repeat statement

with statement

goto statement

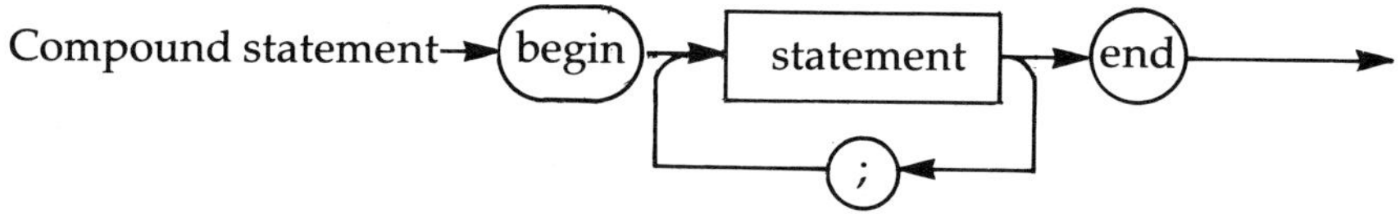

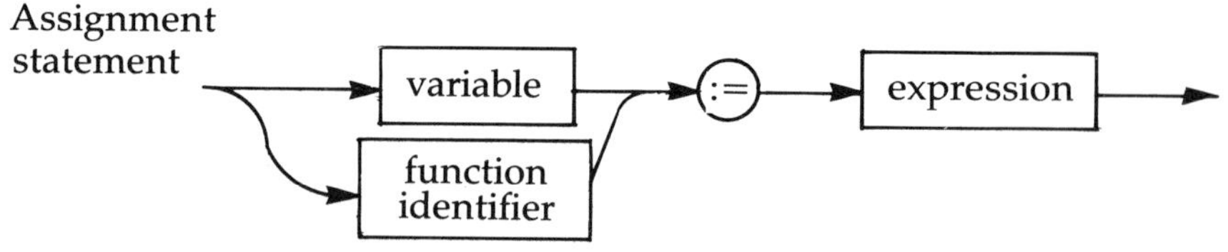

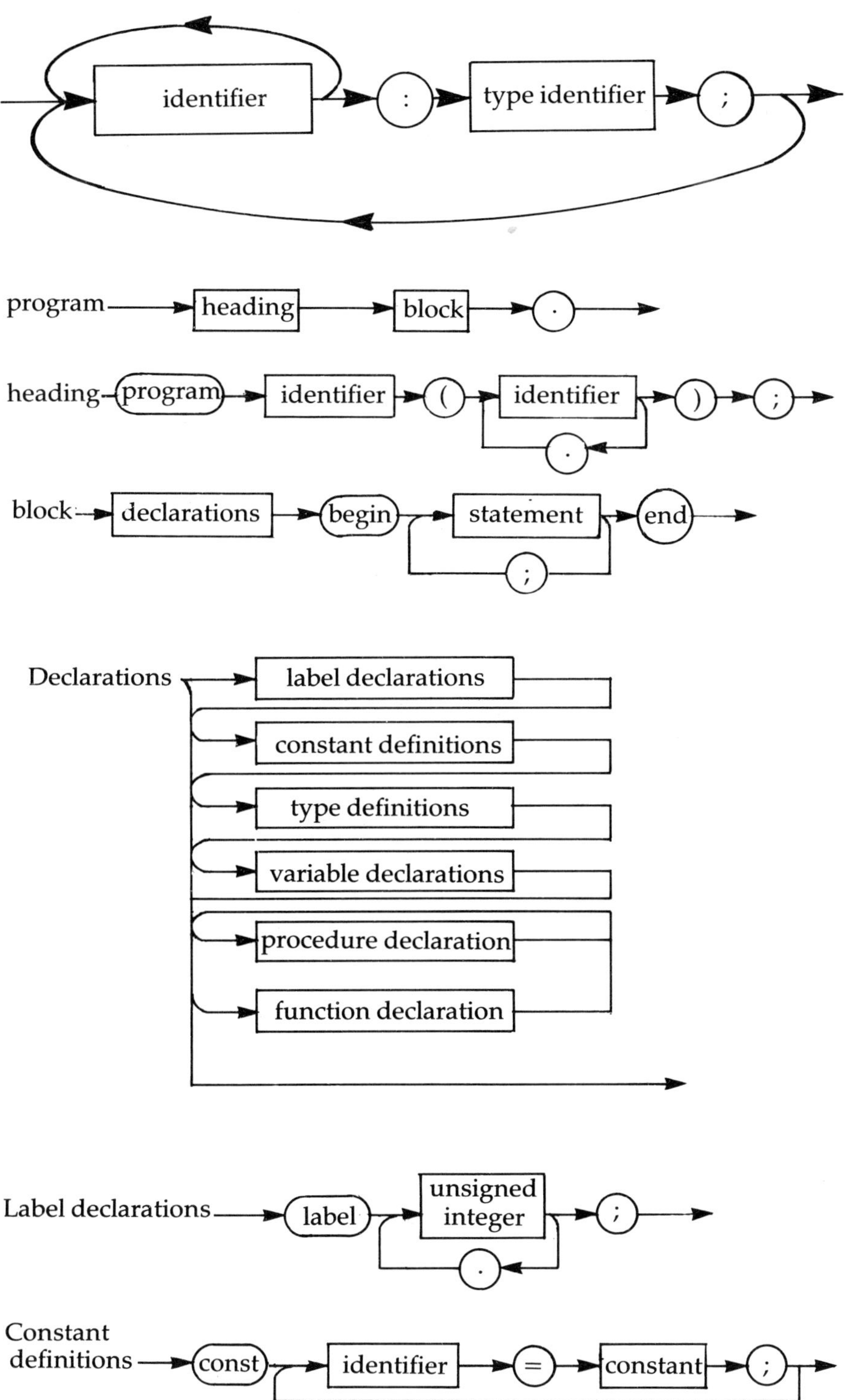
identifier
:
type identifier
;
program
heading
block
.
heading
program
identifier
(
identifier
)
;
,
block
declarations
begin
statement
end
;
Declarations
label declarations
constant definitions
type definitions
variable declarations
procedure declaration
function declaration
Label declarations
label
unsigned integer
;
,
Constant definitions
const
identifier
=
constant
;

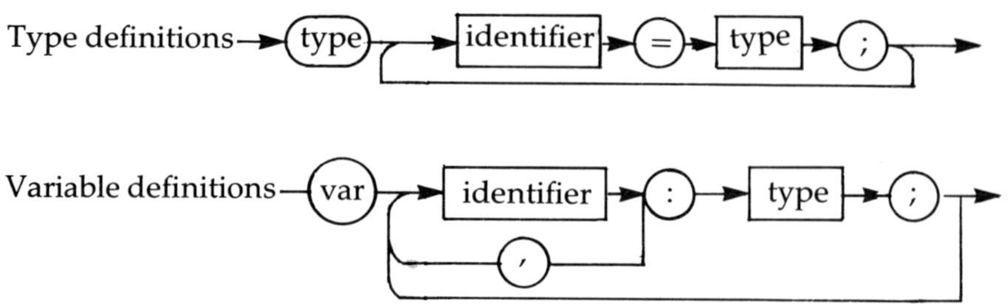
Type definitions
type
identifier
=
type
;
Variable definitions
var
identifier
:
type
;
,

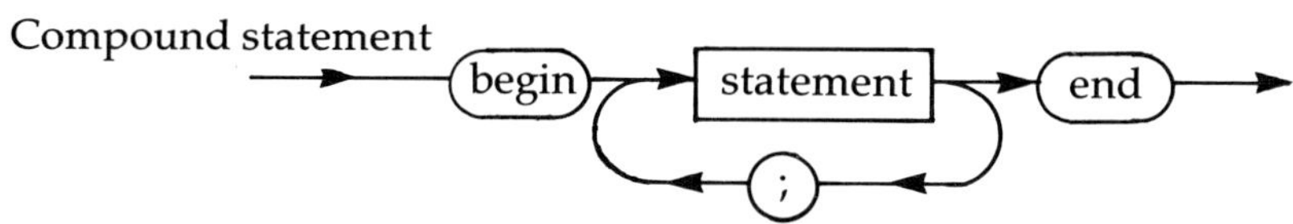
Compound statement
begin
statement
end
;

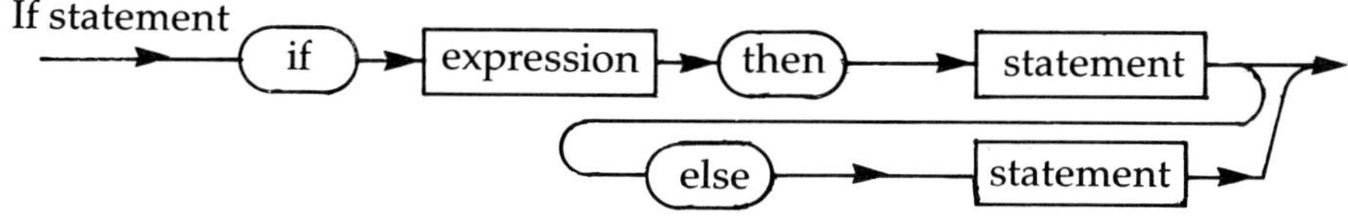
If statement
if
expression
then
statement
else
statement

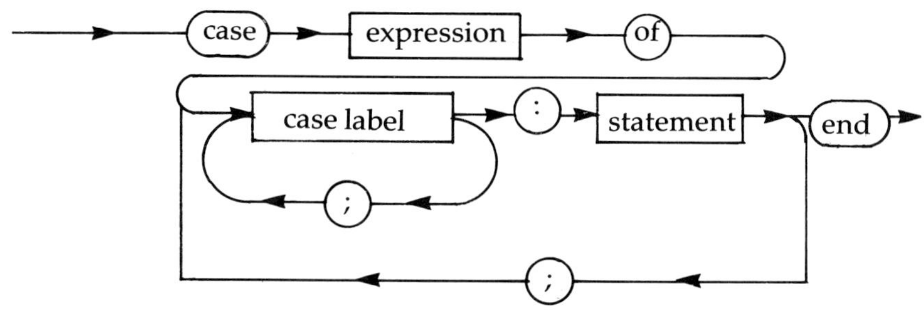
case
expression
of
case label
:
statement
end
;
;

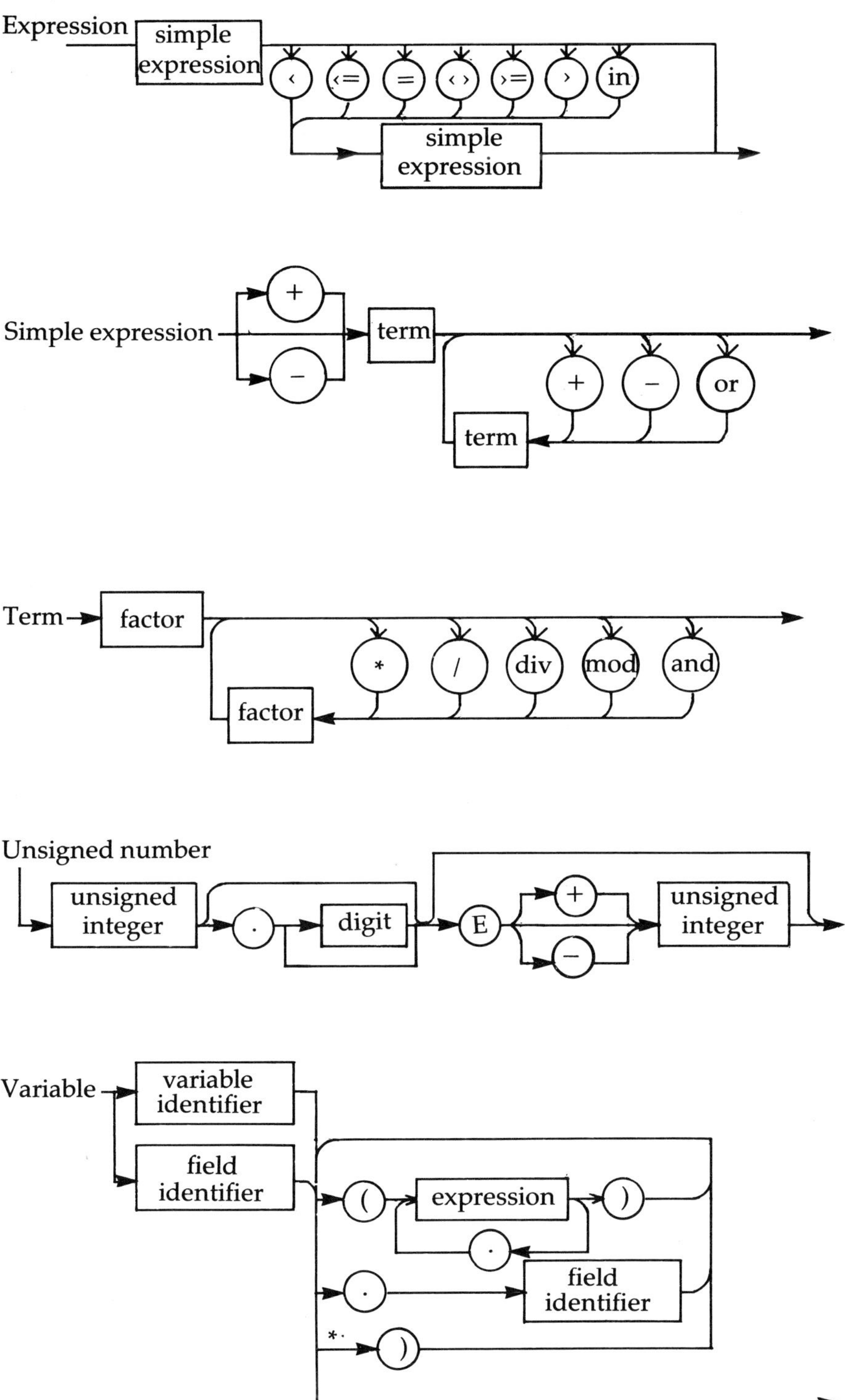
Expression
simple expression
<
<=
=
<>
>=
>
in
simple expression
Simple expression
+
−
term
+
−
or
term
Term
factor
*
/
div
mod
and
factor
Unsigned number
unsigned integer
.
digit
E
+
−
unsigned integer
Variable
variable identifier
field identifier
(
expression
)
.
.
field identifier
)

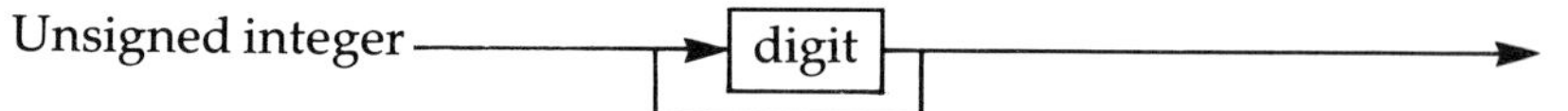

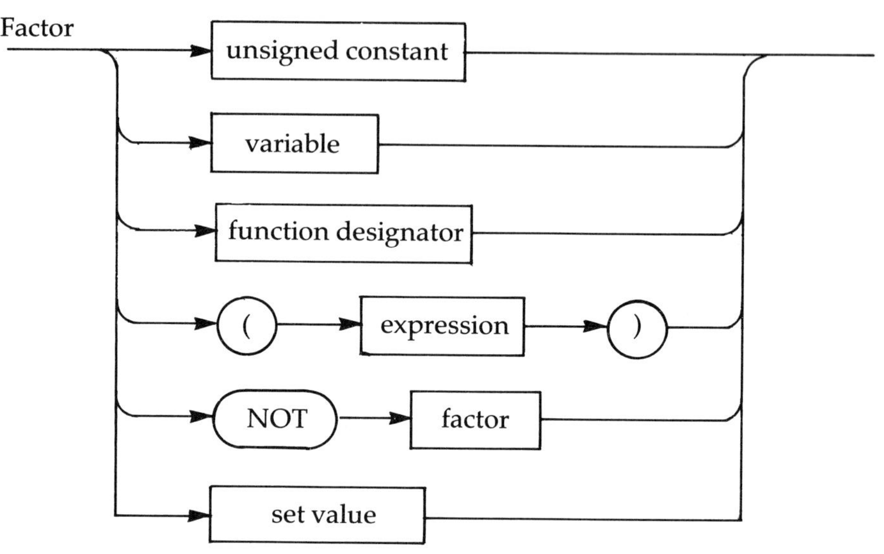

Function designator

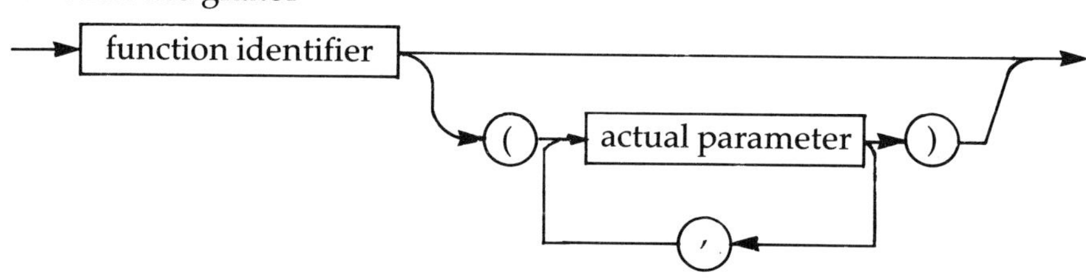

Set value

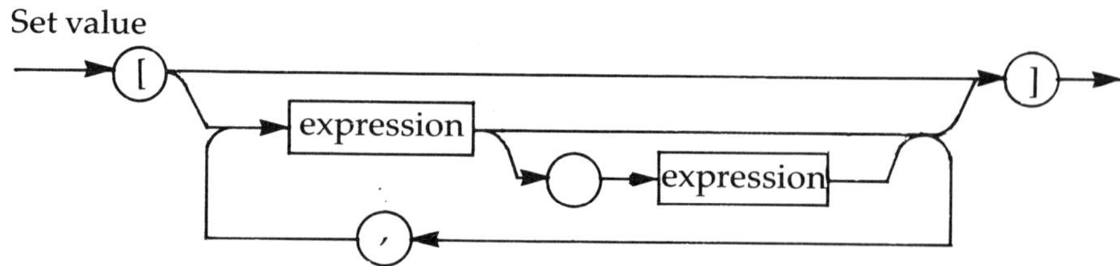

Procedure statement

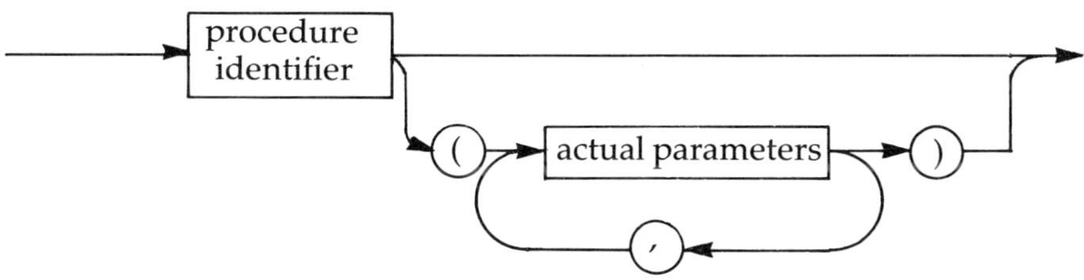

Identifier

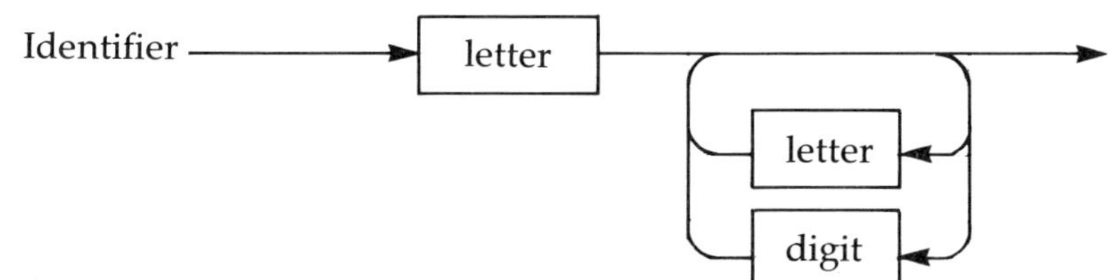

Unsigned constant

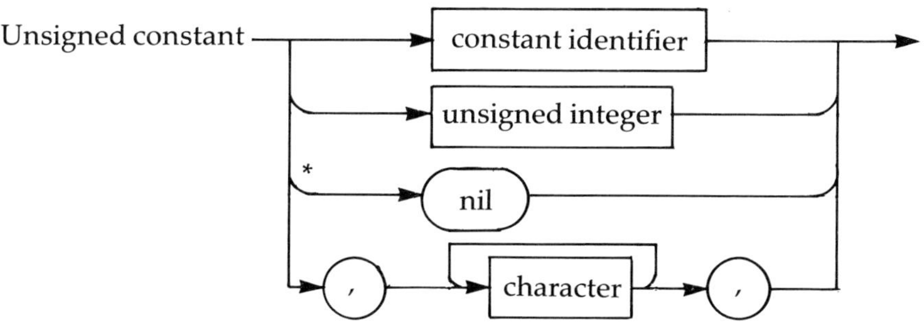

Constant

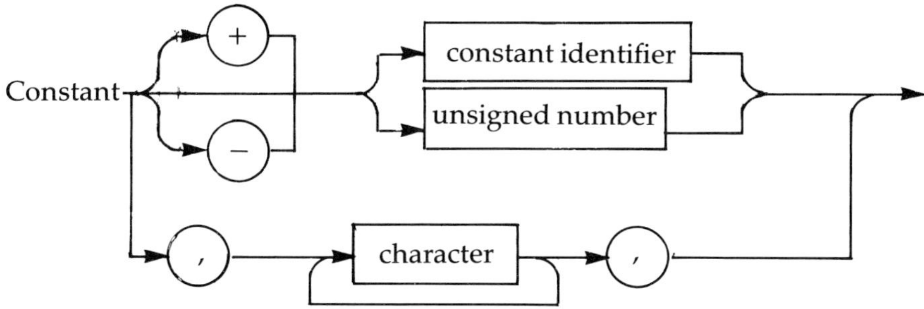

Field list

identifier
:
type
.
:
*
case
identifier
:
type identifier
of
variant
:

Simple type
type identifier
constant
..
constant
*
(
identifier
)

Variant
*
constant
:
(
field list
)

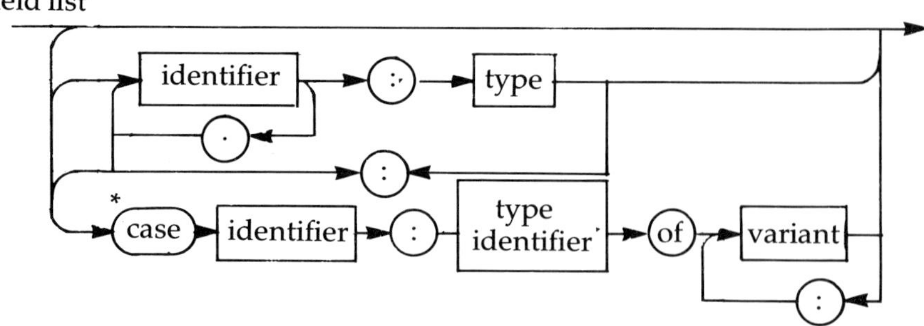

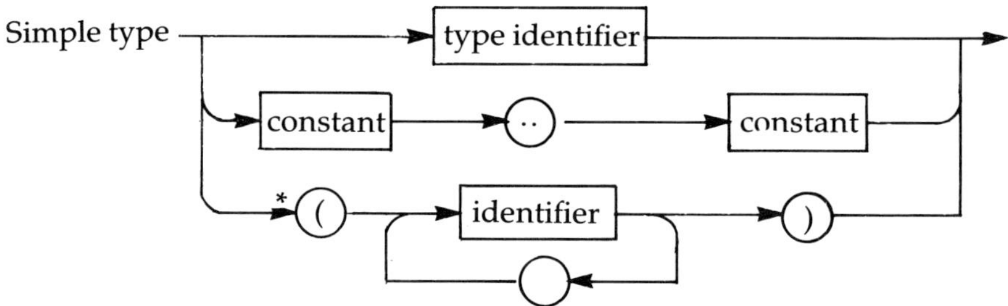

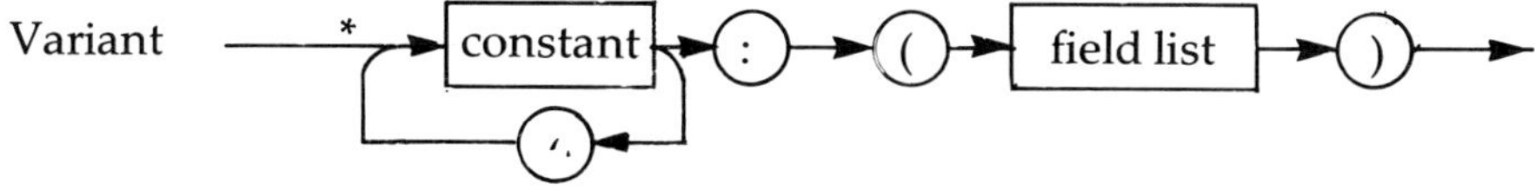

Appendix 2

KEYWORDS

Pascal recognises certain keywords which have a predefined meaning. These words are:

AND	END	NOT	THEN
ARRAY	FILE	OF	TO
BEGIN	FOR	OR	TYPE
CASE	FUNCTION	PACKED	UNTIL
CONST	GOTO	PROCEDURE	VALUEXXX
DIV	IF	PROGRAM	VAR
DO	IN	RECORD	WHILE
DOWNTO	LABEL	REPEAT	WITH
ELSE	MOD	SET	

Appendix 3

ASCII TABLE

AMERICAN STANDARD CODE FOR INFORMATION INTERCHANGE

ROW	COLUMN	0	1	2	3	4	5	6	7
	BITS $^{765}_{4321}$	000	001	010	011	100	101	110	111
0	0000	NUL	DEL	SP	∩	@	P	\	p
1	0001	SOH	DC1	!	1	A	Q	a	q
2	0010	STX	DC2	″	2	B	R	b	r
3	0011	ETX	DC3	#	3	C	S	c	s
4	0100	EOT	DC4	$	4	D	T	d	t
5	0101	ENQ	NAK	%	5	E	U	e	u
6	0110	ACK	SYN	&	6	F	V	f	v
7	0111	BEL	ETB	′	7	G	W	g	w
8	1000	BS	CAN	(	8	H	X	h	x
9	1001	HT	EM	)	9	I	Y	i	y
10	1010	LF	SUB	*	:	J	Z	j	z
11	1011	VT	ESC	+	;	K	[	k	{
12	1100	FF	FS	,	›	L	\	l	¦
13	1101	CR	GS	-	=	M	]	m	}
14	1110	SO	RS	.	‹	N	^	n	~
15	1111	SI	US	/	?	O	—	o	DEL

Explanation of special control functions in columns 0, 1, 2 and 7.

NUL	*Null*	*DLE*	*Data Link Escape*
SOH	*Start of Heading*	*DC1*	*Device Control 1*
STX	*Start of Text*	*DC2*	*Device Control 2*
ETX	*End of Text*	*DC3*	*Device Control 3*
EOT	*End of Transmission*	*DC4*	*Device Control 4*
ENQ	*Enquiry*	*NAK*	*Negative Acknowledge*
ACK	*Acknowledge*	*SYN*	*Synchronous Idle*

BEL	*Bell (audible signal)*	*ETB*	*End of Transmission Block*
BS	*Backspace*	*CAN*	*Cancel*
HT	*Horizontal Tabulation (punched card skip)*	*EM*	*End of Medium*
LF	*Line Feed*	*SUB*	*Substitute*
VT	*Vertical Tabulation*	*ESC*	*Escape*
FF	*Form Feed*	*FS*	*File Separator*
CR	*Carriage Return*	*GS*	*Group Separator*
SO	*Shift Out*	*RS*	*Record Separator*
SI	*Shift In*	*US*	*Unit Separator*
SP	*Space (blank)*	*DEL*	*Delete*

Appendix 4

SPECIAL SYMBOLS

Certain characters and character pairs are recognised as special symbols. These symbols are:

CHARACTER	SYMBOL NAME	GENERAL USAGE
+	plus	arithmetic operators
–	minus	
*	asterisk	
/	slash	
<	less than	relational operators
>	greater than	
=	equals	
< >	not equal	
#	not equal	
<=	less than or equal	
>=	greater than or equal	
:=	assignment operator	variable assignment
(	left parenthesis	enclose parameters and
)	right parenthesis	expressions
[	left bracket	enclose indexes
]	right bracket	

(*	left brace	enclose comments
*)	right brace	enclose comments
{	left brace	enclose comments
}	right brace	enclose comments
.	period	decimal point, program terminator
..	double period	upper/lower range delimiter
:	colon	label separator
;	semicolon	statement separator
'	single quote	enclose string
^	circumflex	pointers
@	at-sign	

Appendix 5

DATA STRUCTURES

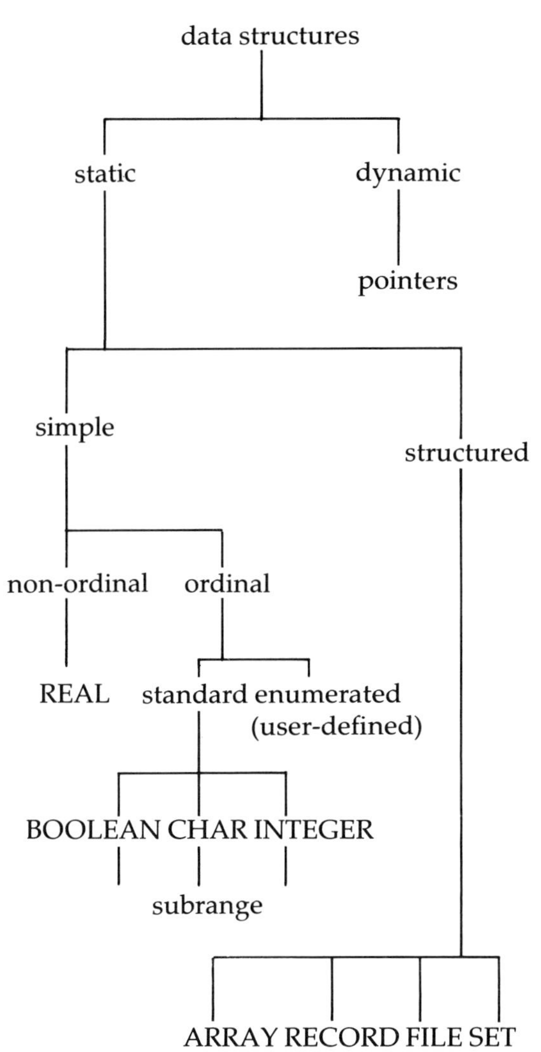

A data specification is:

- 1. A description of the values that may be used and hence the storage requirements.
- 2. A description of the way the elements of the data structure are related.
- 3. A specification of the methods of access to the elements.
- 4. A specification of the permitted operations.

Appendix 6

ARITHMETIC OPERATORS

OPERATOR	OPERATION	OPERAND'S TYPE	RESULT TYPE
*	multiplication	INTEGER and/or REAL	INTEGER if both operands are INTEGER, else REAL
/	real division	INTEGER and/or REAL	REAL
DIV	integer division	INTEGER	INTEGER
MOD	modulus	INTEGER	INTEGER
+	addition	INTEGER and/or REAL	INTEGER if both operands are INTEGER, else REAL
–	subtraction	INTEGER and/or REAL	INTEGER if both operands are INTEGER, else REAL

Appendix 7

RELATIONAL OPERATORS

OPERATOR	OPERATION	OPERAND'S TYPE	RESULT
=	equality	simple data type, string, set or pointer	BOOLEAN
›‹ or #	inequality	simple data type, string, set or pointer	BOOLEAN
›	greater than	simple data type or string	BOOLEAN
‹	less than	simple data type or string	BOOLEAN
›=	greater or equals	simple data type or string	BOOLEAN
‹=	less or equals	simple data type or string	BOOLEAN
IN	set membership	first is simple data type, second is set type	BOOLEAN

Appendix 8

SIMPLE STATEMENTS

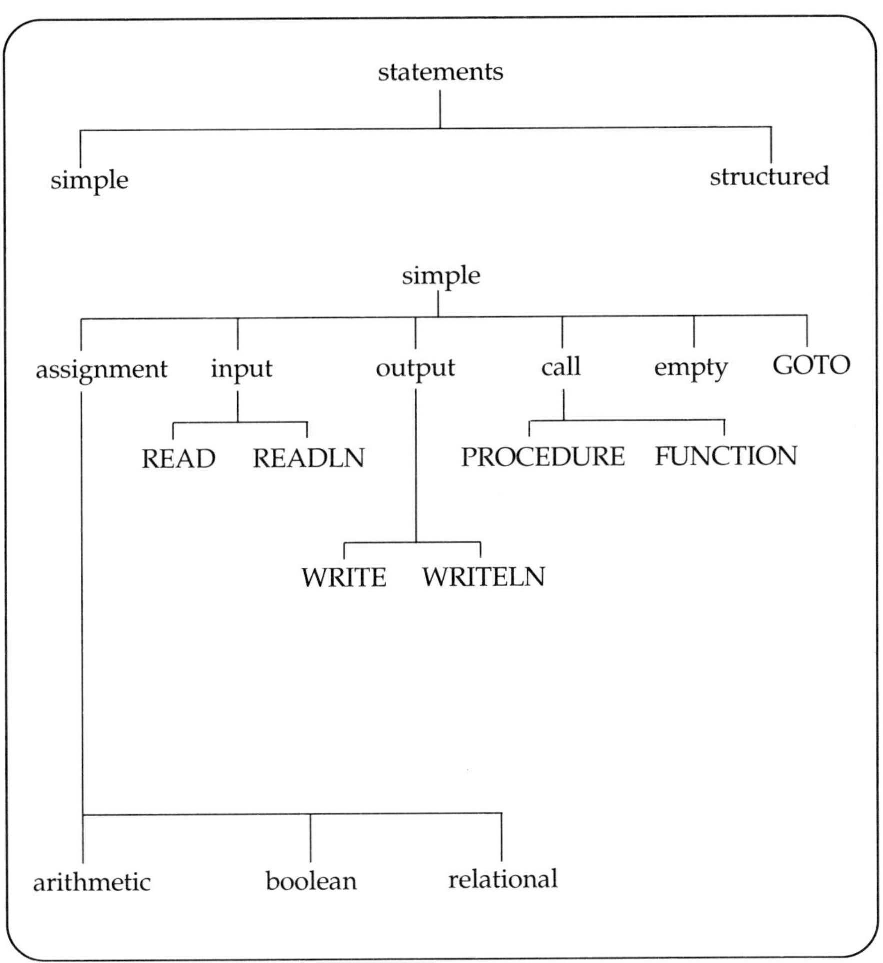

Appendix 9

STRUCTURED STATEMENTS

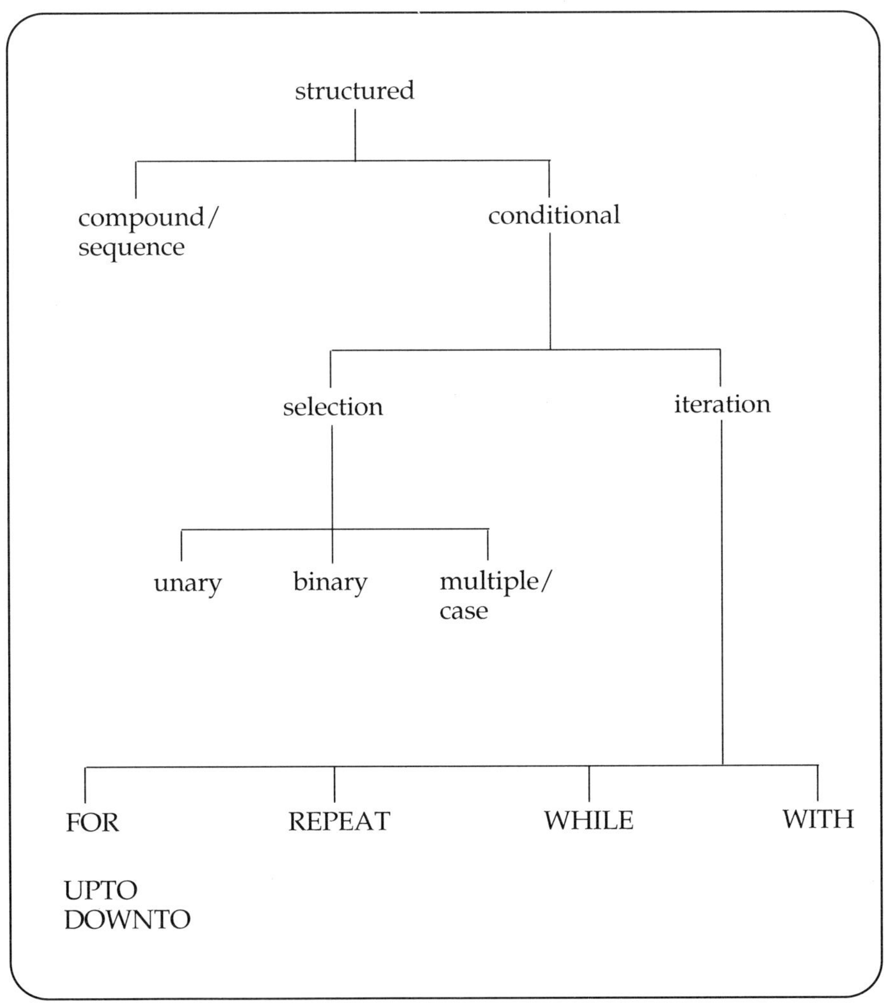

Index